IMAGES
of America

WAKEMAN AND FLORENCE TOWNSHIPS

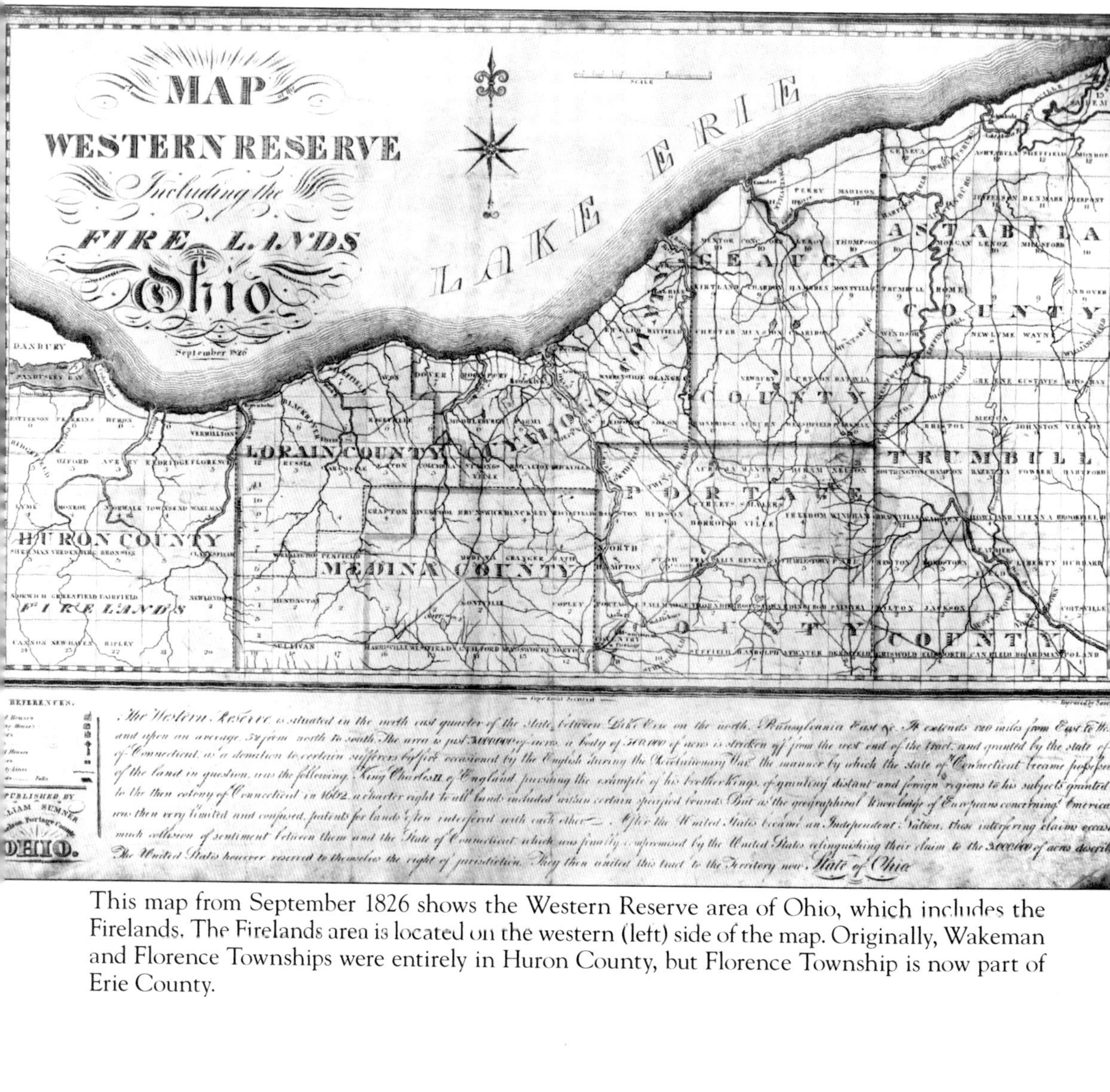

This map from September 1826 shows the Western Reserve area of Ohio, which includes the Firelands. The Firelands area is located on the western (left) side of the map. Originally, Wakeman and Florence Townships were entirely in Huron County, but Florence Township is now part of Erie County.

On the Cover: This c. 1900 photograph of downtown Wakeman shows horses and buggies conveying their owners to shops, the bank, or lunch. This part of the downtown block included the Wakeman Bank (later moved a block west), M.T. Scott's general store, a meat market, and a lunchroom. Judging from the blanket on the horse tied to the hitching post, it must have been a cold day in Wakeman.

IMAGES
of America

Wakeman and Florence Townships

David Graves and Amie Swope

ARCADIA
PUBLISHING

ISBN 978-0-7385-9353-1

Published by Arcadia Publishing
Charleston, South Carolina

Printed in the United States of America

Library of Congress Control Number:

For all general information, please contact Arcadia Publishing:
Telephone 843-853-2070
Fax 843-853-0044
E-mail sales@arcadiapublishing.com
For customer service and orders:
Toll-Free 1-888-313-2665

Visit us on the Internet at www.arcadiapublishing.com

To F.A. Denman, whose dedication to preserving information and photographs is greatly appreciated by his grandson and great-granddaughter, who are the authors of this book

Contents

Acknowledgments

Creating a book that covers two villages and two townships would not have been possible without the generous help of fellow community members. We deeply appreciate those who loaned images, told us stories, and helped identify the people in the photographs. Special thanks to the Wakeman Community Library, Elwin and Nancy Sayler, Lois Ross, Jason Gargasz, Ben Brookover, Sue Palmer, Nelson Green, Guy Schieve, Roger Howe, Christine Johannsen, Ross Bethard, Kurt Scholl, the Florence Township Fire Department, and the Wakeman Fire Department. We also want to thank Jeffrey Swope for his patient scanning and computer knowledge and Beverly Graves for the many ways she supported this project. Unless otherwise noted, all images came from the collection of the authors.

INTRODUCTION

Wakeman and Florence Townships are joined by a common history, a number of common ancestors, at least one major road, and a beautiful river. This region in Northern Ohio was originally part of the Western Reserve, which was land set aside for the Fire Sufferers of the American Revolution. The government of Connecticut attempted to make retribution to residents whose land was destroyed in a series of British raids, but because it took so many years for the land grants to actually materialize, most Fire Sufferers did not make the trip to Ohio. Their children did, however, and the Firelands began to be populated after the War of 1812.

In 1817, Jessup Wakeman founded the Village of Wakeman. Also that year, Florence Township was organized, elected its first officers, and established its first church. Jessup Wakeman had one of the larger tracts of land in the Firelands and purchased even more, eventually acquiring the unincorporated Village of Birmingham—originally named Jessup—to his holdings. Many groups, organizations, and schools bear the names of the original intent of the land. Western Reserve Local Schools and Firelands Local Schools are an example. Some cities and towns in the Firelands are also named after their counterparts in Connecticut. For example, Norwalk, Greenwich, New Haven, and Danbury are local names that made the move. Other towns, like Wakeman, bear the names of their founders.

The Village of Wakeman's population has stayed remarkably steady over the past century, at about 950 residents. Many of the families in town have been there for generations. The surrounding Wakeman Township comprises many farms and has a population of over 2,500, and it is very common for family farms to be passed down from generation to generation. Wheat, corn, and soybeans are the predominant crops grown, and dairy cattle dot the landscape.

Wakeman Township's farms run into Florence Township, and only a road sign marks the change. Florence Township also has a population of about 2,500 residents. Much like Wakeman Township, farming has always been a primary occupation there. Picturesque Birmingham, situated on the Vermilion River, has a small downtown area of unique shops that have been there for many years. Almost the entire downtown area burned in the fire of 1891, but the community was resilient then, and continues to be that way. Wakeman and Florence Townships both have residents with the hardy attributes of seasoned New Englanders.

Historically, Wakeman and Florence Townships have benefited from the graceful Vermilion River that runs through them. Wakeman and Birmingham both had mills along the river, which were run primarily by waterpower. Interestingly, both villages suffered a fire that burned their mills to the ground, with Wakeman's mill burning in 1899, and Birmingham's in 1906. Bridges and dams are important to towns that exist on a river, and the bridge that carries traffic across the river in Wakeman has been rebuilt three times. In 1827, Philo Sherman and Burton French built the first wooden bridge. A steel bridge that was built in 1878 stood until it was deconstructed and shipped by rail to another local village, eventually being replaced by a concrete bridge in 1908. Increased traffic and the need for work during the Great Depression led to a newer concrete bridge in 1934.

The area around Birmingham had a historic covered bridge and several others that crossed the river. The wooden covered bridge was built in 1820 and replaced by another covered bridge in 1841. In 1900, the covered bridge was replaced by a steel bridge, which itself was replaced in 1931 by a concrete bridge.

The river connects both townships, but it was the railroad that connected the area to the rest of the country. Steam trains with passengers and freight made multiple daily stops in Wakeman, but diesel trains eventually replaced steam. Birmingham was part of an electric rail system, the Green Line, which ran daily from Cleveland.

Recreation and community events are important historical aspects of the area. In Wakeman, the river provided entertainment with several swinging bridges and pleasure boating. Wakeman was also the home to the Wakeman Red Caps, a semiprofessional baseball team that existed for nearly half a century. In 1935, it was one of the first fields in Ohio to have lights installed for playing night games. Crowds of 1,000 people were common, and there were sometimes 2,000 people in attendance at Red Cap Field in Wakeman. Traveling baseball clubs, such as the Ethiopian Clowns, visited once a year.

Schoepfle Gardens, situated on the Vermilion River in Birmingham, is a beautiful attraction that draws 100,000 visitors a year. Visitors can see the shale river bottom up close, walk on the many paths, and view the rose garden. Otto Schoepfle was the longtime editor of a local newspaper who donated his gardens for everyone to enjoy.

Some notable residents of the Wakeman and Florence Township area distinguished themselves with inventions or industry. Garrett Morgan, the inventor of the traffic light, had a summer home in Wakeman. He had plans of creating a summer community along the river south of town, but World War II stalled his plans. Wakeman was one of the first local towns to have a traffic light installed in 1948, and it is still the only traffic light in Wakeman, since it is quiet town where another light is not needed. Dr. Beeman, who was an inventor of chewing gum with pepsin added, had homes in Wakeman and Birmingham. The hardworking C.S. Clark had a seed house in Wakeman that once supplied one fifth of all the seed corn grown and shipped in the United States. His name can still be seen on the old building in downtown Wakeman.

Wakeman and Florence Townships got their start with the American Revolution. People industrious or brave enough to travel to the untamed wilderness of Ohio in the early 1800s must have been captivated by the fertile farmland, vegetation, and peaceful river that flowed through the area. Farming, community, and the enjoyment of the scenery are still important parts of life in Wakeman and Florence Townships, Ohio.

One

Bridges, Rivers, Roads, and Railroads

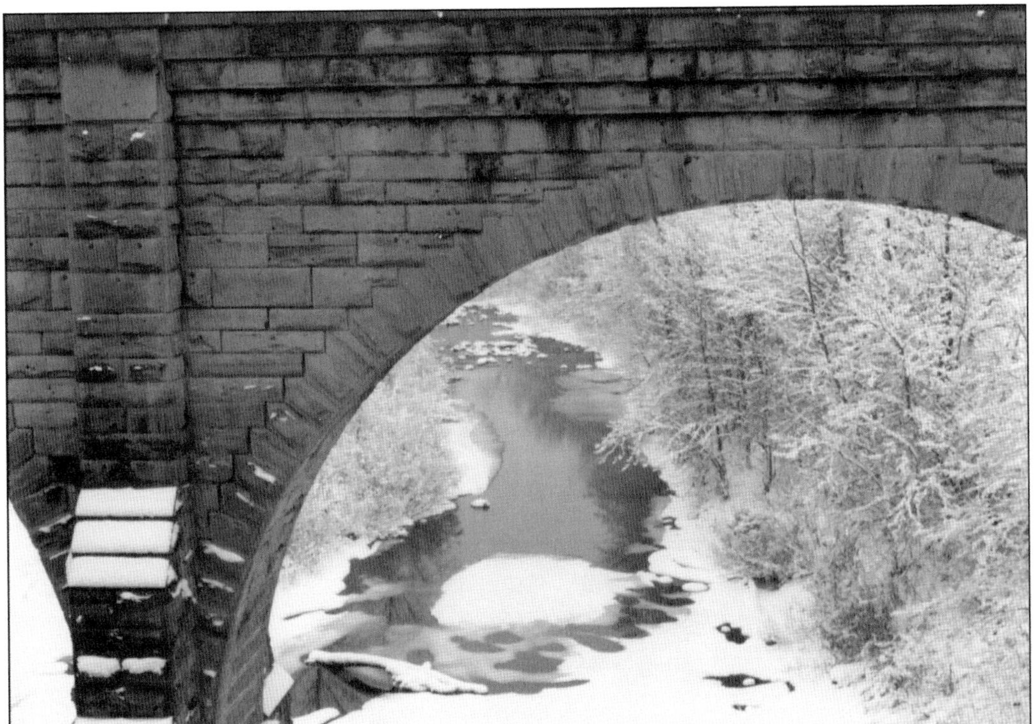

The Vermilion River winds under the stone railroad bridge in Wakeman and heads north. It passes through Birmingham on its way to meet Lake Erie in Vermilion, Ohio. Bridges, rivers, roads, and railroads are very important to small towns because they foster relationships with the outside world. The river has fueled sawmills and gristmills, cooled steam engines, and provided beauty and recreation to local residents for two centuries.

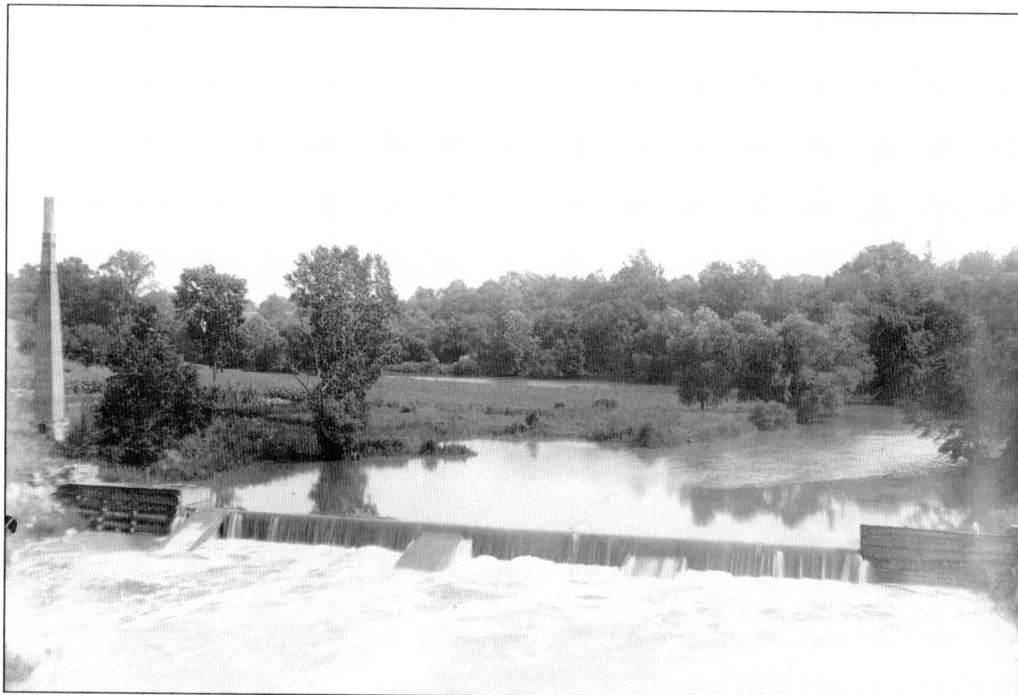

In the 1850s, this wooden dam was built just south of the road and railroad bridges in Wakeman. The sawmill and gristmill owners built the dam in order to harness the power of the Vermilion River. The ramp in the middle of the dam is a fish ladder.

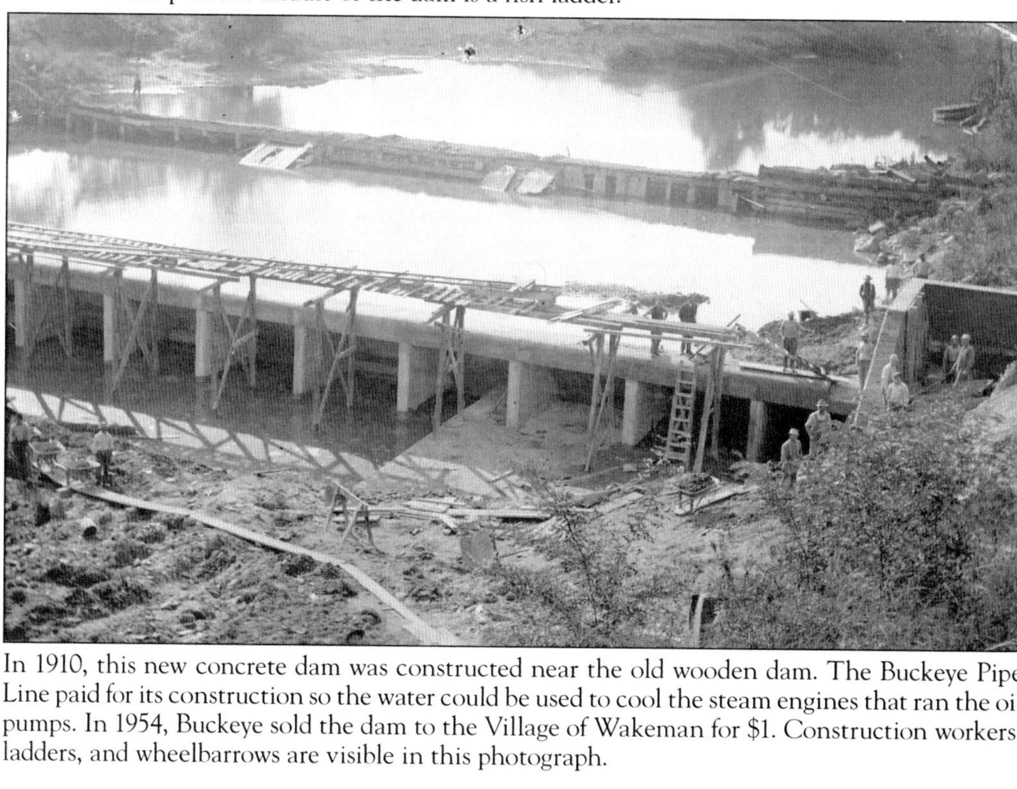

In 1910, this new concrete dam was constructed near the old wooden dam. The Buckeye Pipe Line paid for its construction so the water could be used to cool the steam engines that ran the oil pumps. In 1954, Buckeye sold the dam to the Village of Wakeman for $1. Construction workers, ladders, and wheelbarrows are visible in this photograph.

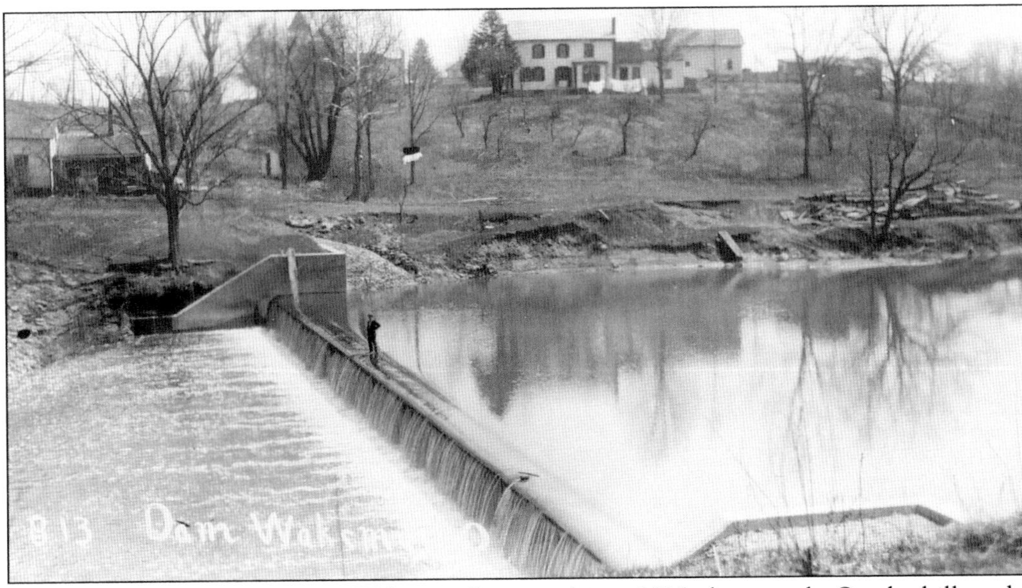

A man stands on the concrete Wakeman Dam in this c. 1915 photograph. On the hill to the left, the steeple of St. Mary's Catholic Church is visible. The Burk family, whose house is visible on the hill, owned the grain elevator in Wakeman. The house was later moved several hundred yards north.

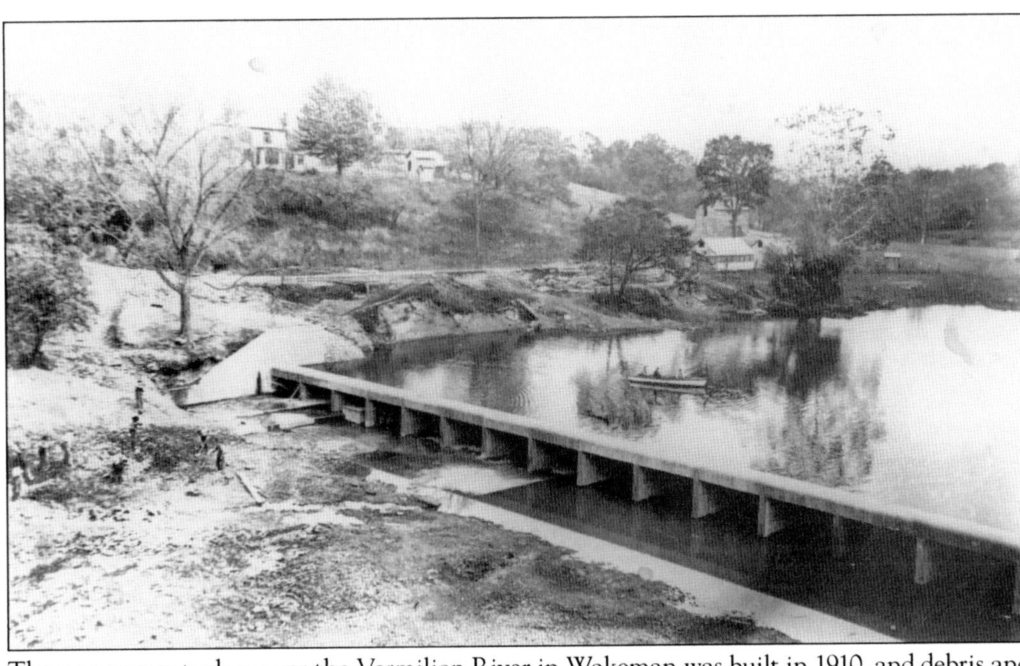

The new concrete dam over the Vermilion River in Wakeman was built in 1910, and debris and construction workers can still be seen to the left of this photograph taken right after construction. Note the pleasure boaters and the icehouse near the riverbank.

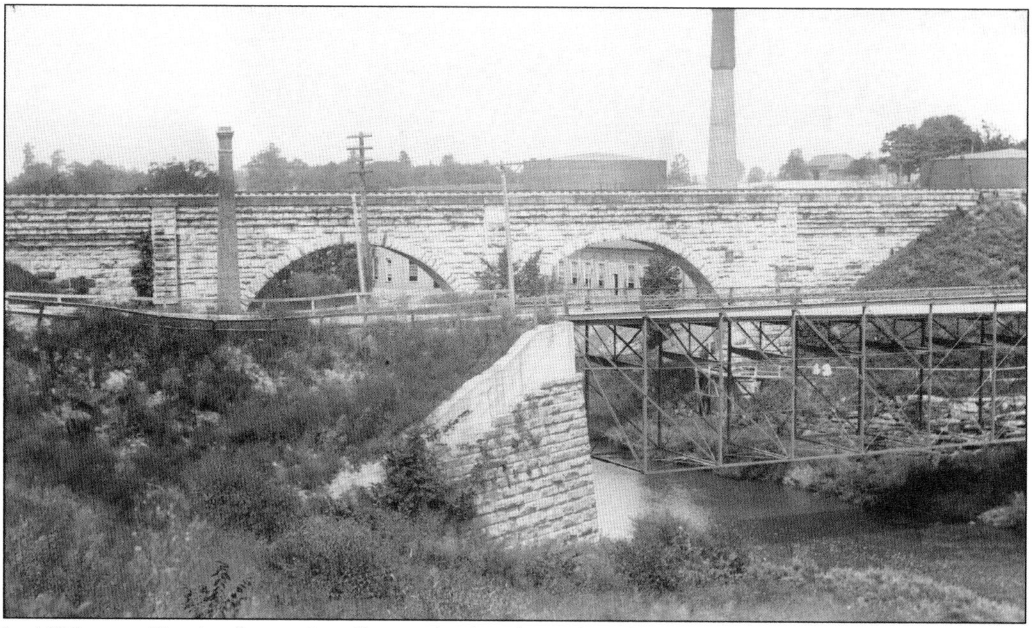

In 1876, a steel bridge for road traffic was built. The railroad bridge, built four years earlier, stands behind it. Smokestacks and circular storage tanks (above right) belonged to the Buckeye Pipe Line storage facility. The Buckeye also maintained a walkway visible below the steel bridge for its employees to check on the dam and its water pipes. The pipes, used for cooling steam pumps at the time, are still in the river and visible when the water is low. This steel bridge is actually the second steel bridge to span the river at this location. The original one was removed and taken by railcar to be used in Monroeville, a village about 20 miles away.

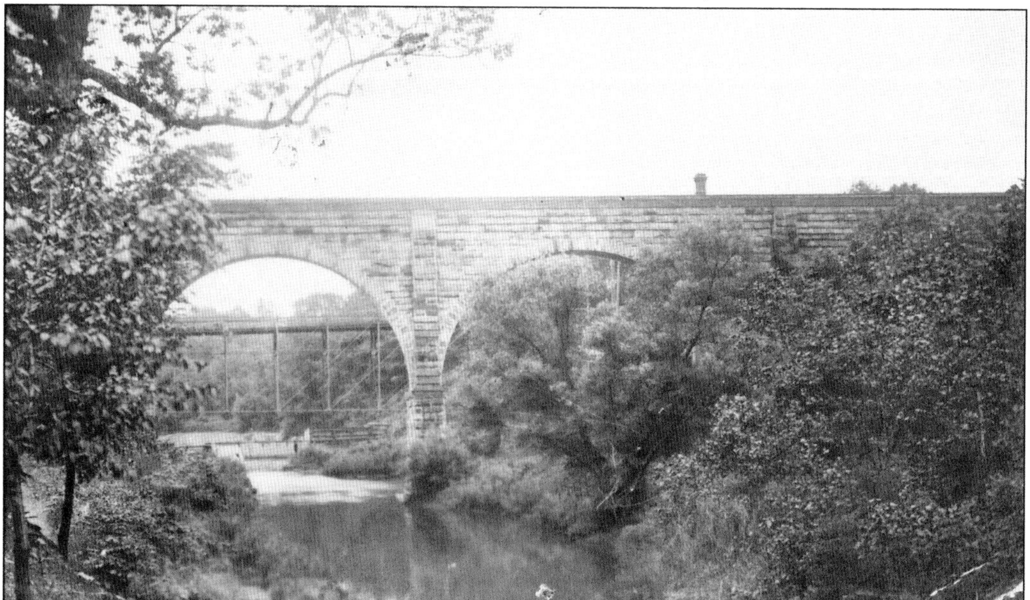

This view looking south along the Vermilion River in Wakeman shows the 1872 railroad bridge, built by the Michigan Southern Railroad, in the foreground. The 1876 steel road bridge is visible behind it. This stone railroad bridge still stands and may be used for a recreational trail in the future.

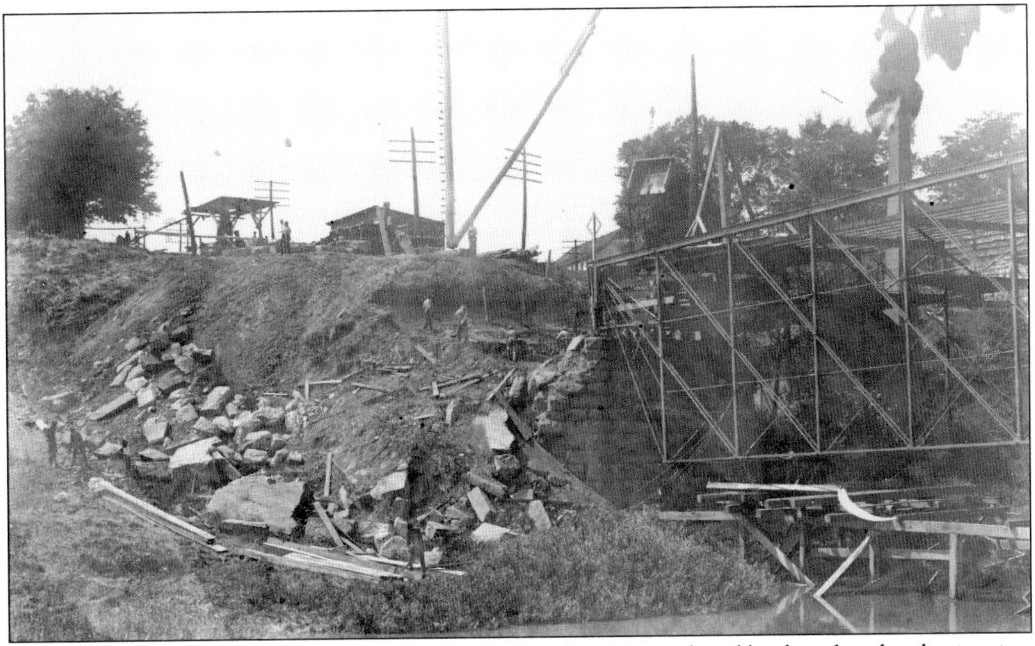

In 1903, the steel bridge was raised to match the height of the railroad bridge, thereby eliminating inclined approaches. At the top of the photograph, a gin pole (an early form of a crane) is used to lift the bridge.

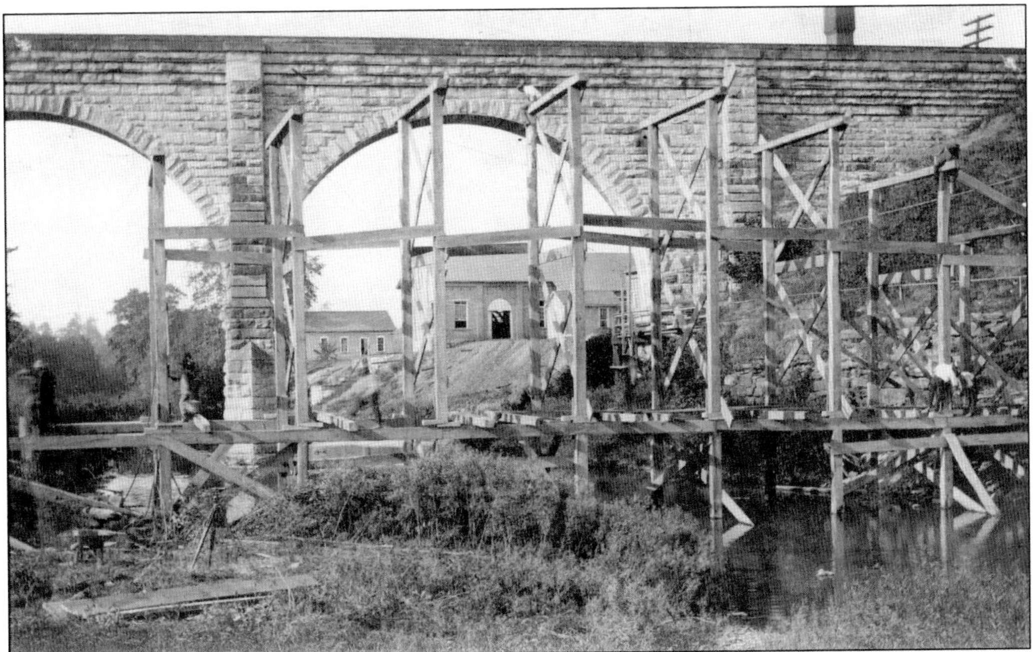

In 1908, a new concrete bridge replaced the existing steel one. This bridge had an arched design similar to the railroad bridge just north of it. The pump houses for the Buckeye Pipe Line are in the background of this summertime construction picture.

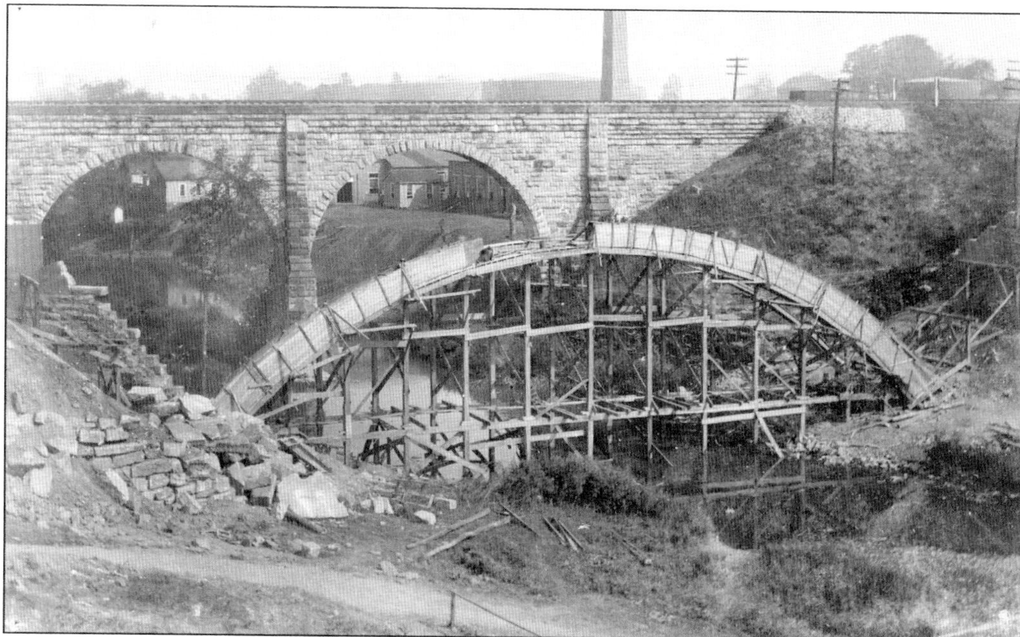

In this 1908 photograph, workers continue to build the new concrete bridge over the Vermilion River in Wakeman. The road that crossed this bridge is now the modern US Route 20, which stretches across the country.

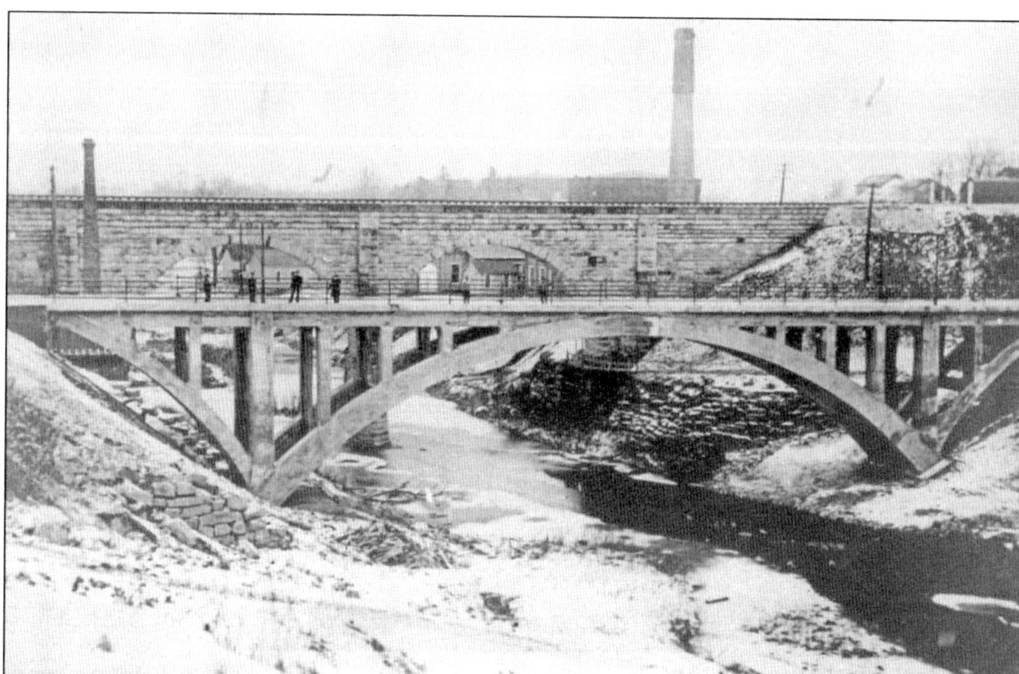

This 1908 winter scene shows the newly completed concrete road bridge in Wakeman. Pipe railings provided safety for pedestrians. Unfortunately, not enough steel was used in the construction of the bridge for it to withstand the road traffic that increased with the 20th century.

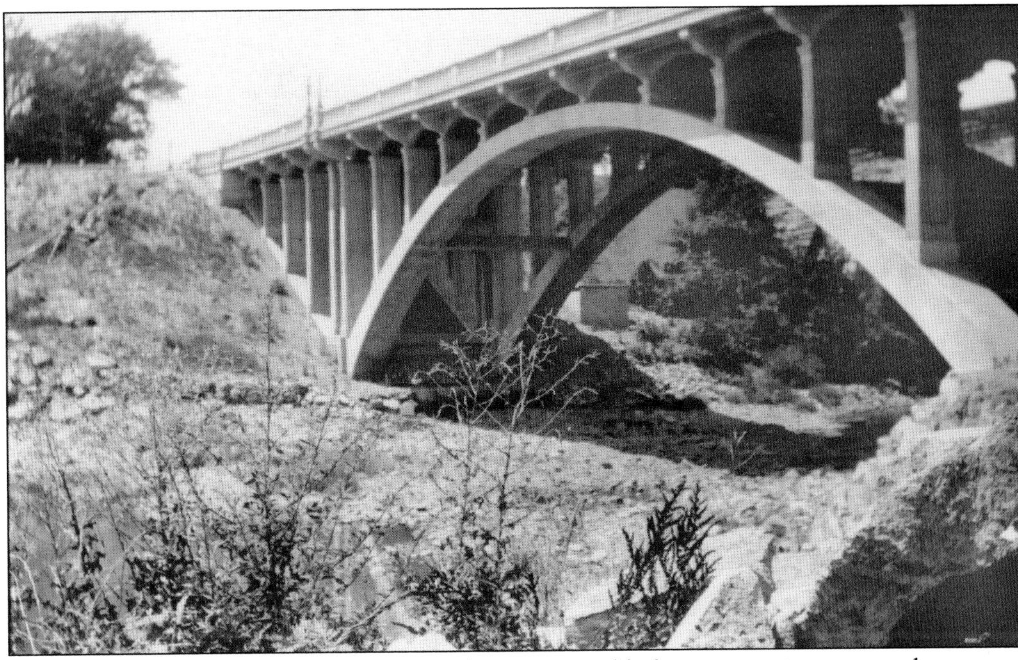

The Works Progress Administration (WPA) was responsible for many projects across the country, and Wakeman was the recipient of at least two of them. In 1937, a new school was completed, and this new concrete bridge replaced the old one in 1934. Many local men were happy to have work during the Great Depression as they trucked in steel and poured concrete on this bridge.

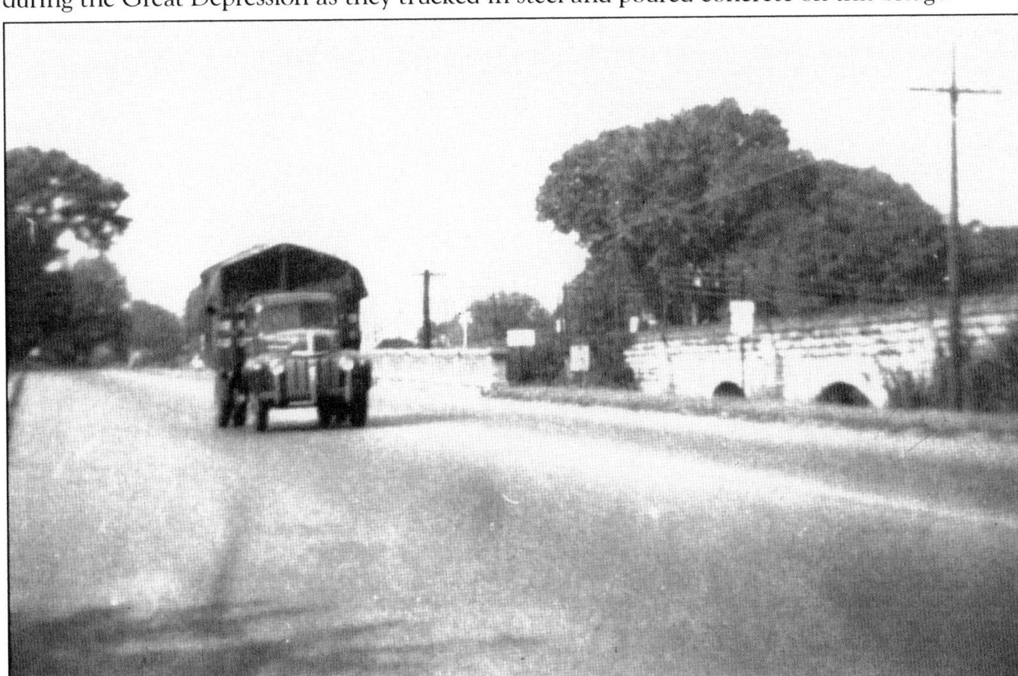

A truck owned by C.S. Clark's Seed House leaves downtown Wakeman and crosses the road bridge in the late 1940s. Clark's seed house delivered seed corn to local farmers and also exported it all over the country.

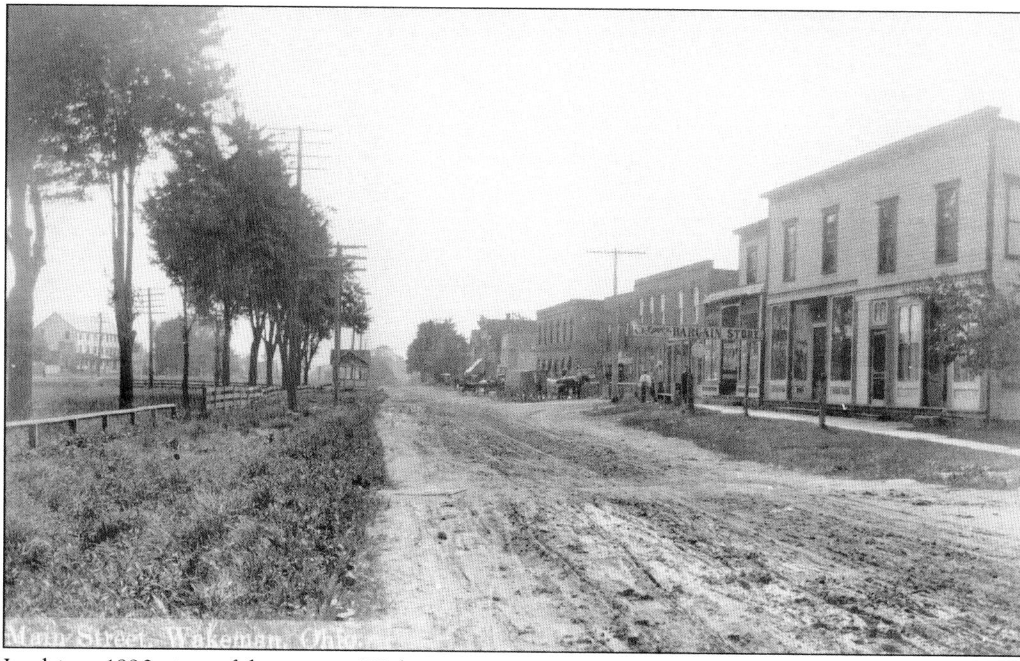

In this c. 1890 view of downtown Wakeman, Main Street is a dirt road. Stores on the right have horses lined up out front, and a community bandstand is just to the left of the dirt road. Telegraph poles line the railroad tracks that run along the left side of the photograph.

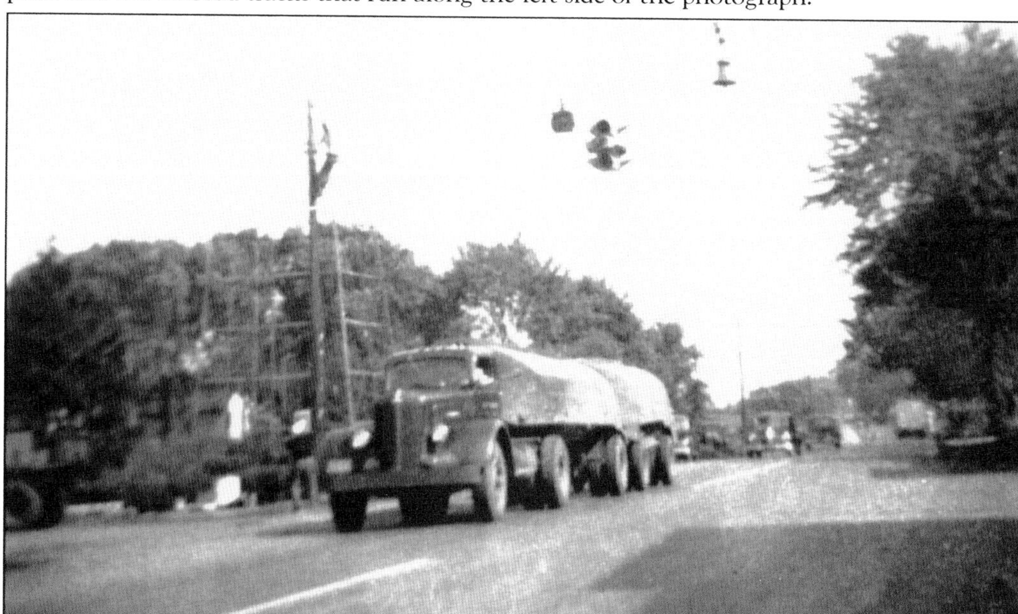
This 1948 photograph, taken by local history enthusiast F.A. Denman, shows the day when the traffic light was installed in downtown Wakeman. The inventor of the traffic light, Garrett Morgan, had a summer home along the river in Wakeman, which may be the reason Wakeman was one of the first small towns in Ohio to have a traffic light. The road pictured is Main Street, which is now US Route 20. The flag tower on the left was erected in 1917 to commemorate the town's centennial.

The Vermilion River bisects Birmingham, Ohio, in Florence Township. This photograph shows construction of a very early bridge in Birmingham. (Courtesy of Jason Gargasz.)

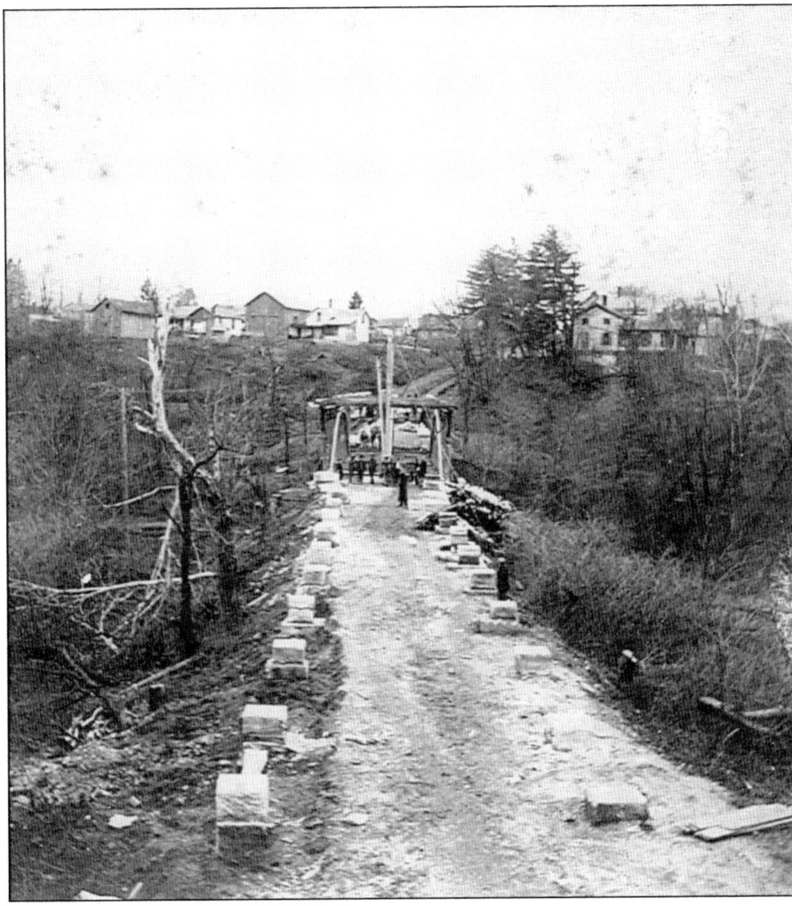

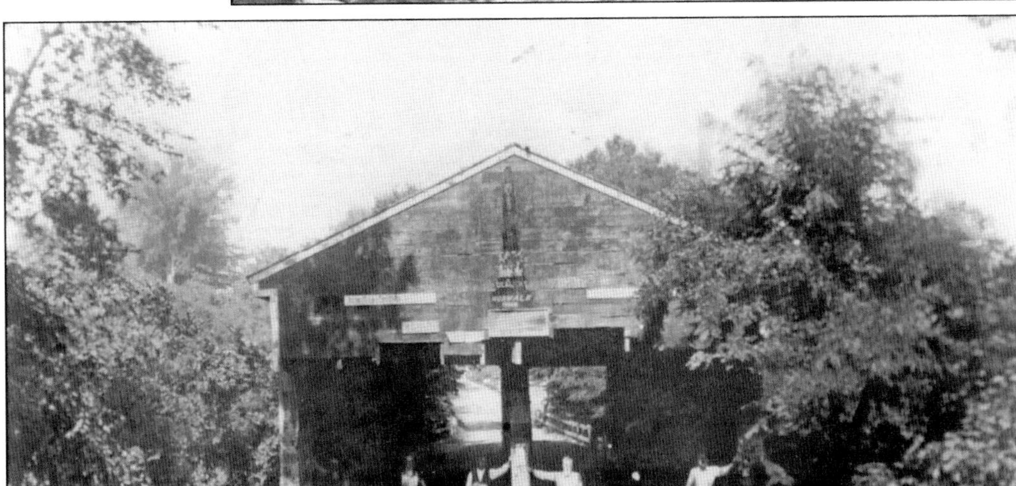

In 1841, Edward and Murari Durand built this covered bridge in Birmingham. It served until an iron bridge replaced it in 1900. Farmers donated the oak for the bridge. (Courtesy of Jason Gargasz.)

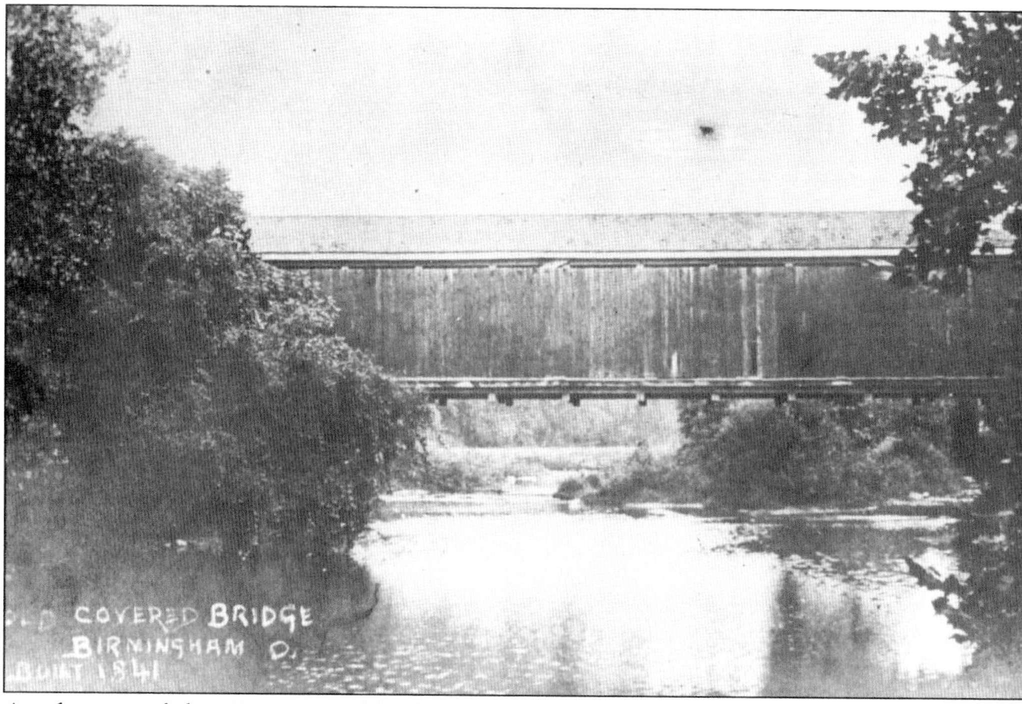

A side view of the 1841 covered bridge in Birmingham shows the river flowing peacefully beneath it. (Courtesy of Jason Gargasz.)

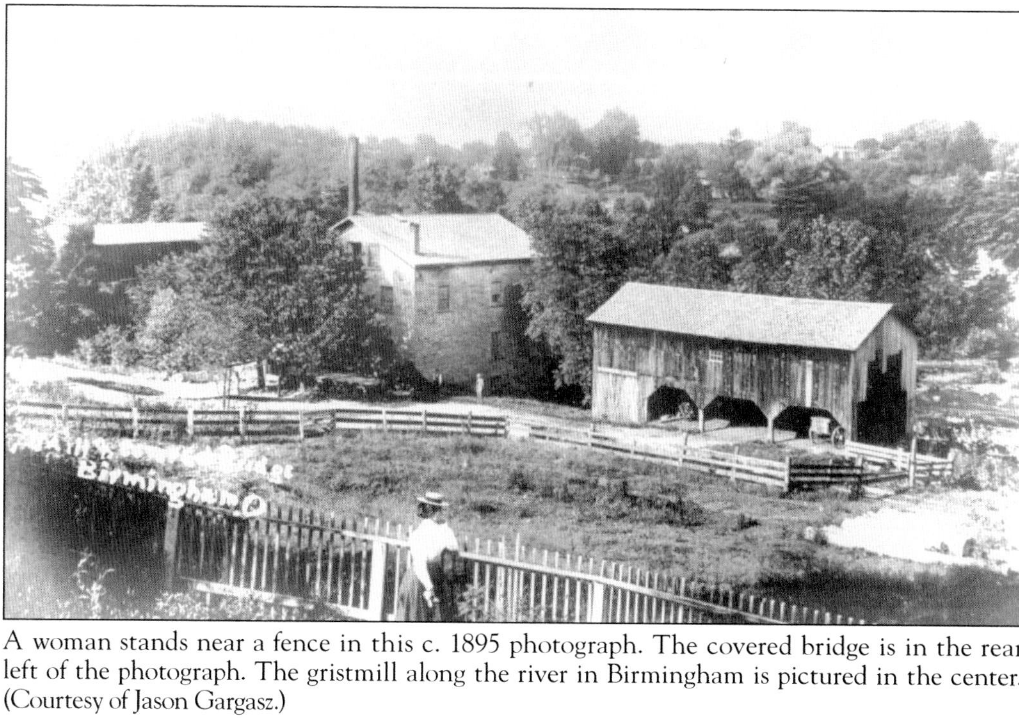

A woman stands near a fence in this c. 1895 photograph. The covered bridge is in the rear left of the photograph. The gristmill along the river in Birmingham is pictured in the center. (Courtesy of Jason Gargasz.)

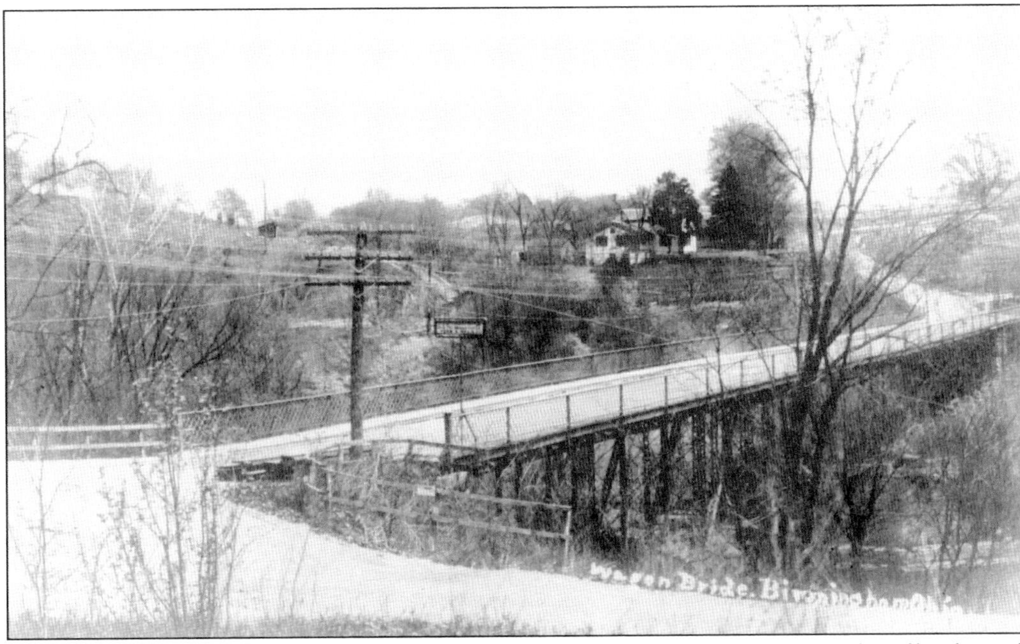

In 1900, an iron bridge replaced the covered wooden one. This bridge carried traffic through Birmingham on the road that is now State Route 113. (Courtesy of Jason Gargasz.)

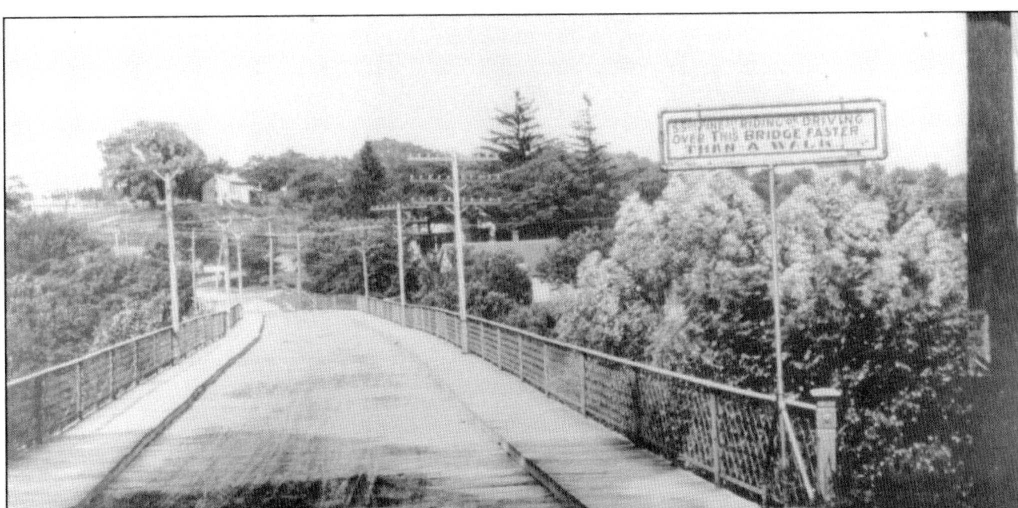

The iron bridge in Birmingham has a curious sign that reads, "$5.00 fine for riding or driving over this bridge faster than a walk." Wooden bridge decking is piled in the foreground of the photograph, perhaps waiting to replace damaged parts of the bridge. (Courtesy of Jason Gargasz.)

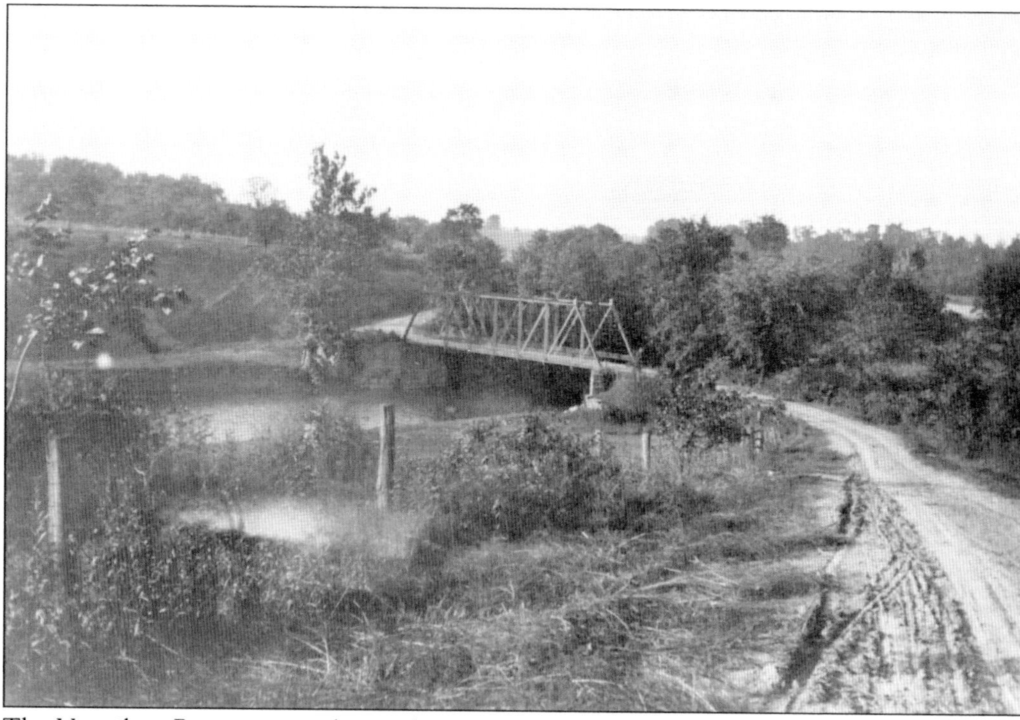

The Vermilion River crosses the road just south of the Village of Birmingham. This c. 1890 photograph shows an iron bridge. This hill is commonly referred to as Terryville Hill, and the road is State Route 60. There have been many bridges over the river at this location, one of them notoriously washed away in a large flood on July 4, 1969. (Courtesy of Jason Gargasz.)

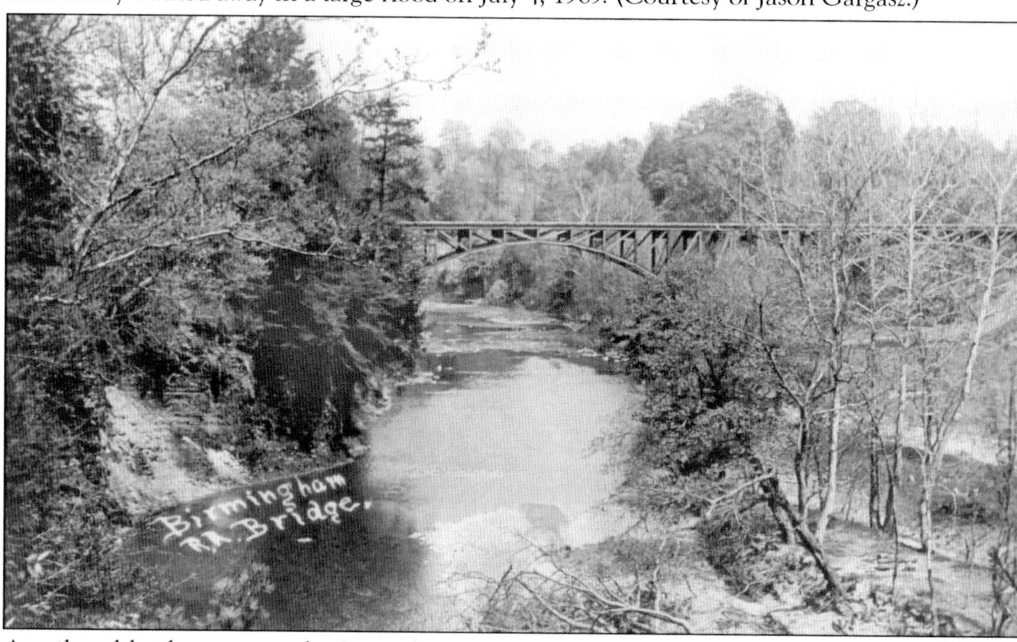

A railroad bridge crosses the Vermilion River on what is now the property of Schoepfle Gardens in Birmingham. The stone foundations are still visible, but the iron trestle was sold for scrap in 1924. (Courtesy of Jason Gargasz.)

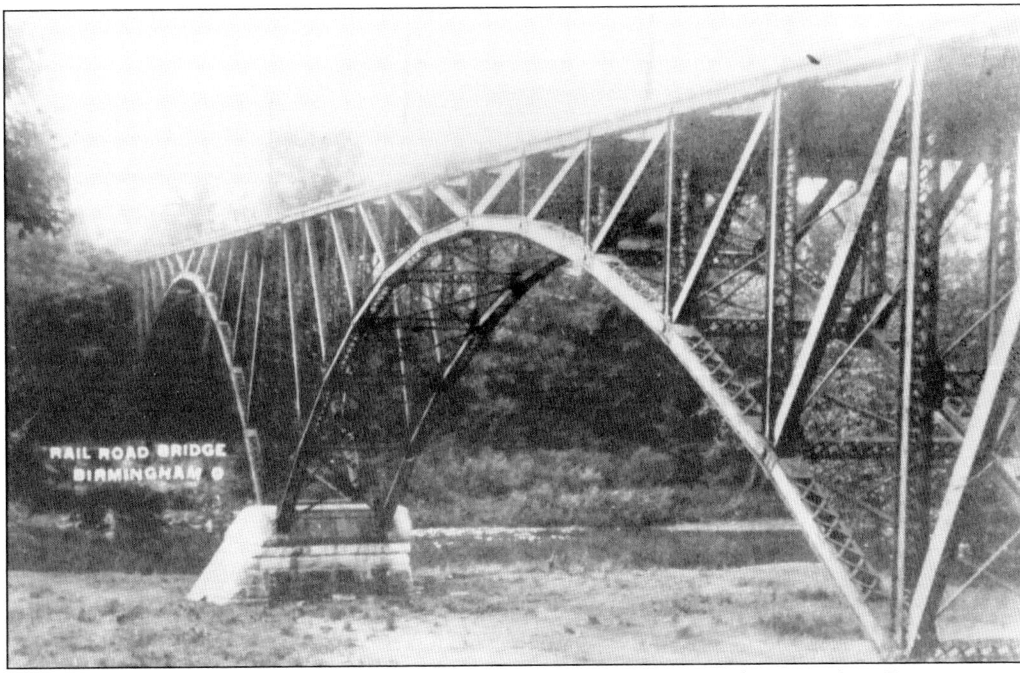

This photograph shows another view of the railroad bridge crossing the Vermilion River to serve passengers in Birmingham. The river under the bridge has a shale bottom and many interesting rock formations. (Courtesy of Jason Gargasz.)

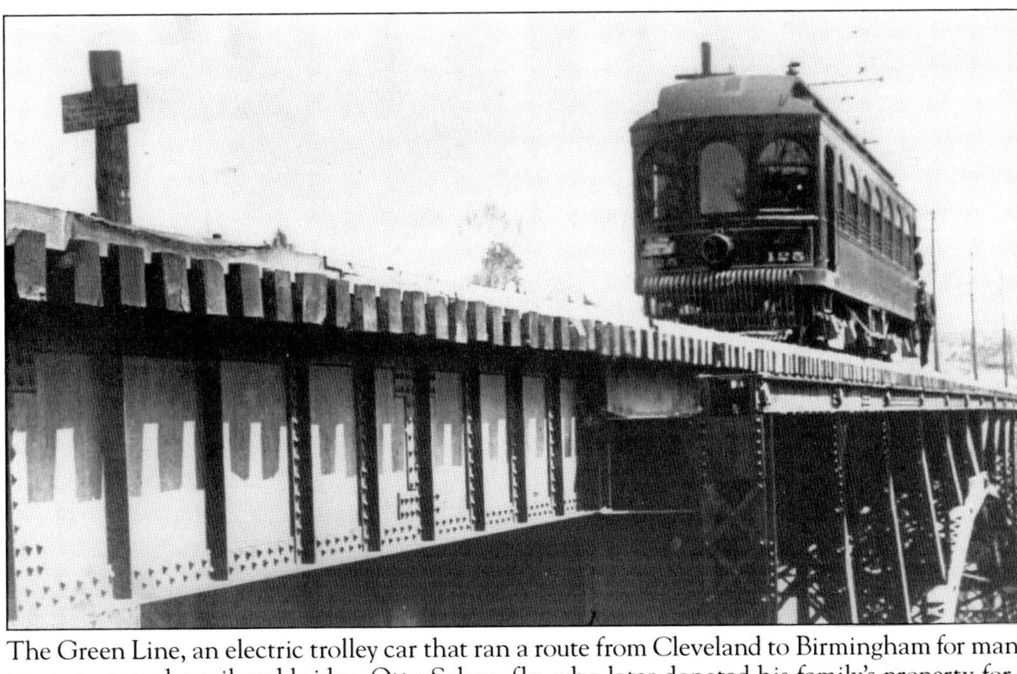

The Green Line, an electric trolley car that ran a route from Cleveland to Birmingham for many years, crosses the railroad bridge. Otto Schoepfle, who later donated his family's property for a public garden and park, used the Green Line to travel to his grandparents' home for a visit when he was a young boy. (Courtesy of Jason Gargasz.)

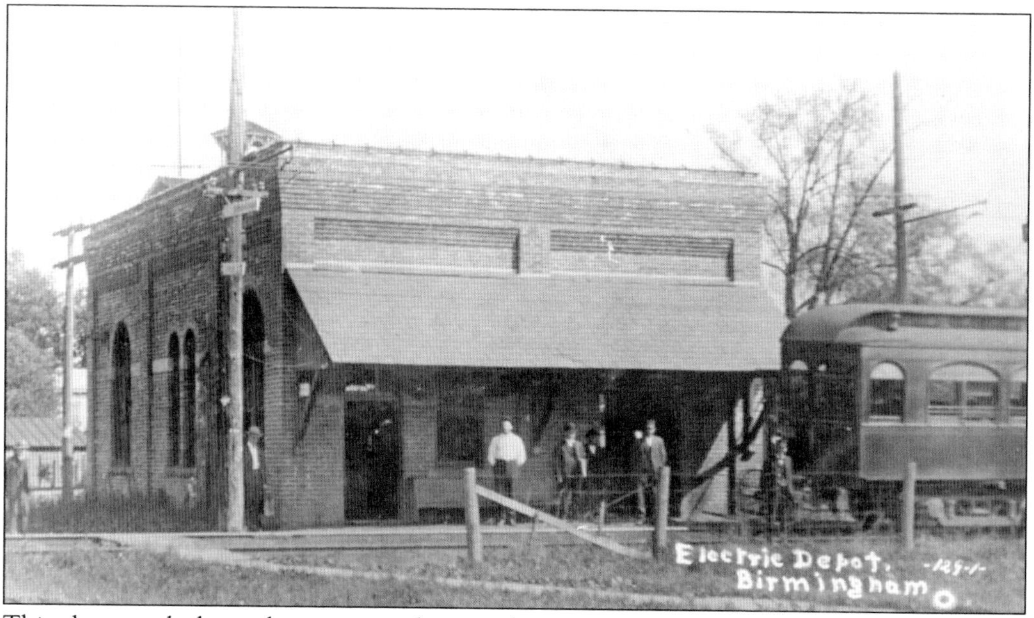

This photograph shows the passenger depot and waiting area for the Green Line electric trolley in Birmingham. (Courtesy of Jason Gargasz.)

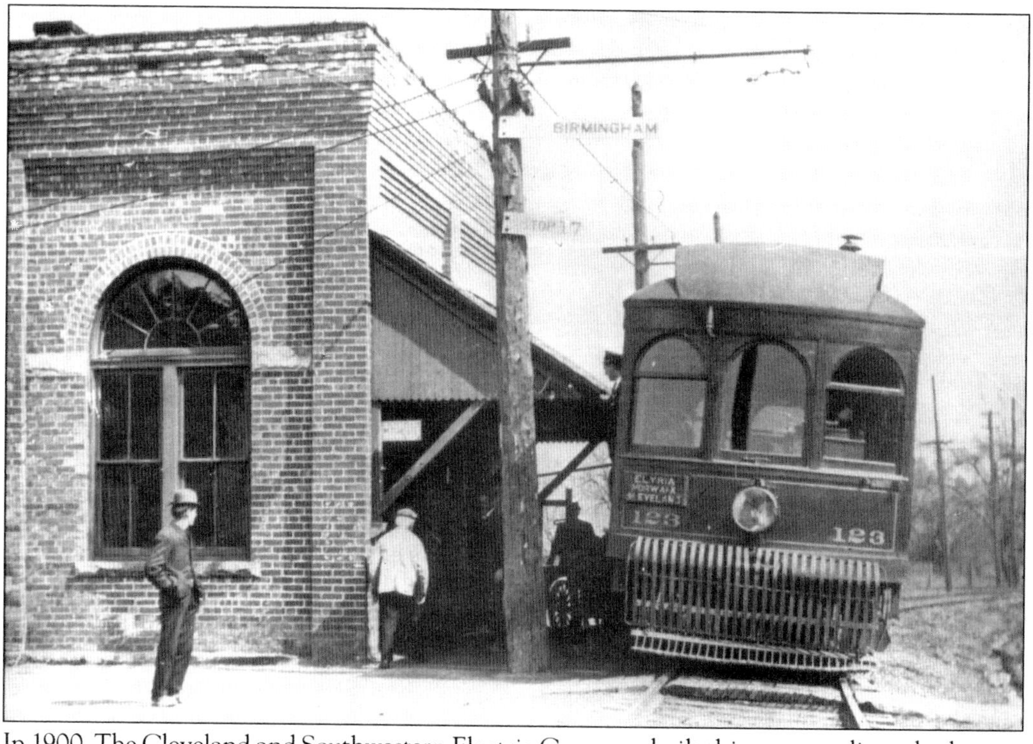

In 1900, The Cleveland and Southwestern Electric Company built this streetcar line, also known as the Green Line, through Birmingham. The brick depot and waiting room (pictured) was on Third Street. The streetcar operated until it went bankrupt in 1920, put out of business by the automobile. Note the signs that say "Birmingham, Stop 17." The streetcar traveled from Cleveland to Elyria to Norwalk, Ohio. (Courtesy of Jason Gargasz.)

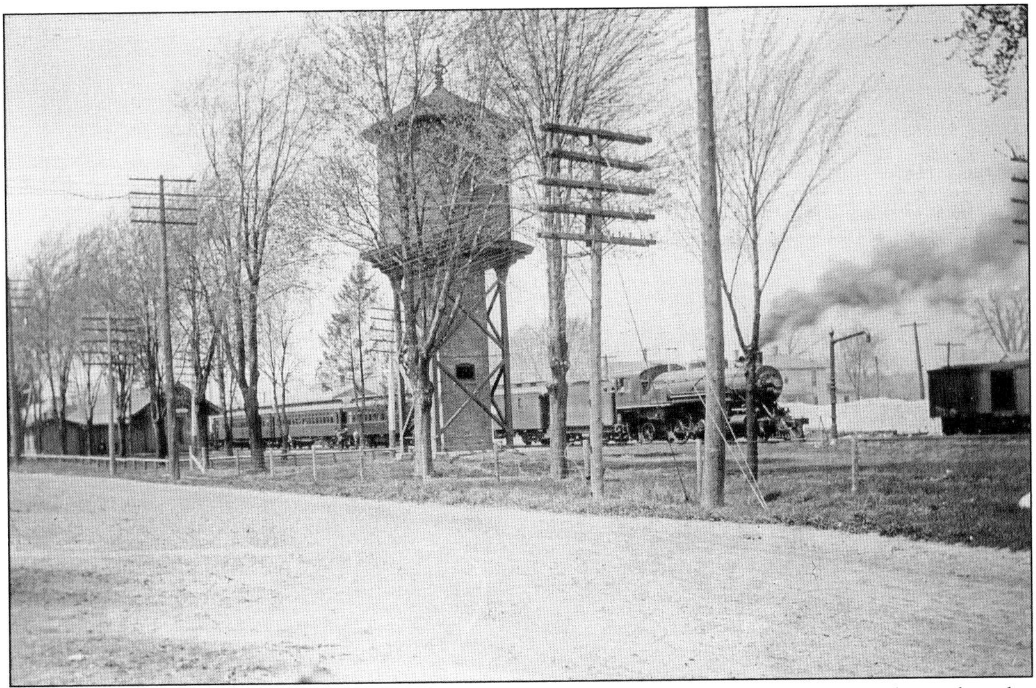

A steam train passes the depot and brick water tower in downtown Wakeman. Telegraph poles line the tracks. The depot was a busy place. Every day for many years, seven passenger trains went through town.

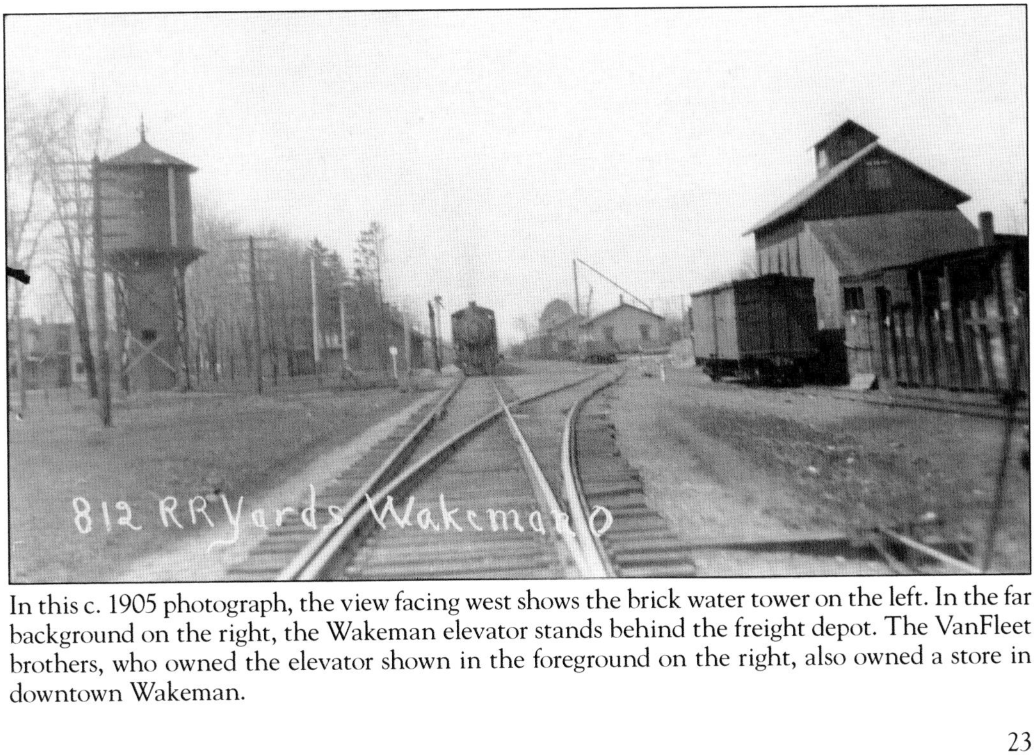

In this c. 1905 photograph, the view facing west shows the brick water tower on the left. In the far background on the right, the Wakeman elevator stands behind the freight depot. The VanFleet brothers, who owned the elevator shown in the foreground on the right, also owned a store in downtown Wakeman.

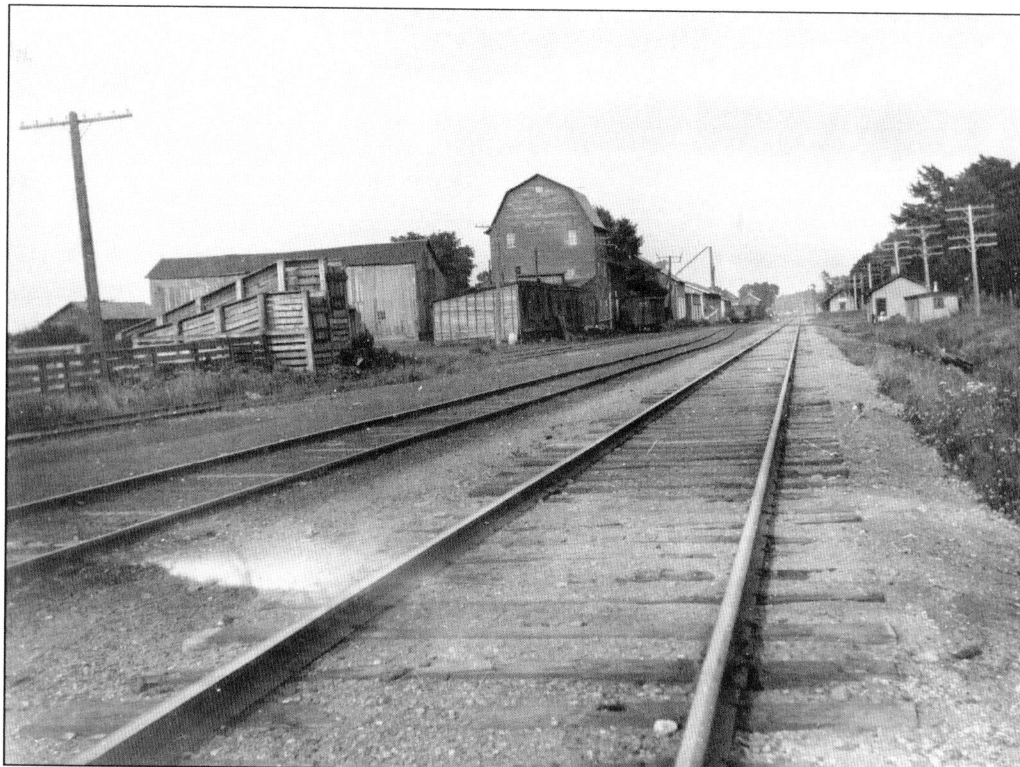

This view facing east shows the Wakeman elevator and its rail sidings on the left. The tracks stretch far ahead, taking passengers across the Vermilion River and on to Cleveland.

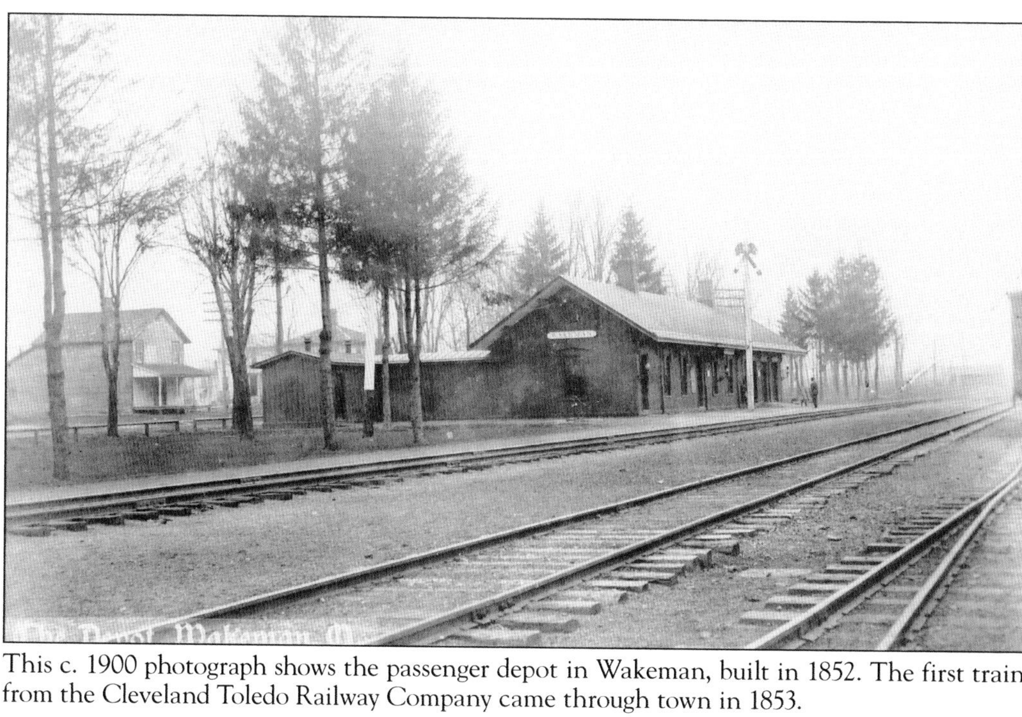

This c. 1900 photograph shows the passenger depot in Wakeman, built in 1852. The first train from the Cleveland Toledo Railway Company came through town in 1853.

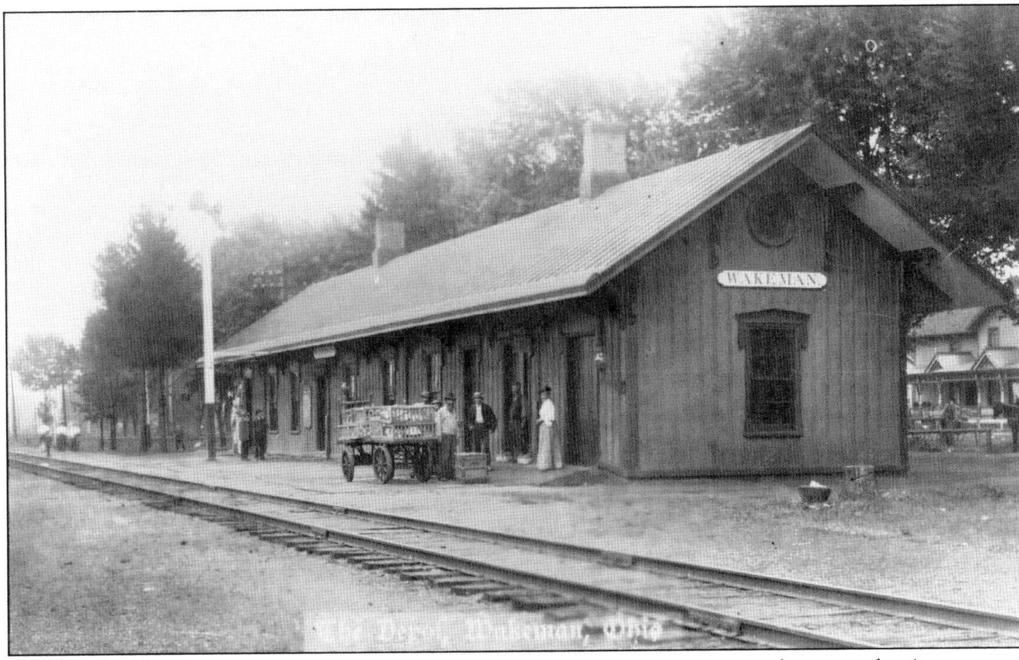

People were not the only passengers using the depot in this c. 1900 photograph. A wagon of chickens, owned by Ab Todd, sits outside the station. He was also known as "Chicken Todd" and used the railroad to ship his chickens.

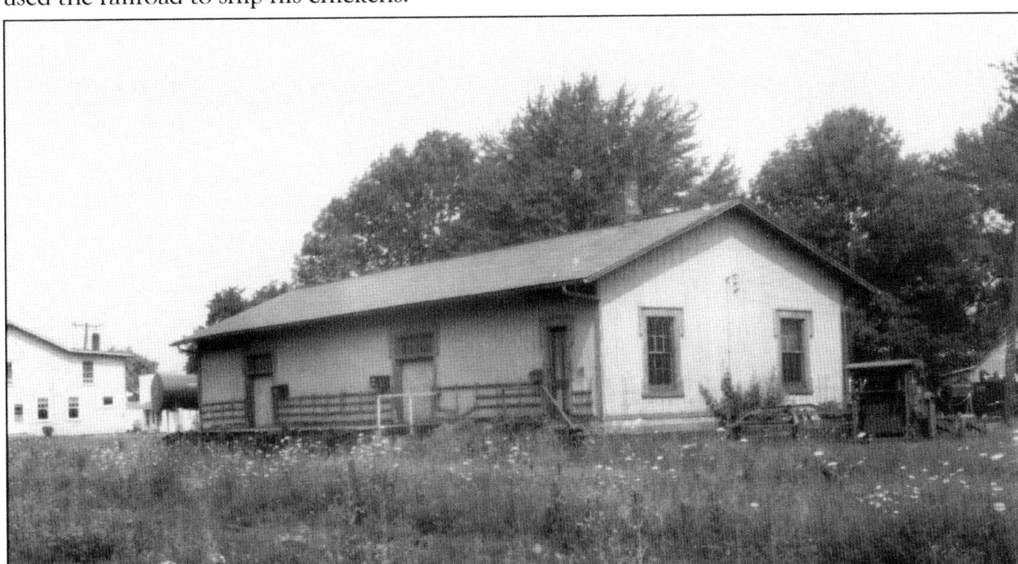
This c. 1950 close-up view of the freight depot in Wakeman shows weeds growing up through unused siding. The depot is located just north of the railroad tracks and still stands. It has had many owners and uses over the years.

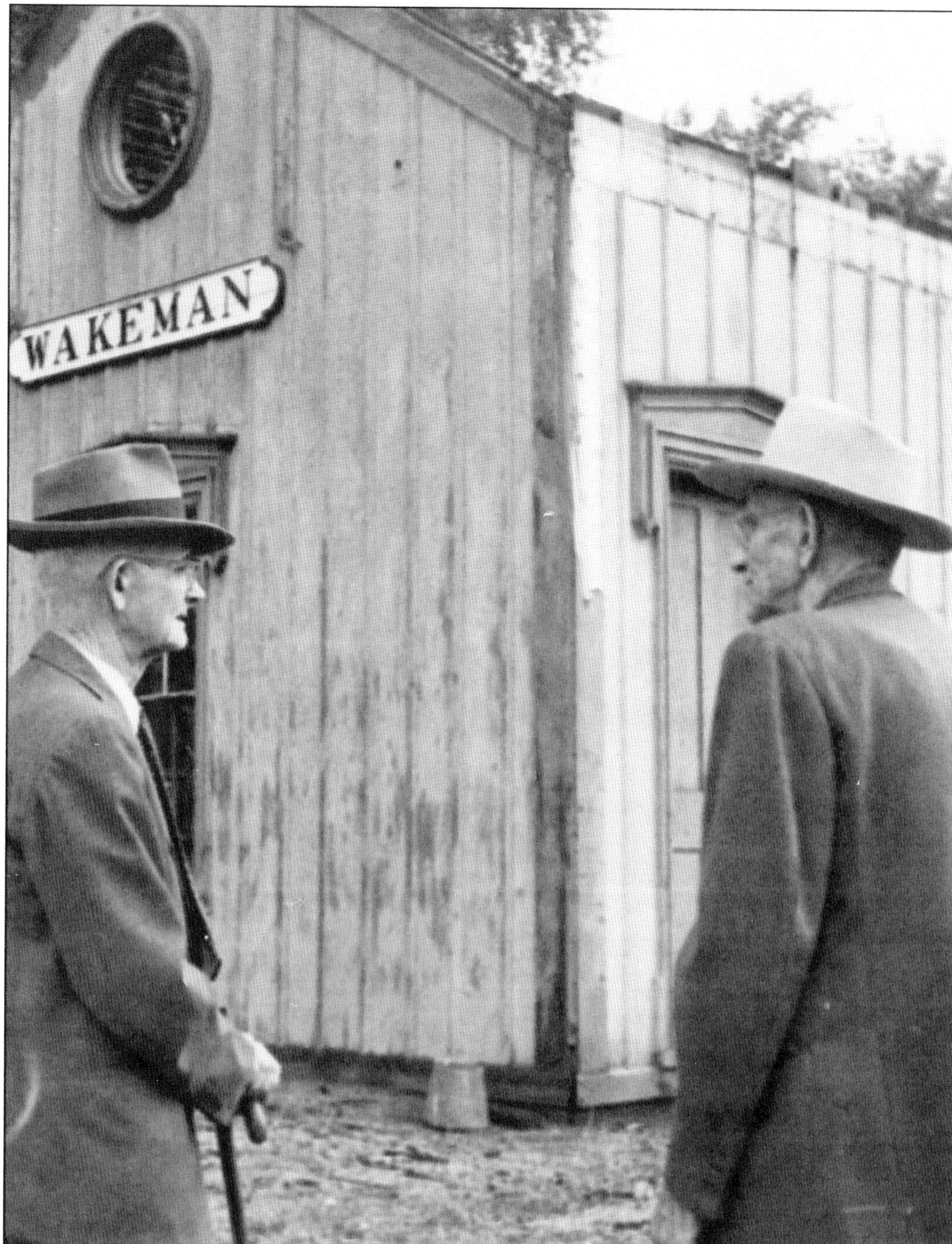

The passenger depot in Wakeman was built in 1852 and stood for more than 100 years. In 1956, the building was dismantled and some of its timbers were used in other projects. Two local residents visited the site daily to watch the depot being torn down. On the left is Carl Ketchum, who was the station agent for more than 30 years. F.A. Denman, a local historian and lifelong resident of Wakeman, is on the right. In his diary entry dated June 8, 1956, Denman wrote, "Earl E. Smith from 424 Williams Street in Huron bought the old passenger depot and is taking it down and selling the lumber and some relics." He mentions the depot in many entries, adding that he talked with Mr. Smith or Mr. Ketchum. On June 23, 1956, he notes, "The old depot was nearly all down this forenoon."

Two

FARMS AND FARMERS

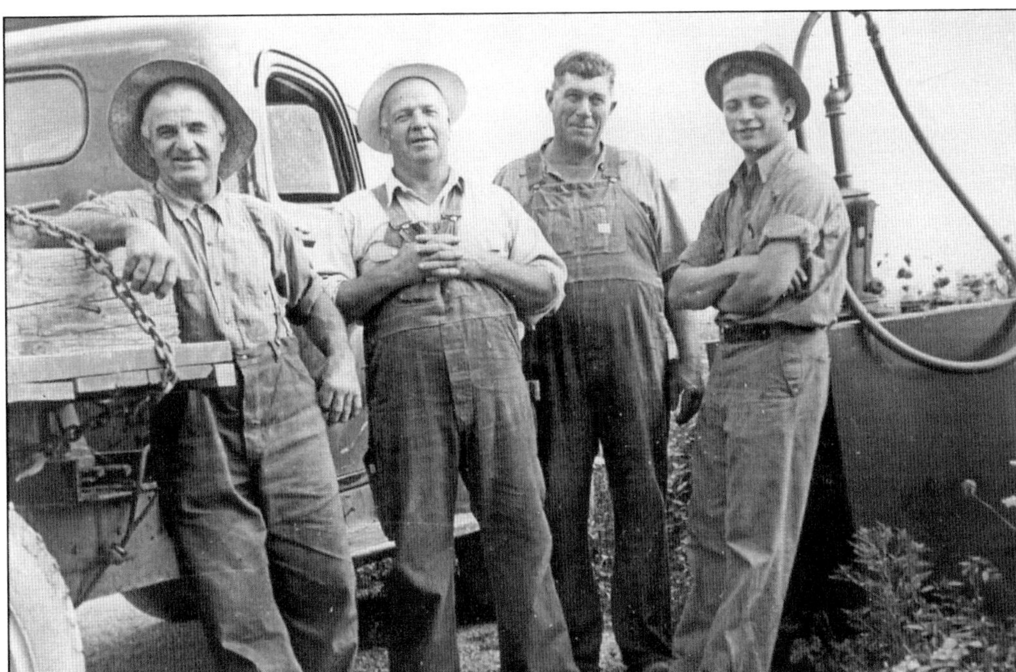

Farmers standing by their truck are, from left to right, Art Flew, J.C. (James) Parsons, Fred Arnett, and J.R. (Richard) Parsons. In addition to being a farmer, James Parsons was a member of the school board when the 1937 WPA project school was built. When a new school was built years later, in 1963, he planted the lawn for the new building. He was also a local legend as a mover of houses and barns. Richard Parsons, his son, served in World War II. This photograph was taken shortly after the war.

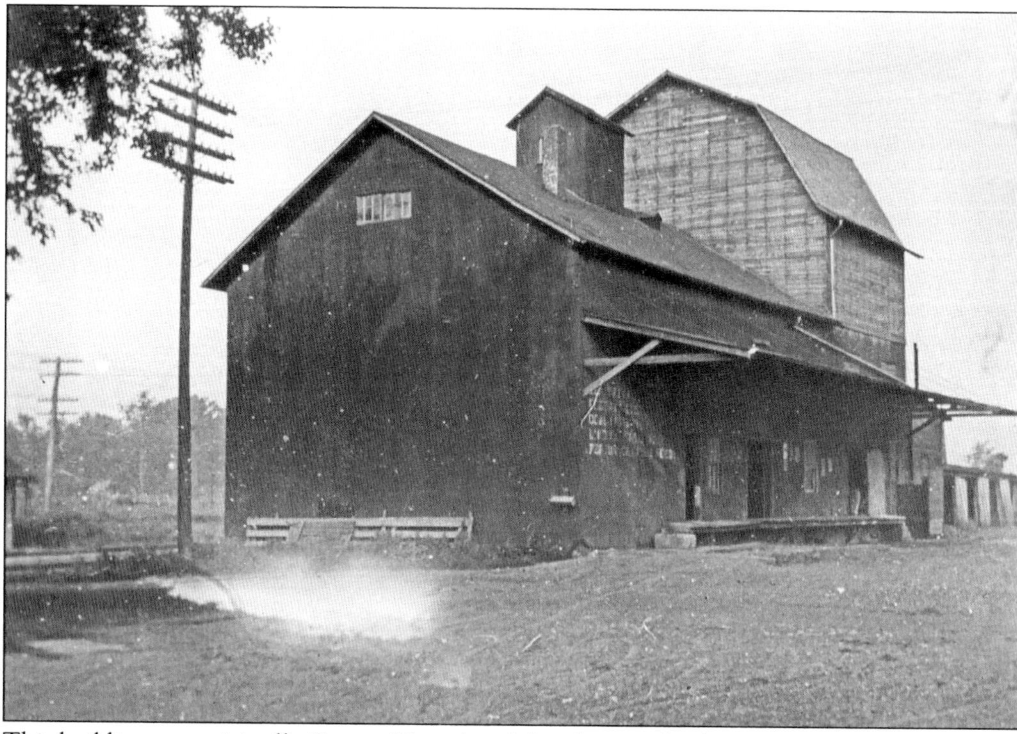

This building was originally George Humphrey's bending works, but F.A. Denman converted it to a flour mill in 1900. It served the community by grinding feed until it burned in 1918. The fire was considered suspicious because when it burned, the brothers who owned this mill also owned another mill that burned down the same year.

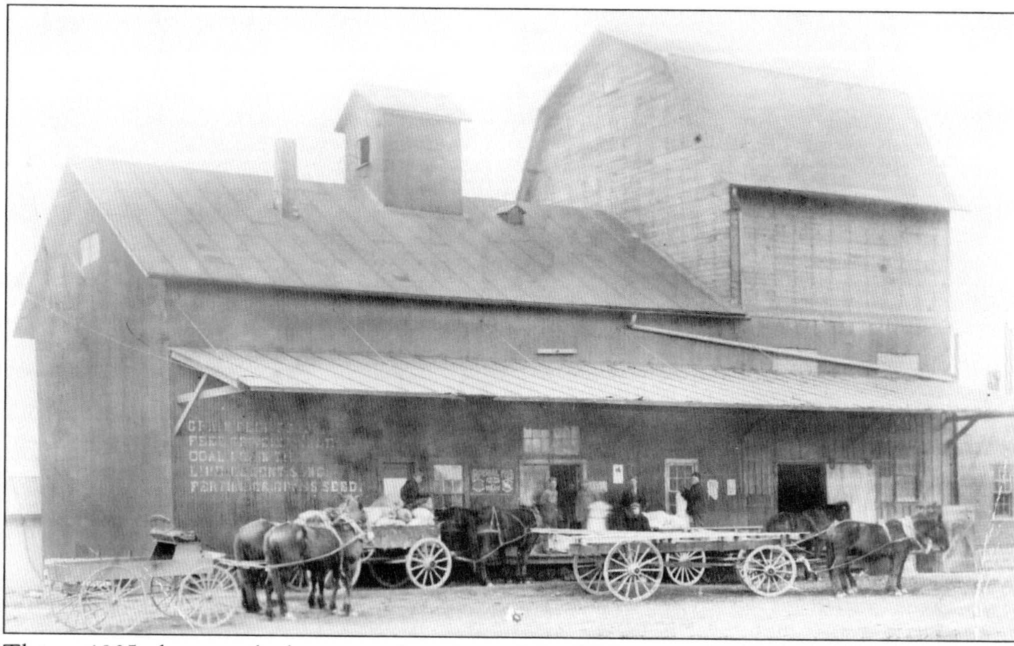

This c. 1905 photograph shows another view of the Wakeman elevator with farmers lined up with wagons and sacks of grain.

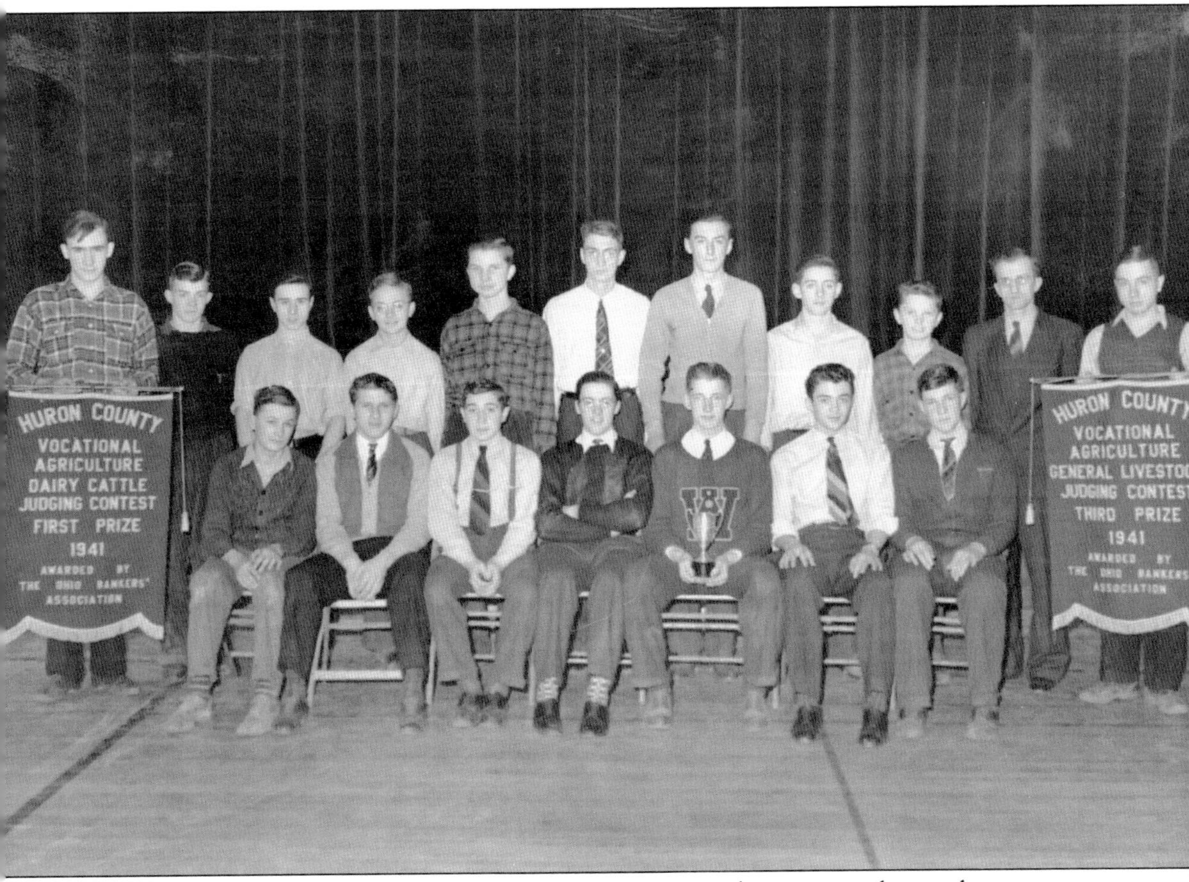

An important element of building a farming community is the vocational agriculture program at the school, commonly known as the Future Farmers of America. In this 1941 photograph, the team is shown with its first-place and third-place banners from the county fair. From left to right are (first row) Robert Stewart, Howard Stacker, Donald Butler, Walter Tuttle, Richard Green, Bill Davis, and Floyd Garner; (second row) Harold Divers, Bill Welch, Oscar Kinat, Richard French, Zygmont Gawron, Lynn Green, Ken Waldron, A. Ward, Ed Gawron, Mr. Bachelder, and Don Worcester. Interestingly, both of the boys holding the banners farmed, drove the school bus, and worked for the local farm implement dealership, Graves Implement, for many years.

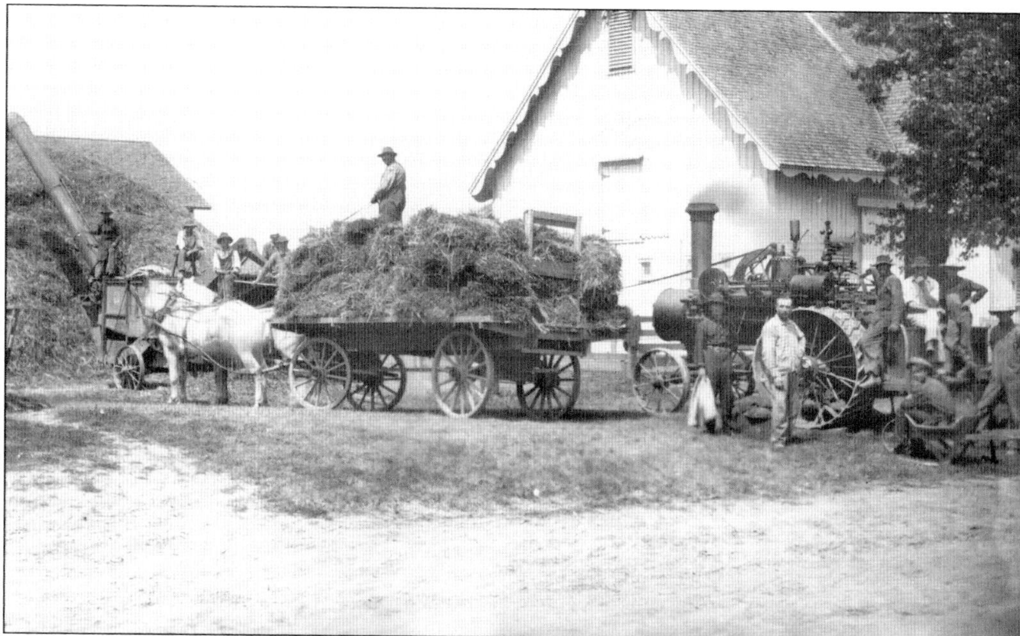

Farmers thresh wheat using a steam tractor on the Loretz farm, around 1895. The barn in the background burned in 1951. It is now the home of the Sean Nolan family.

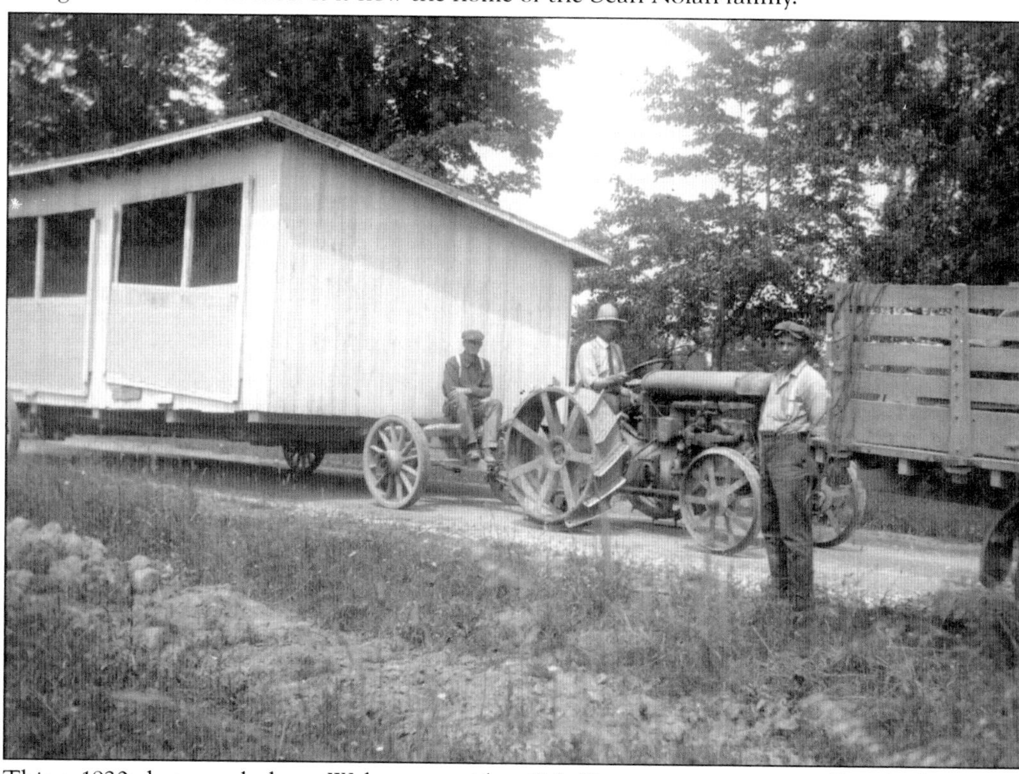

This c. 1920 photograph shows Wakeman resident F.A. Denman moving one of his chicken coops with a Fordson tractor. Seated on the trailer is Vern Johns, and Bryant Pettiford is standing. It is unknown why F.A. was moving his chicken coop.

Pictured around 1940, farmer James Parsons drives a steel-wheeled Farmall H down the road. Rubber tires were rationed during World War II, which may explain why this tractor has steel wheels.

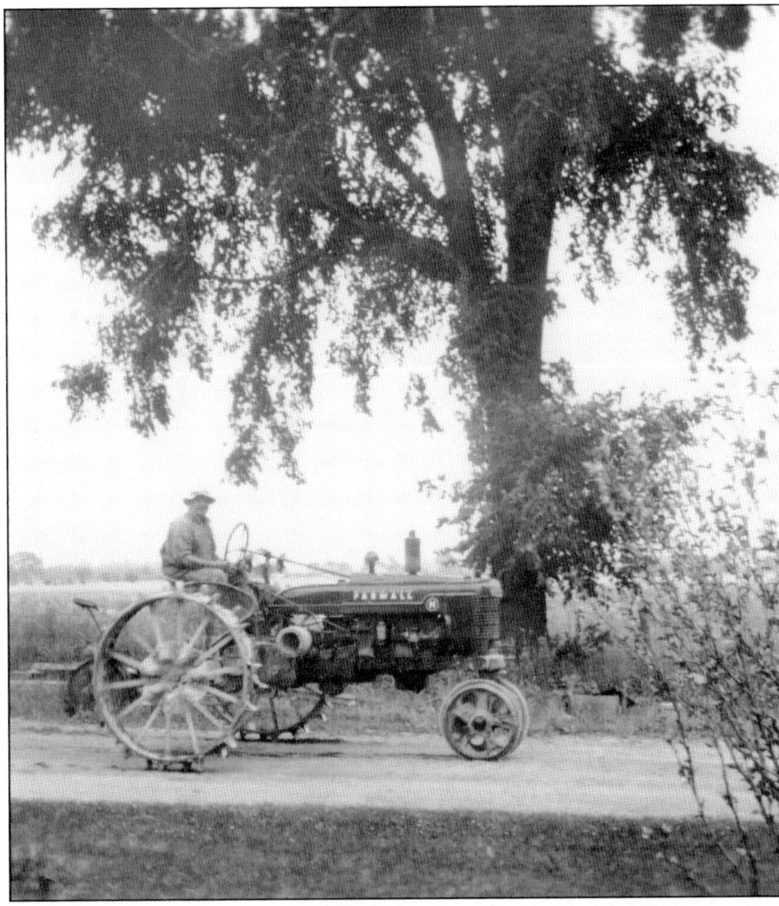

Charles Parsons, below (father of James Parsons, pictured right), sits on his horse-drawn wagon at his family farm west of Wakeman. A split-rail fence is behind him, and his left hand rests upon a basket used for gathering produce.

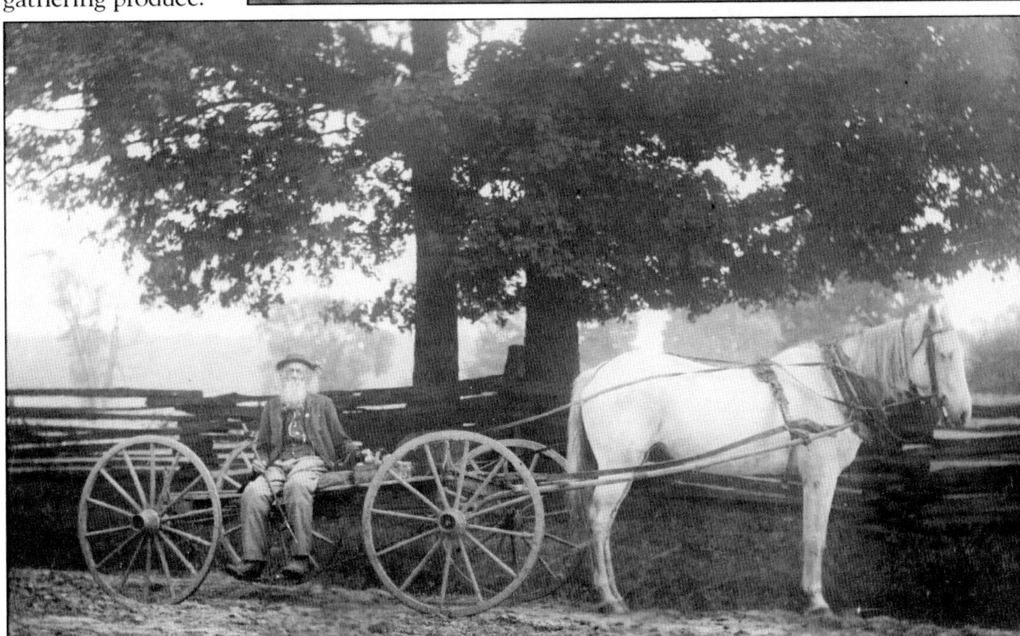

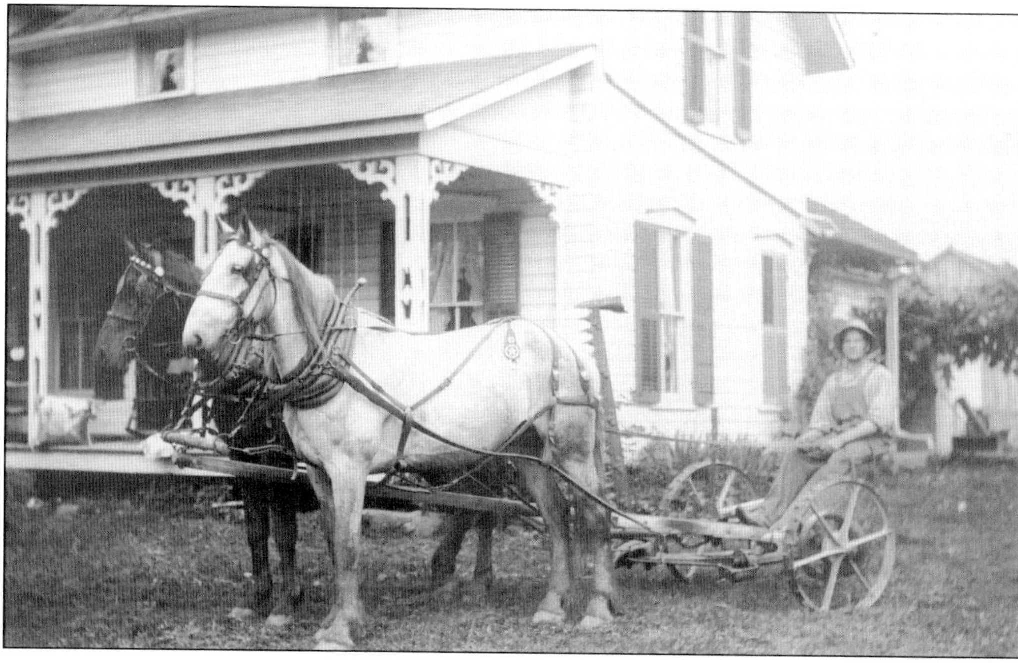

These two photographs, probably taken between 1900 and 1910, show the Parsons farm. Rose, a teacher in a one-room schoolhouse, is pictured below with a horse and dog. Her husband, James, is pictured above on a horse-drawn mower behind horses identified as Ben and Prince. James Parsons farmed and was also locally known for moving houses. Later, he had a horse named "Arnry Jim," who quit for lunch at 11:30 every day, whether his owner wanted him to or not.

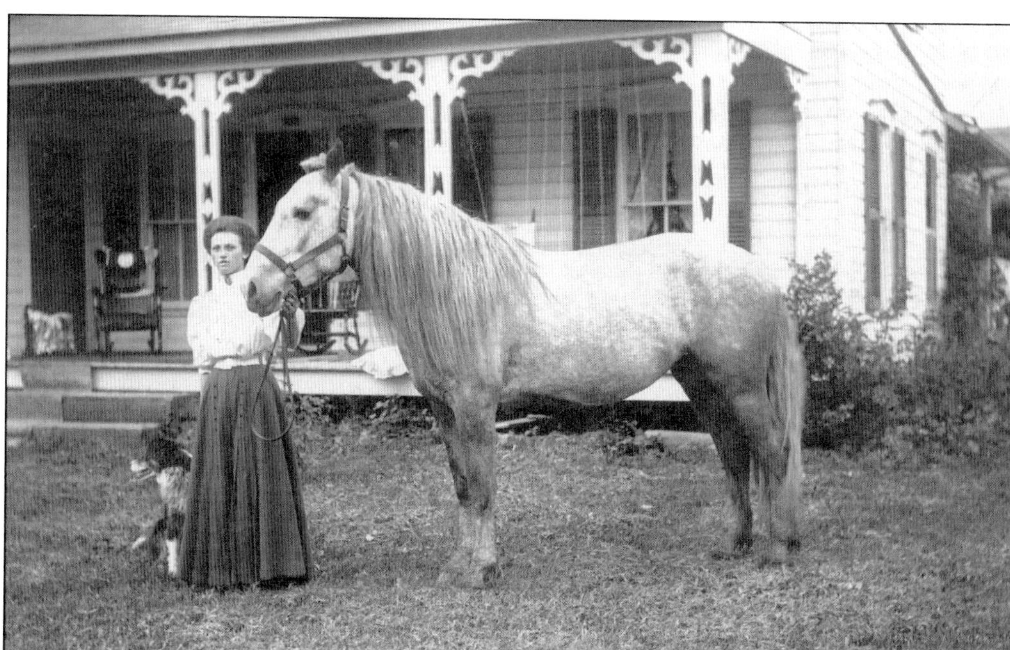

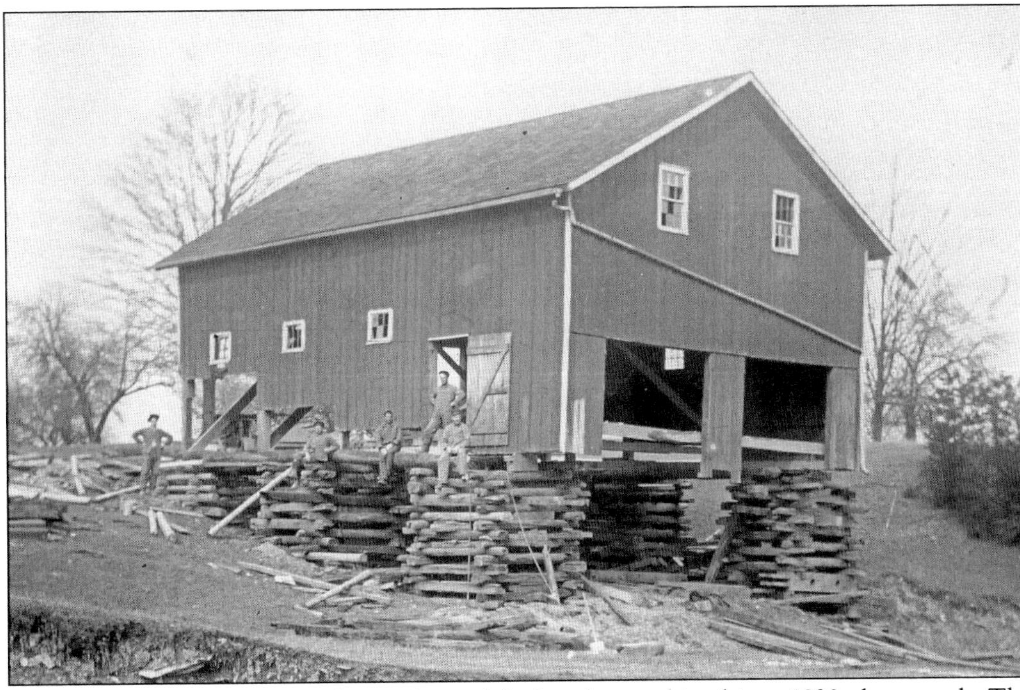

A barn owned by Bernie Haskins is being lifted and moved in this c. 1930 photograph. The Haskins farm was on West River Road north of Wakeman. The owner wanted this section of the barn to connect with another barn on his property. The altered barn still stands.

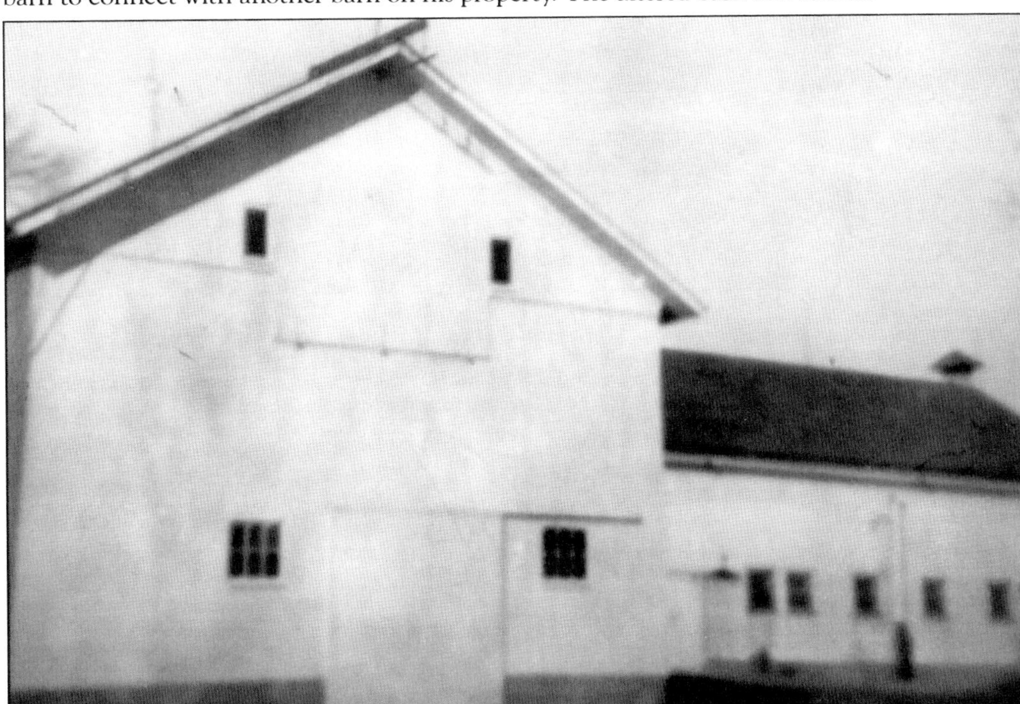

This 1950 photograph shows the section of barn that was moved two decades earlier. The farm is now the property of Elmer Dalton.

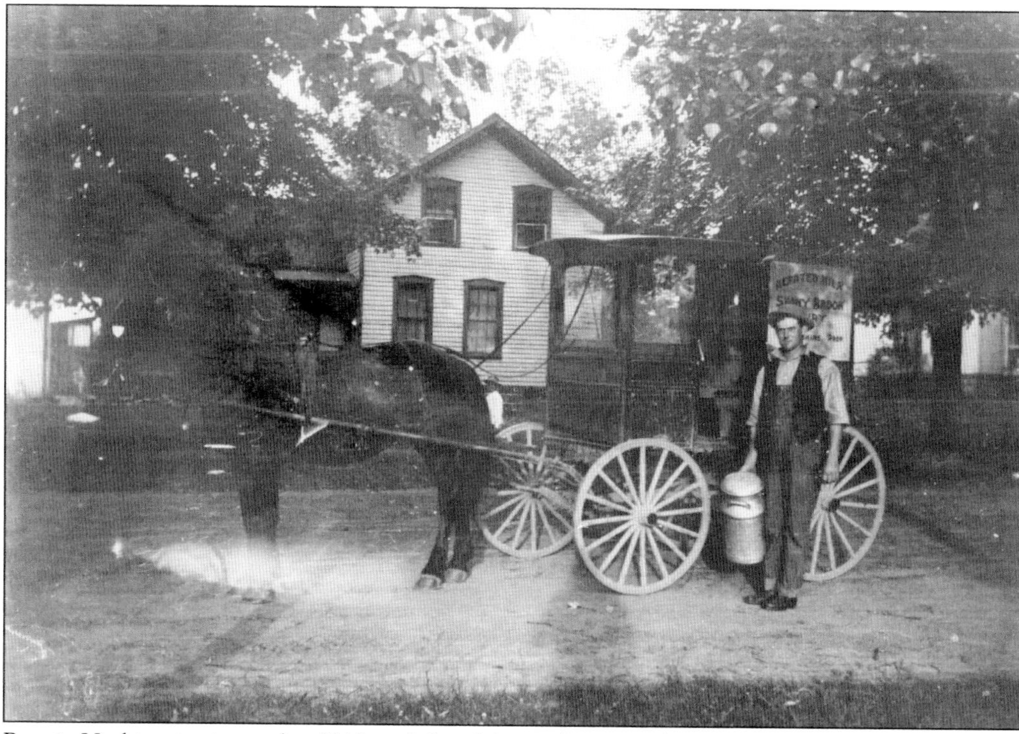

Bernie Haskins is pictured c. 1915 with his delivery horse and milk wagon. Wakeman residents hung buckets in their front yards every day to be filled with milk. On one occasion around the time of this photograph, the National Guard was encamped in town, and residents were surprised to find that all their buckets had been drained by thirsty soldiers.

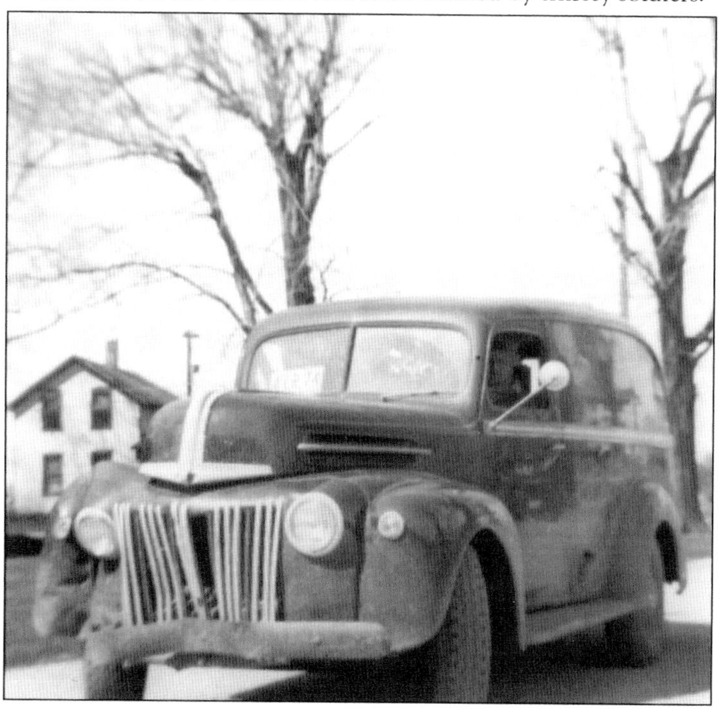

The Dalton family purchased the Haskins' dairy farm and continued to deliver milk in Wakeman. Bill Dalton and his delivery truck are shown in this c. 1940 photograph. Bill Dalton was reputed to know every front porch in town.

Platt Henry Beecher had a farm on Route 60 north of Wakeman and a route selling eggs and produce in town. Sadly, his horse failed him one day when it suddenly lay down and died. He reportedly commented, "Well, it's the first time she ever did that." He is pictured on his farm with his dog in this c. 1920 photograph.

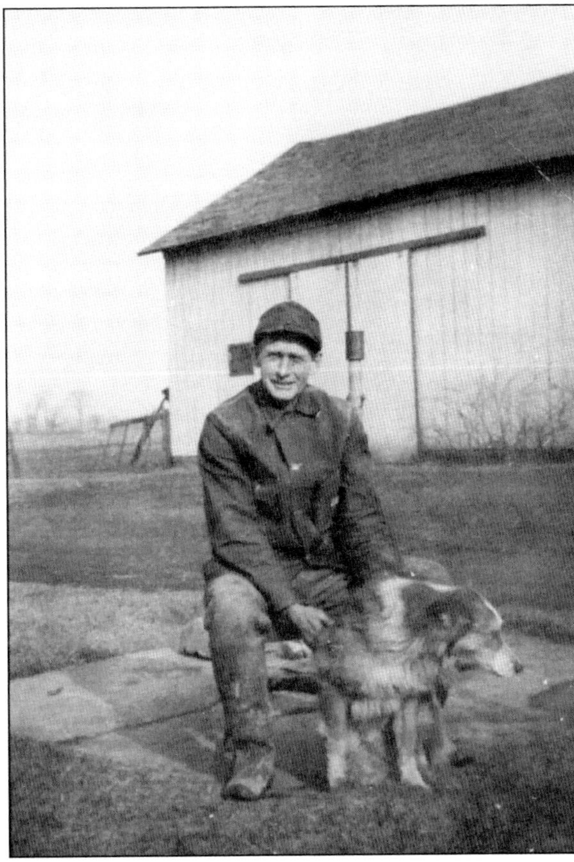

A 1954 Farmall C tractor is being used to demonstrate a fast hitch on the farm of Les Coy. Pictured from left to right are George Parker, Les Coy, ? Vanderbosch, Don Crow, unidentified, Edward Pippert, Jess Worthington, and Fred Graves.

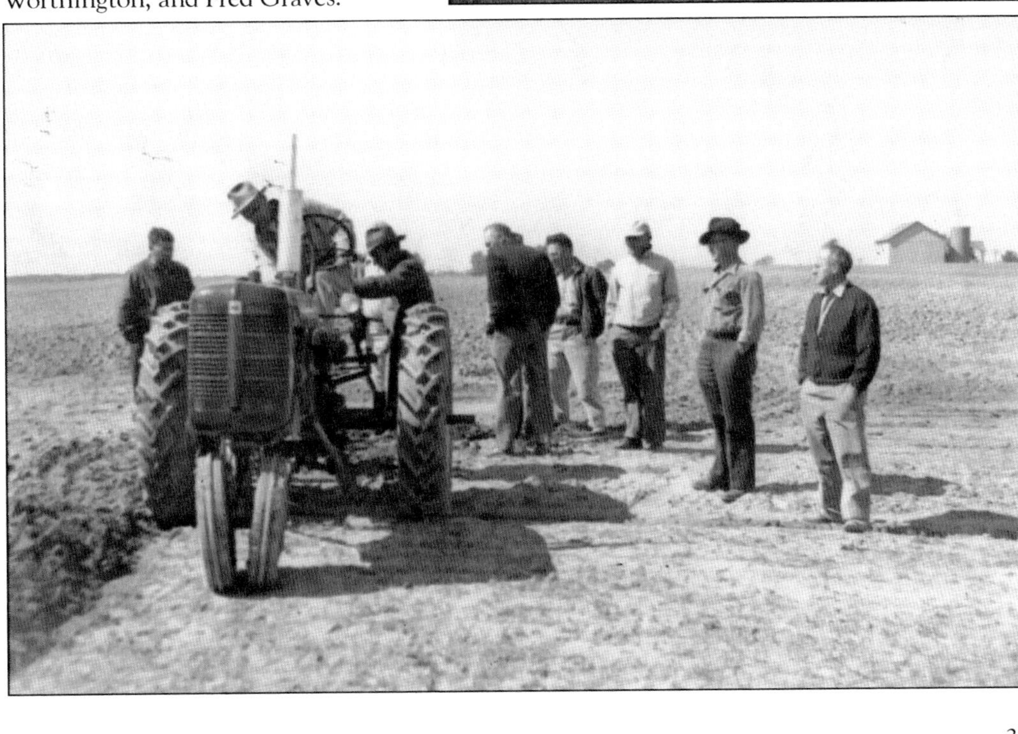

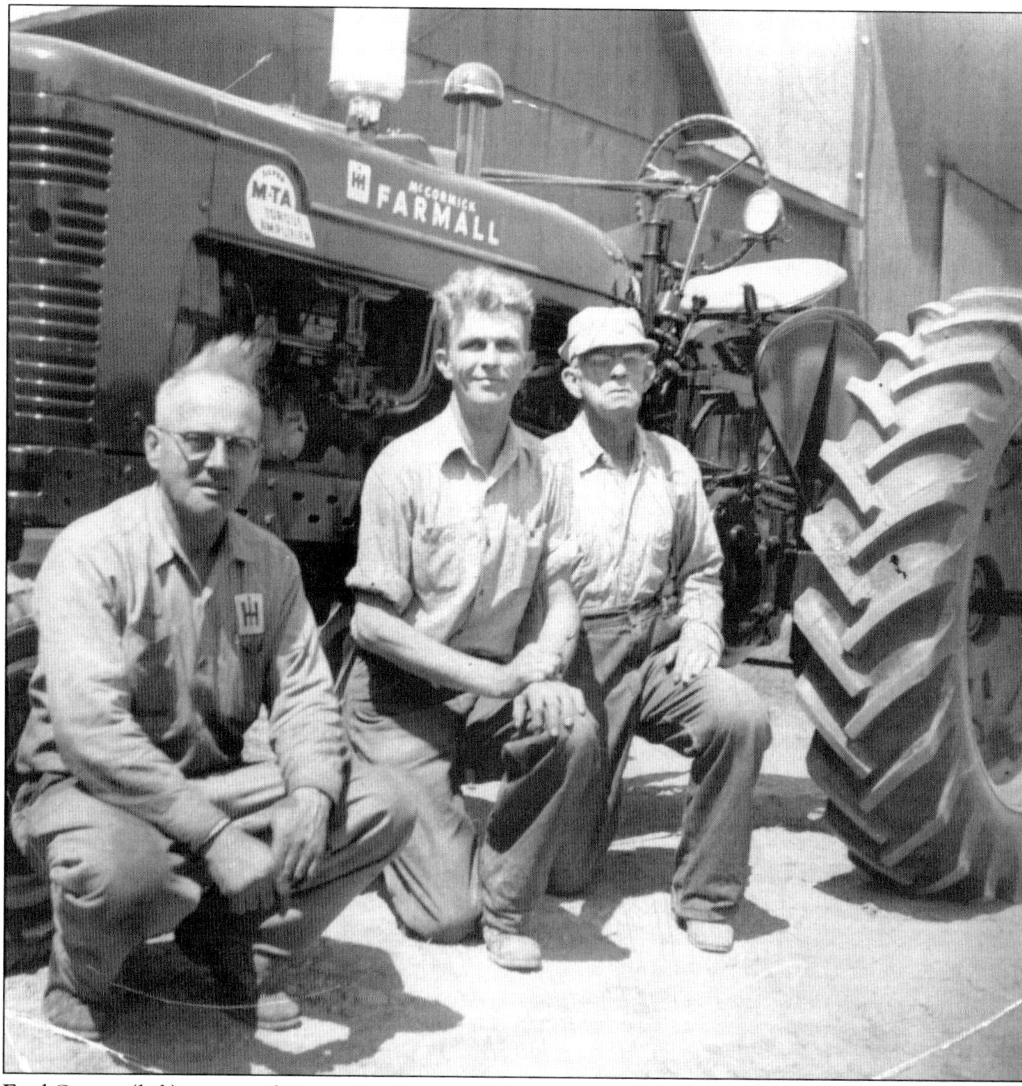

Fred Graves (left), owner of Graves Implement, delivers a new 1954 Farmall Super M-TA to customers Forrest and Earl Fletcher. Forrest Fletcher (center) became mayor of Wakeman in later years. Fred Graves opened the business selling International Harvester tractors in 1936, and his son took over the business in 1969. It remains in the same location on Pleasant Street in Wakeman.

Three

People of Interest

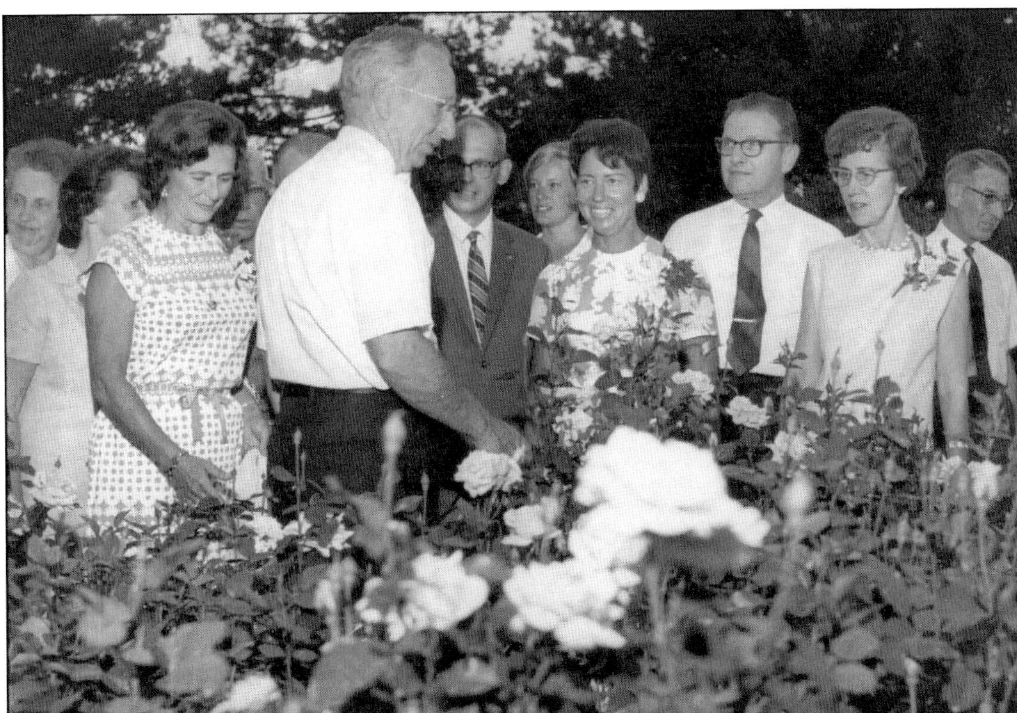

Birmingham resident Otto Schoepfle gives a group tour of his gardens in the 1960s. Schoepfle (1910–1992) was the chief executive officer of a local paper, the *Elyria Chronicle Telegram*, for many years. The gardens are on property that used to be owned by Schoepfle's grandparents, and when he purchased the property in 1936, he demonstrated his research and knowledge of plants by cultivating formal gardens. He donated the gardens to the Lorain County Metroparks in 1969. The Vermilion River borders one side of the 70-acre garden. (Courtesy of Jason Gargasz.)

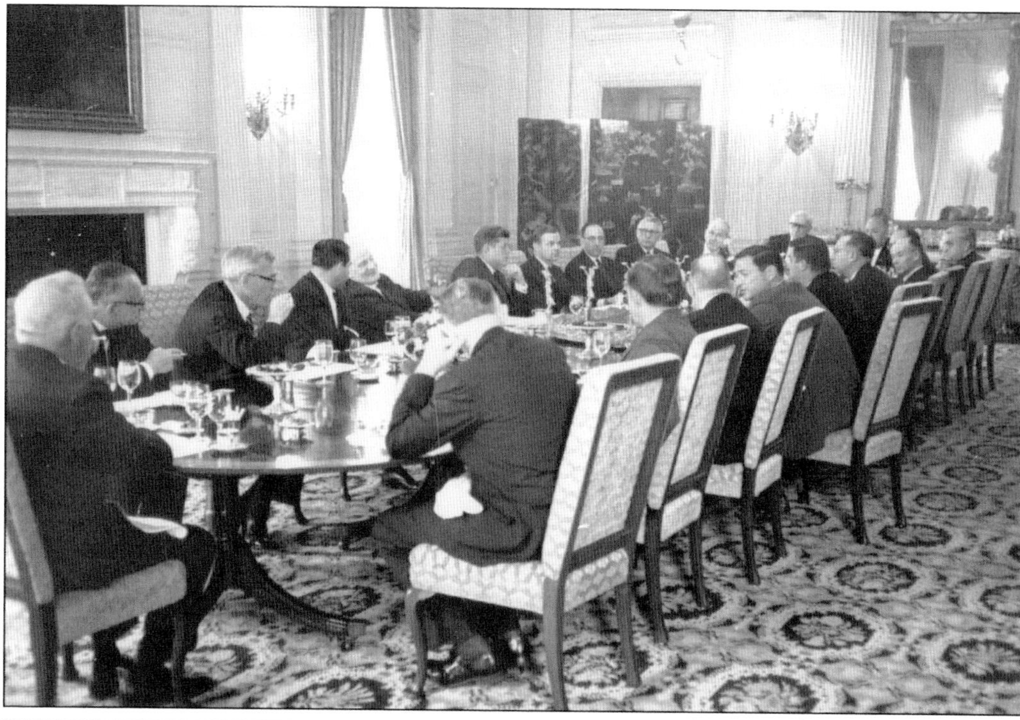

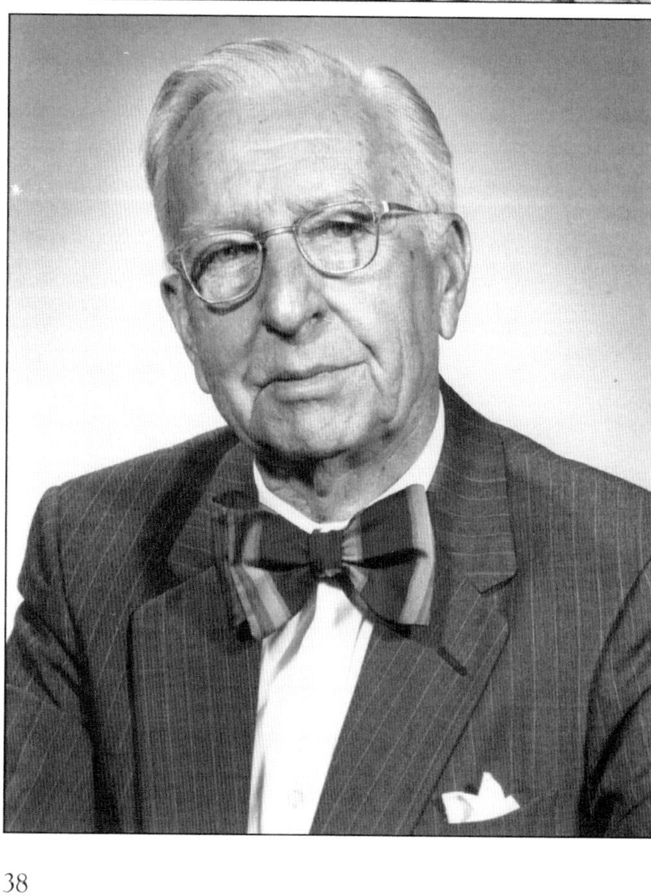

In November 1963, a group of newspaper editors was invited to the White House to meet with President Kennedy. Otto Schoepfle is pictured seated directly across from the president. (Courtesy of Jason Gargasz.)

This formal portrait of Otto Schoepfle was taken during the 1960s. His dedication to the community through his work with the newspaper and the donation of his family's land is an important part of Birmingham's history. (Courtesy of Jason Gargasz.)

Dr. C.J. Cranston was a World War I veteran who reenlisted and served as a physician in World War II. He was in Pearl Harbor, Hawaii, the day it was bombed. More importantly to Wakeman, Ohio, he was the town doctor. Ironically, he delivered a baby when he first came to town and then died on the living room floor of that same house many years later.

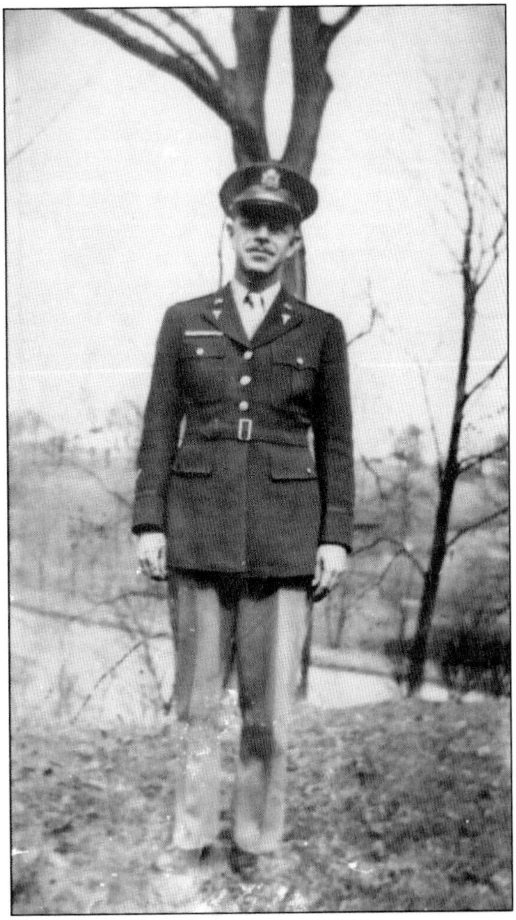

Wakeman resident Bill Pease is pictured with the Vermilion River in the background. He loved the town and the river, and was a friend to everyone. People often sought his advice and counsel. When he died, his funeral was held in the Wakeman Congregational Church. Organist Blaine Hurst played "Home on the Range" as a final request.

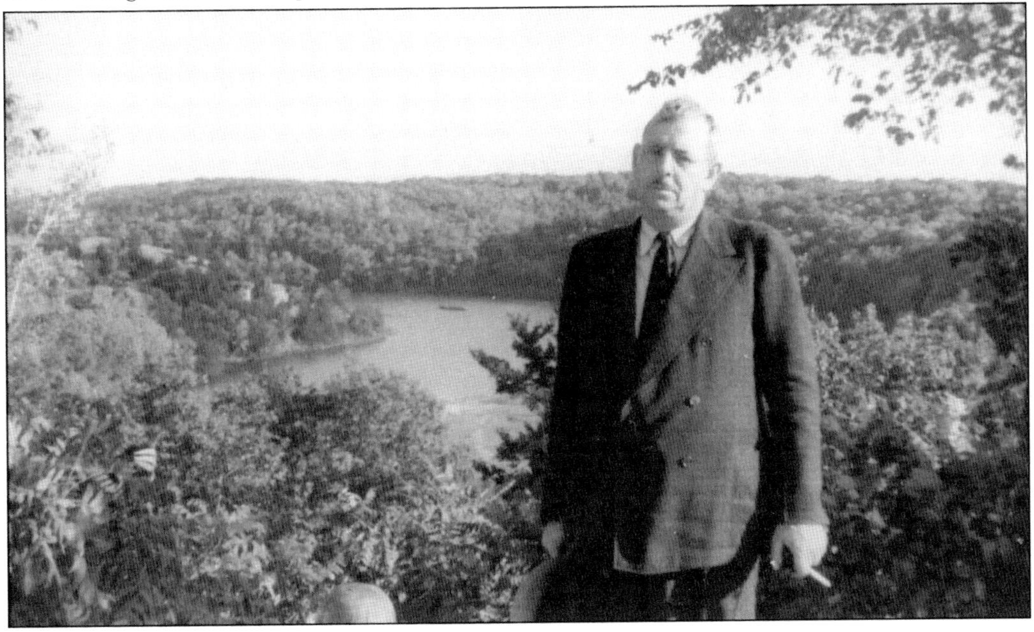

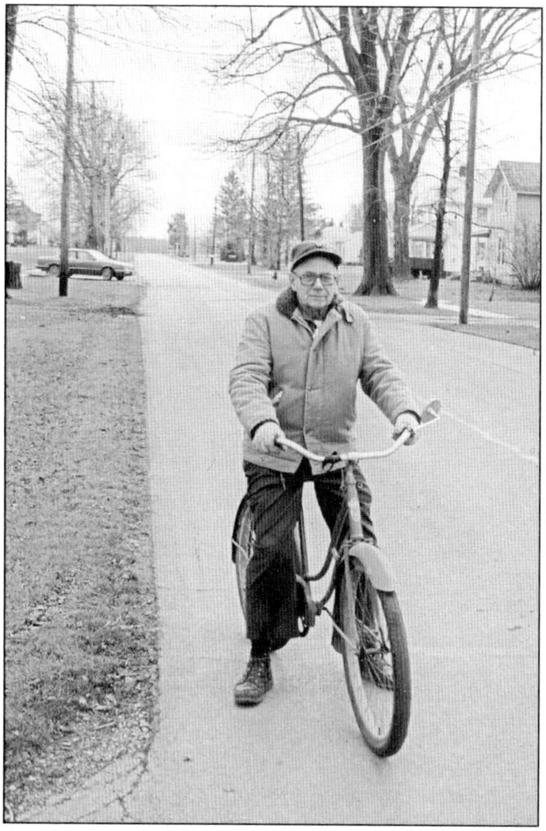

Bob Brucker rides "Big Red" down Pleasant Street in Wakeman. He claimed the street was uphill both directions, but he was known for coasting. He owned a garage downtown and was simply known as "Bees" to the young men who loafed there and learned from him. He believed that growing old was mandatory, but growing up was optional.

Pictured around 1950 at a Kiwanis event, from left to right are Bob Brucker, Art Witzlaben Jr., a Kiwanis International representative, and Gerald Ross.

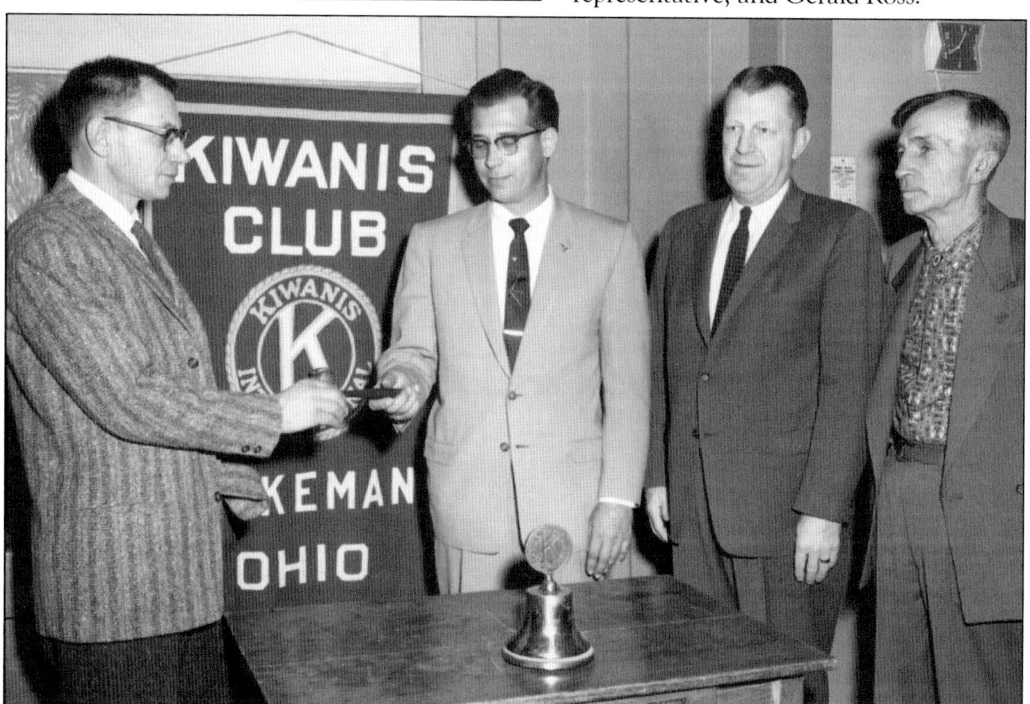

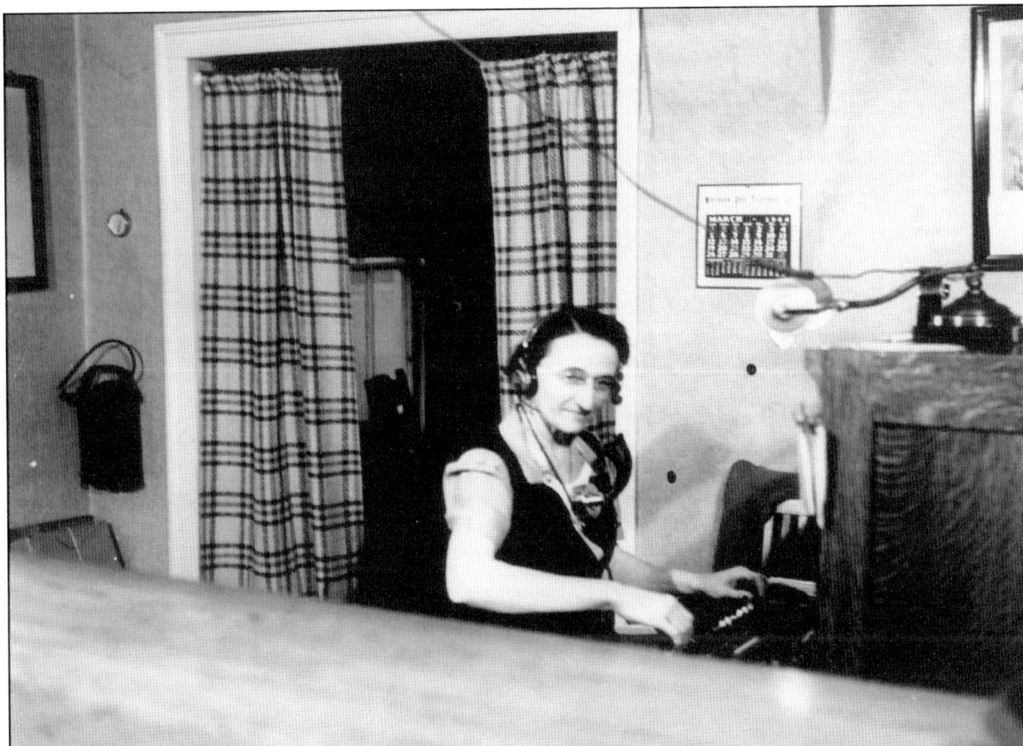

Bertha Keith, a widow, operated the town's telephones from her house. It was typical for the local telephone operator to have the equipment in his or her home, often connecting calls at any hour of the day. The wall calendar reveals the date as March 1944.

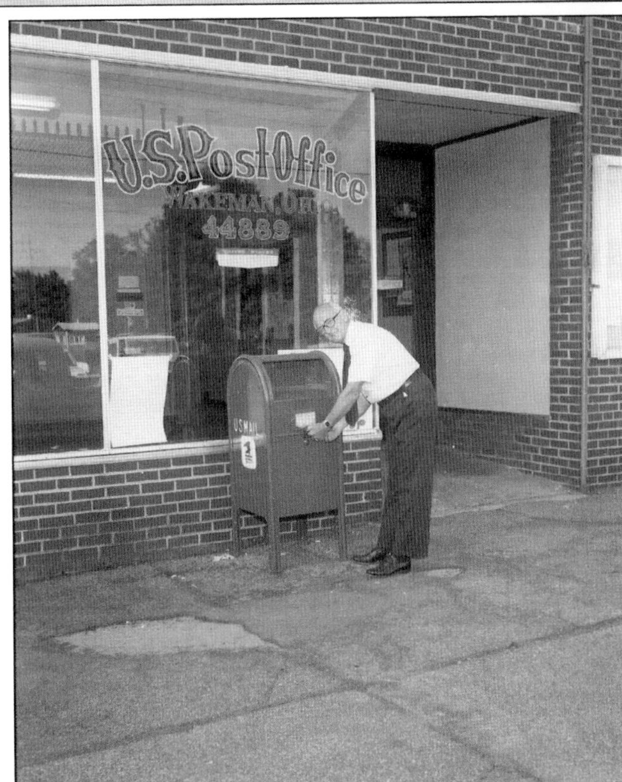

Burton Keith, son of Bertha pictured above, was Wakeman's postmaster for many years. Keeping Wakeman connected to the world was a family tradition. Burton was known to joke that his name was "There" because people typically entered the post office and said, "Hi, there."

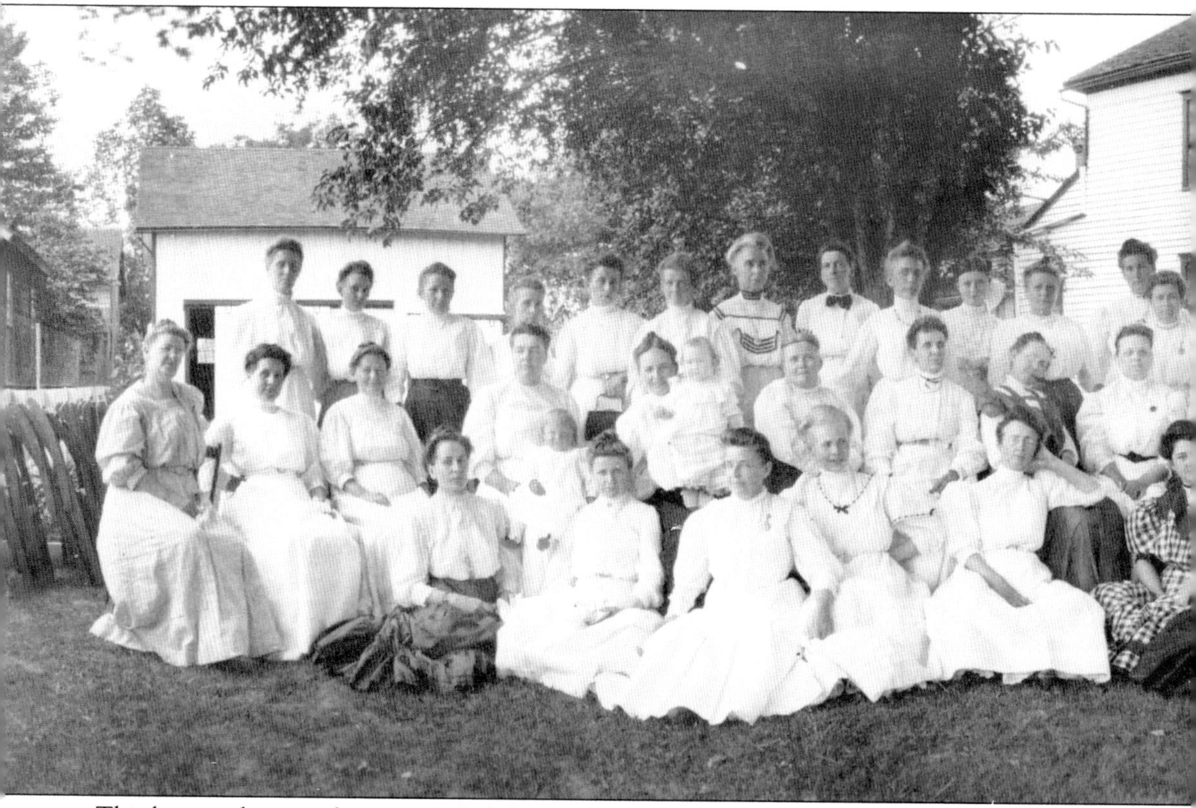

This large gathering of women included members of the Daughters of the American Revolution, pictured in downtown Wakeman around 1905. To be included in the group, a woman needed to be a direct descendant of someone involved in the Revolutionary War. The group had a large presence in the Firelands because the area was originally set aside for the Fire Sufferers, whose land in Connecticut was burned out or destroyed as a result of the Revolutionary War. Train

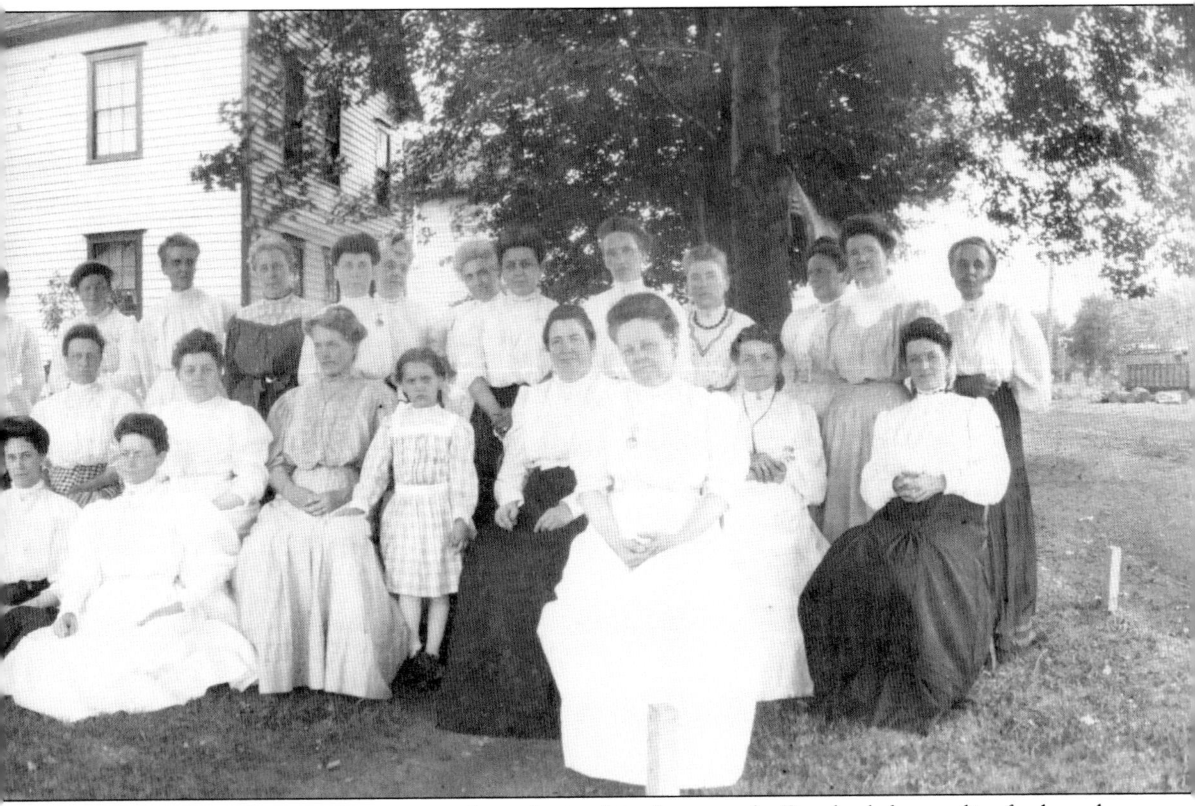

tracks and a railcar can be seen on the right in this photograph. On the left, supplies for barrel making are lined up along a fence. This photograph was taken near Cooper Street in Wakeman, which had a cooperage on it. The women are wearing their finest summer apparel, and there are a few daughters also included.

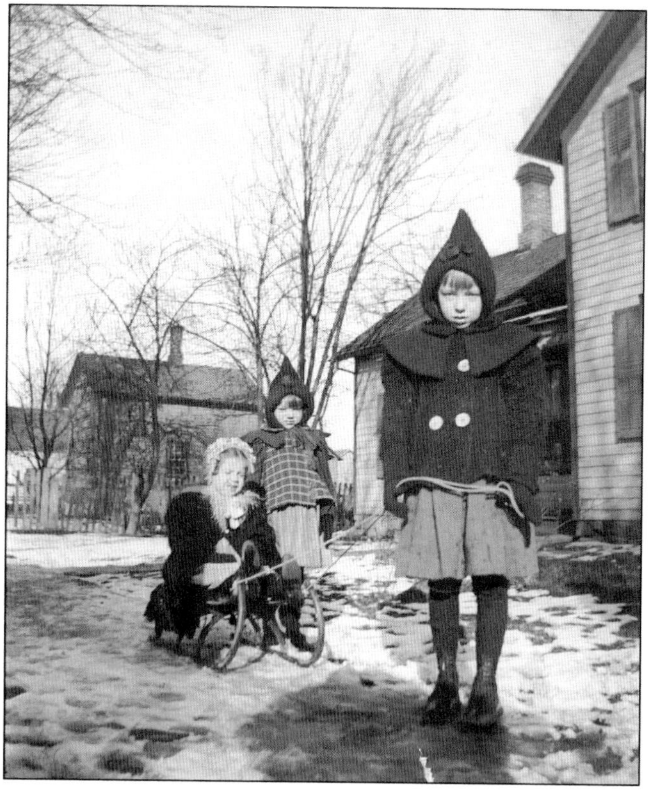

Doris Denman Graves is on a sled in this photograph from the winter of 1910. Her friend Toots Cooley is next to her, and her sister Helen Denman Cunningham holds the ropes for the sled.

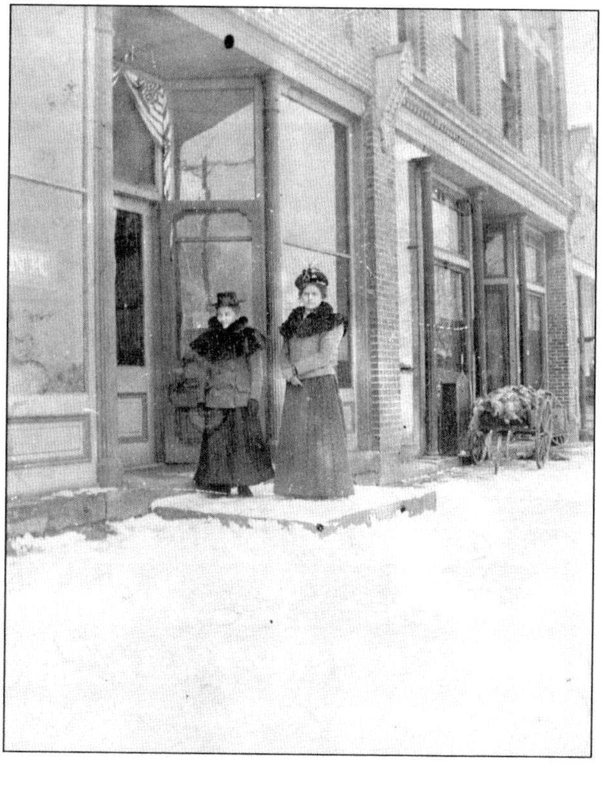

These two ladies, pictured c. 1895, are identified as Mrs. Pierce (left) and Mrs. Wood. They are standing in front of the first bank in Wakeman, which was established in 1892. Mutt Scott's General Store is in the background.

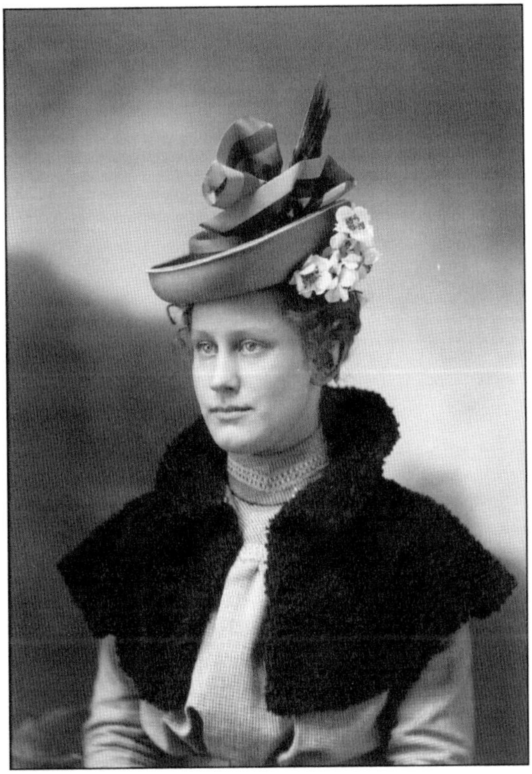

The young lady in this photograph, taken August 1900, is Amy Todd. The back of the photo lists her birthday as August 7, 1880. Perhaps it was on the occasion of her 20th birthday, or her wedding. (Courtesy of the Wakeman Community Library.)

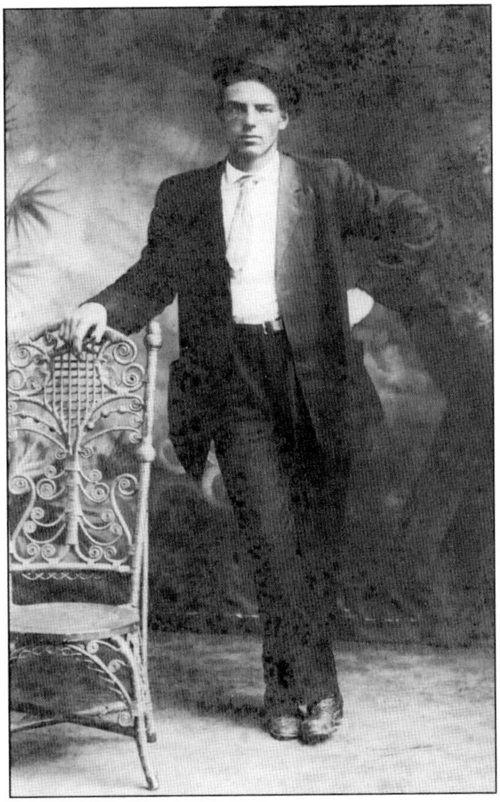

Wakeman resident Herb French poses in this c. 1905 photograph taken by the Haines Studio in Wakeman. He is remembered for planning a recreational area to be called French Lake; however, the plans were never completed. (Courtesy of the Wakeman Community Library.)

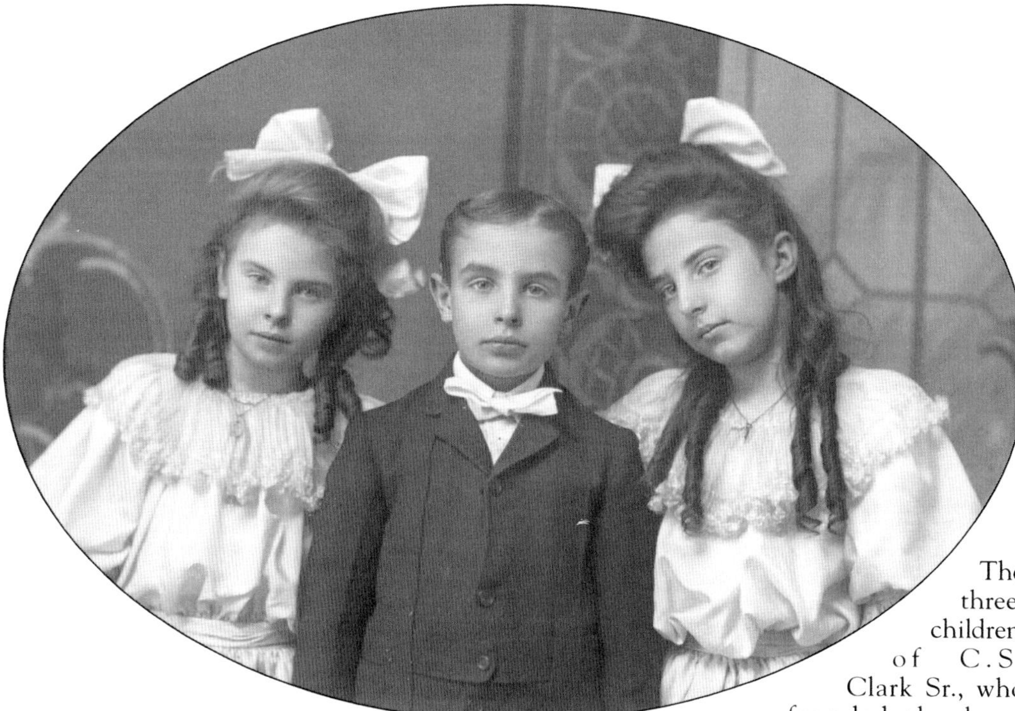

The three children of C.S. Clark Sr., who founded the large seed company in Wakeman, are pictured around 1900. From left to right are Hazel Clark, Charles Clark, and Harriet Clark. (Courtesy of the Wakeman Community Library.)

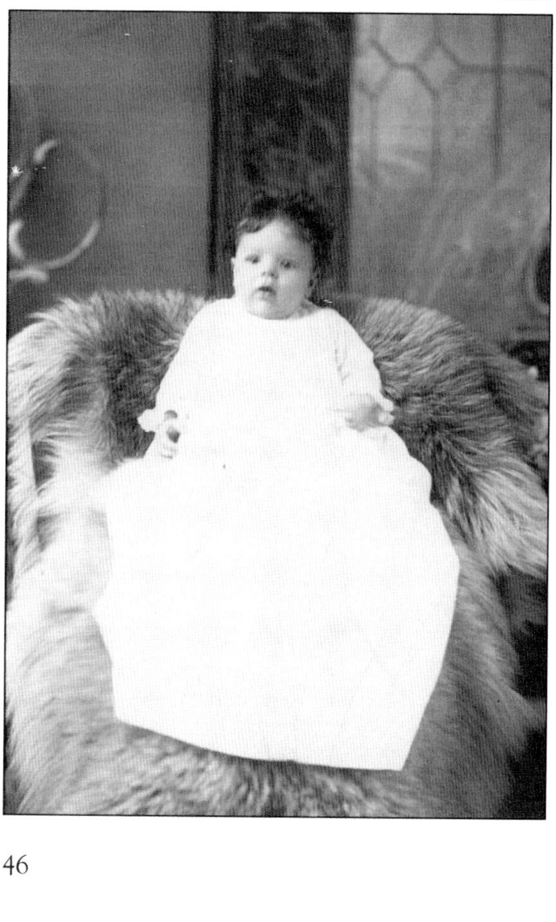

The Haines Photography studio in Wakeman captured many local children and adults around the turn of the 20th century. This photograph is identified as five-month-old Ortense French, and is dated September 12, 1901. (Courtesy of the Wakeman Community Library.)

Leonard Gerber, known as L.D., operated Gerber's funeral home in Wakeman from 1939 to 1966. At that time, the funeral director also ran the ambulance service. He is remembered for driving his hearse very quickly in many medical emergencies.

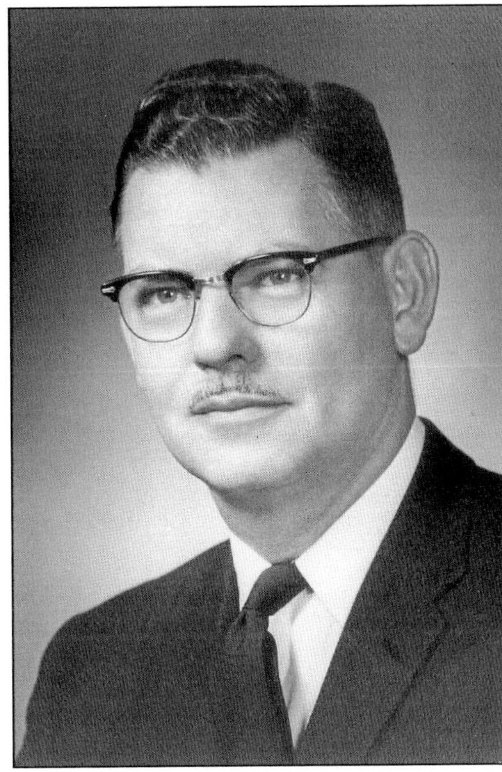

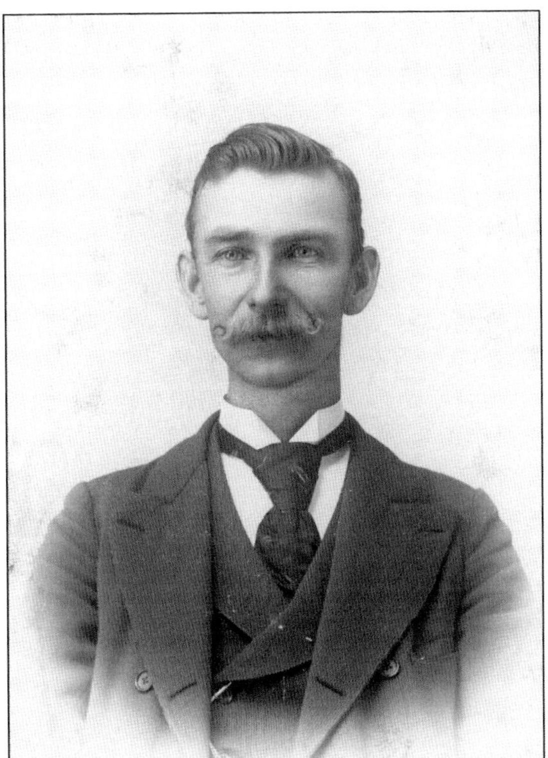

J.J. McMann, pictured around 1895, owned the lumberyard in Wakeman and also sponsored local baseball teams. (Courtesy of the Wakeman Community Library.)

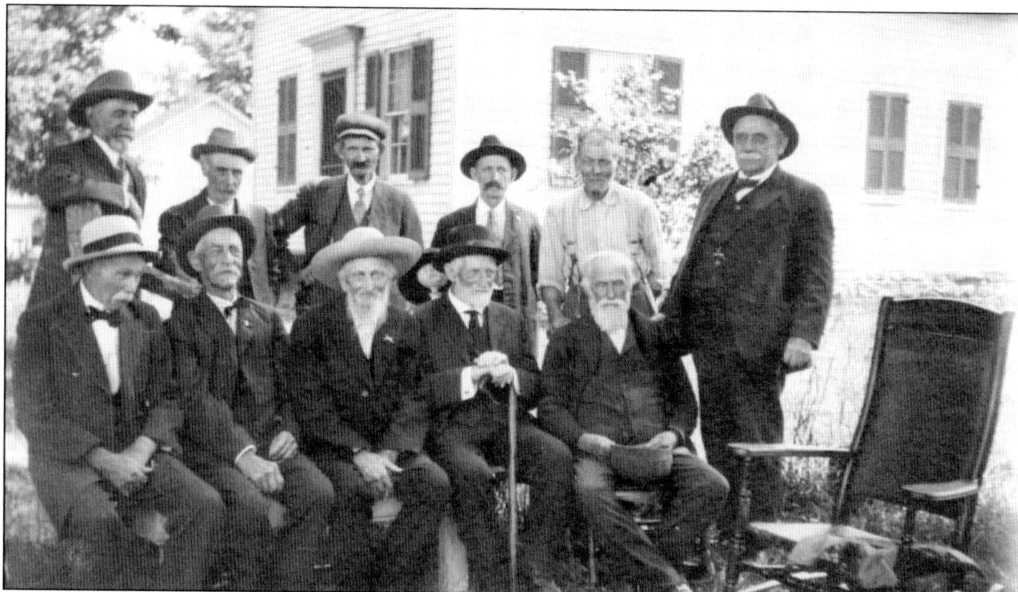

This 1917 photograph has a curiously empty chair. The Octogenarians of the Masonic Lodge are pictured on the lawn of the Ennis residence on Market Street in Birmingham. From left to right are (first row) Dan Blanchard, George Blanden, Jim Aumend, Dan Chandler, and Norman Andrews; (second row) Will Olds, George Denman, George Bentley, John Burkmeyer, Henry McDaniel, and Mark Denman. (Courtesy of Jason Gargasz.)

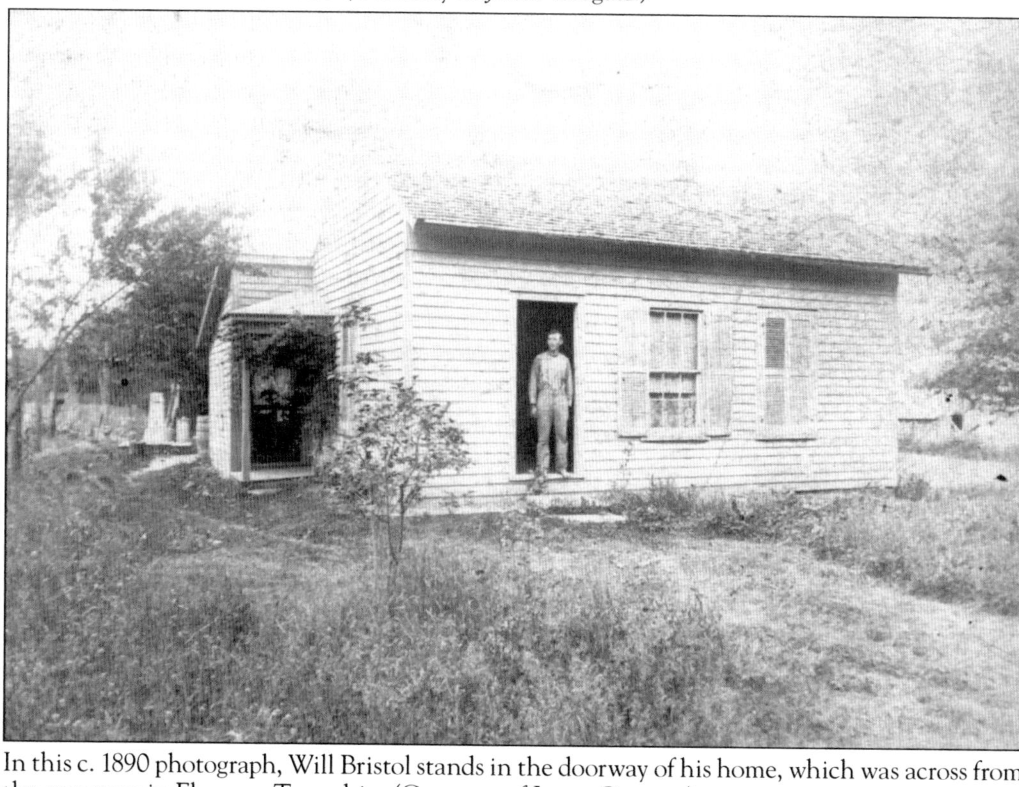

In this c. 1890 photograph, Will Bristol stands in the doorway of his home, which was across from the cemetery in Florence Township. (Courtesy of Jason Gargasz.)

Four

SCHOOLS AND CHURCHES

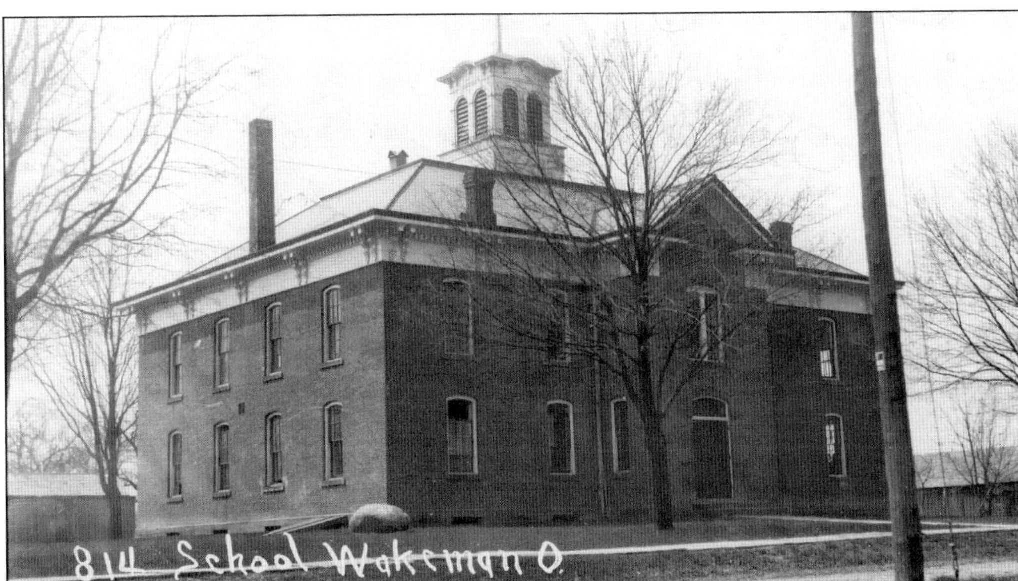

There have been several school buildings in Wakeman, Ohio. The first large brick school was built in 1868 and doubled in 1881. This photograph shows the building after it was doubled, and was probably taken c. 1900. The building was removed in 1935 and replaced by a WPA project building that opened in 1937. Students attended class in the town hall during the interim. The 1937 building housed grades K–12 until 1963, when a new junior high and high school was built outside of town. Grades K–4 continued to use the 1937 building until the 1990s, when a centralized campus was completed at the location of the junior high and high school. The 1937 building was torn down and the lot is currently vacant.

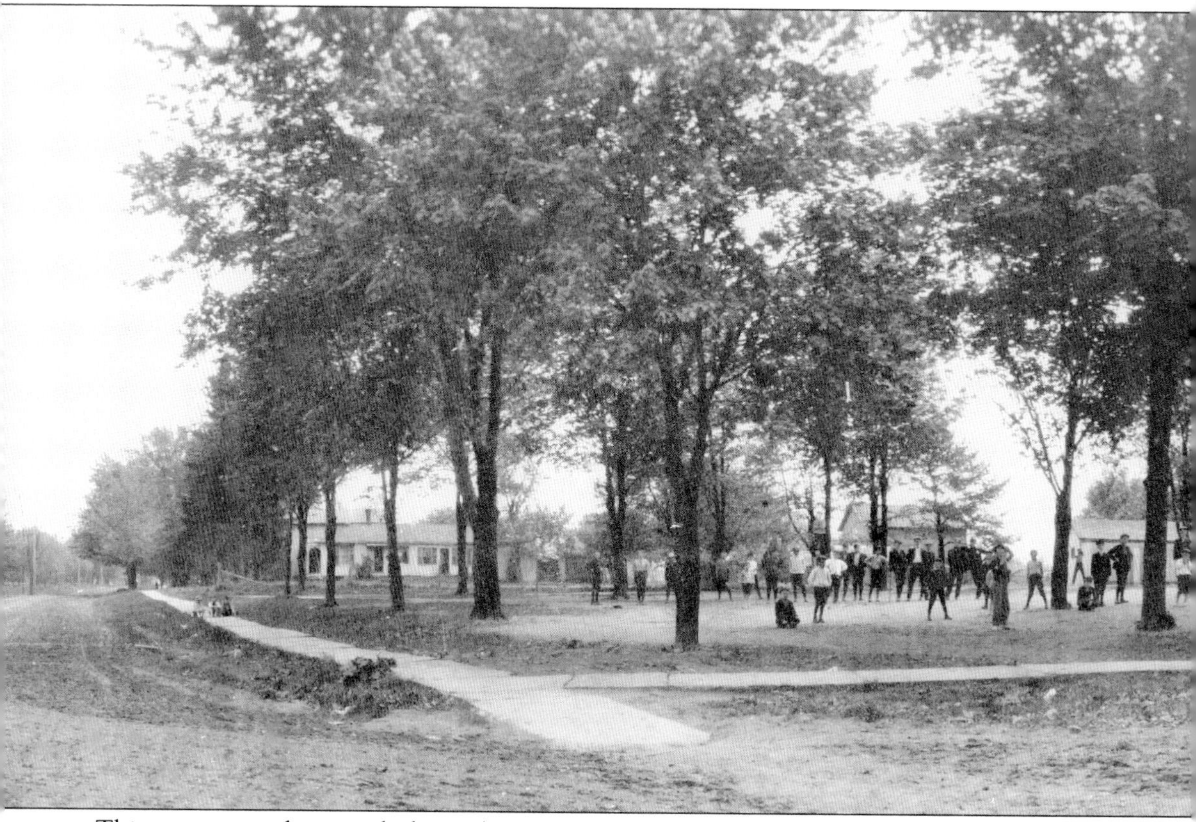

This panoramic photograph shows the 1868 school building on the corner of Abbott and River Streets in Wakeman. Students and teachers are pictured on the front lawn. Two men are holding a banner that says "WHS" near the corner of the building, although the building housed all grades,

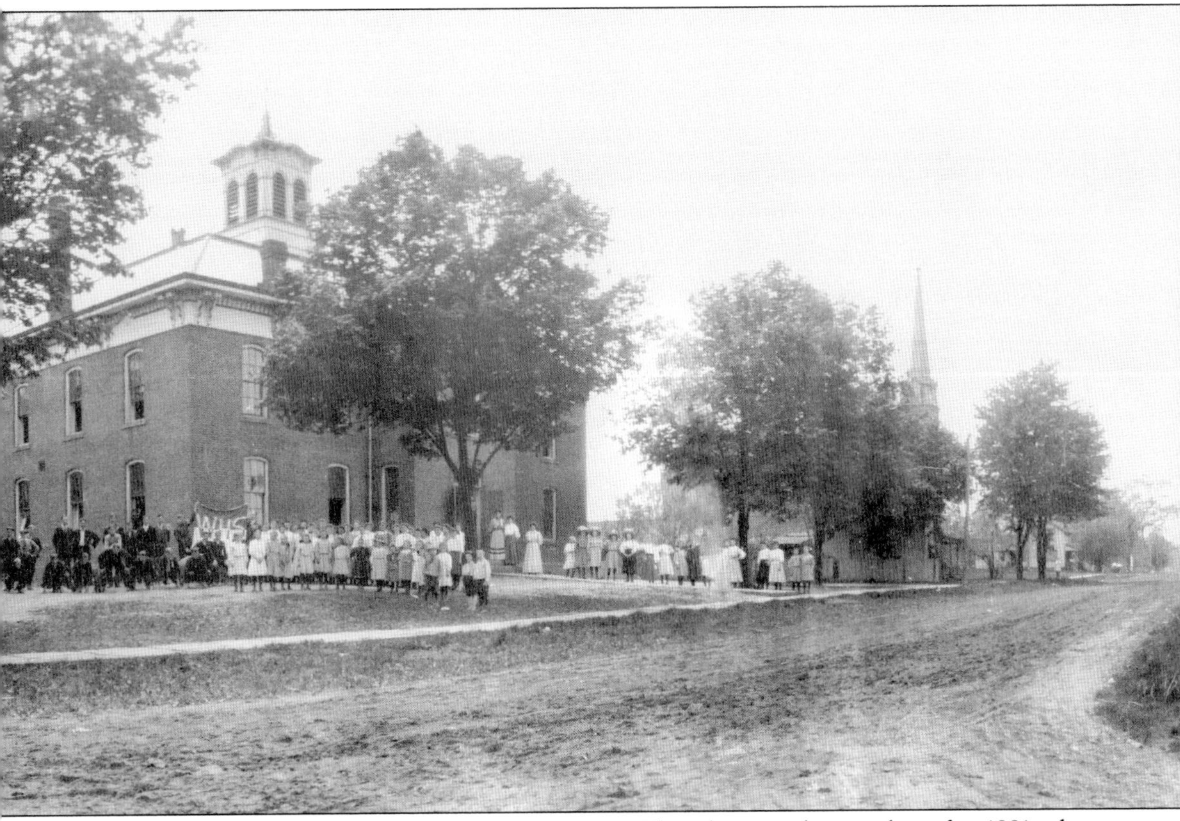

not just the high school. Note the dirt streets in town. This photograph was taken after 1881, when the building doubled in size. On the right, the steeple of the Congregational church, built in 1879, can be seen. On the far left, the white house is the parsonage for the Congregational church.

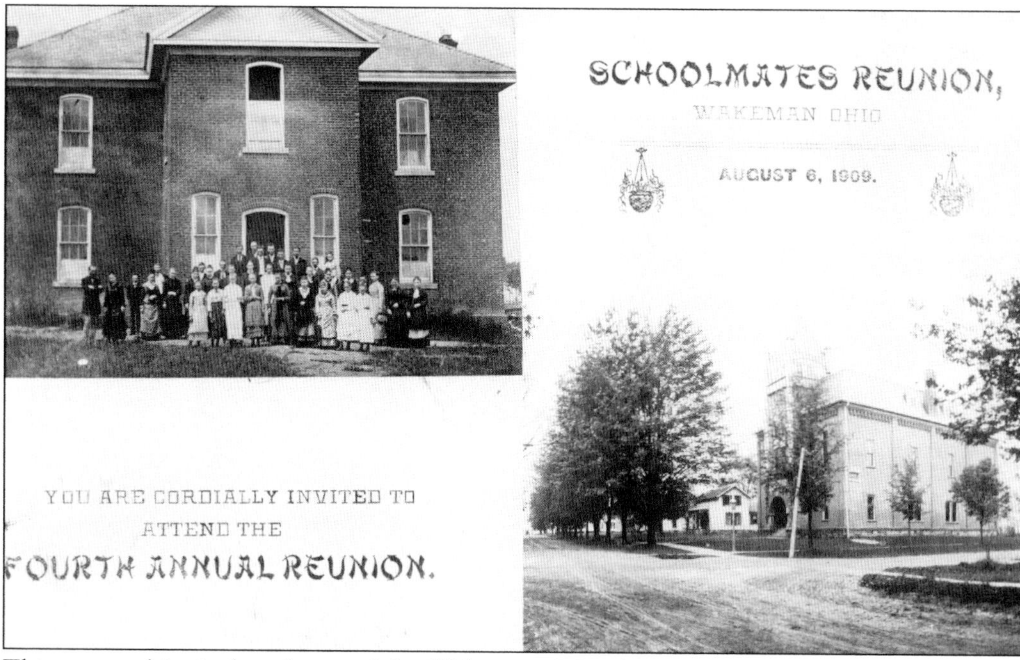

This postcard invited graduates of the Wakeman School to an August 9, 1909, reunion. The original school, built in 1868, is pictured in the upper left corner before it was doubled. The town hall is pictured lower right because it was used for events and overflow classrooms. Although the card calls the reunion the "Fourth Annual," there had been many graduating classes by 1909.

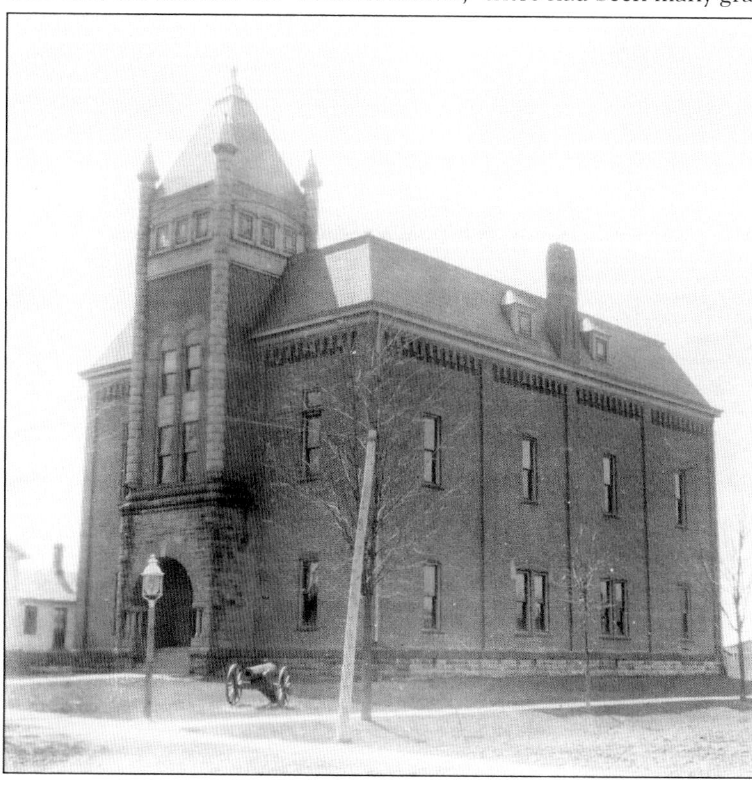

This imposing building on the corner of Abbott and Pleasant Streets in Wakeman was built as a town hall in 1894. It was sold to the Masons in 1949 for $2,550. Over the years, it was used for school basketball games, class plays, graduation, and extra classroom space. It is sometimes called "the opera house" because it has a theater on the upper floor. Note the gaslight on the corner and the Civil War cannon in the yard. The cannon was sold for scrap during World War II.

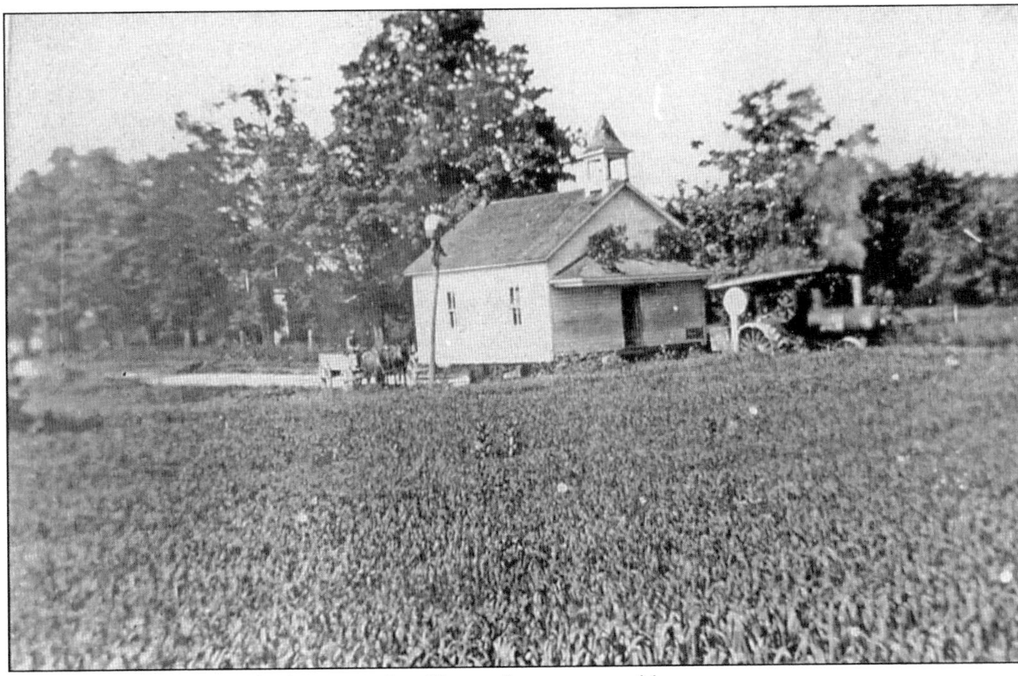

This c. 1890 photograph shows a schoolhouse being moved by a steam tractor.

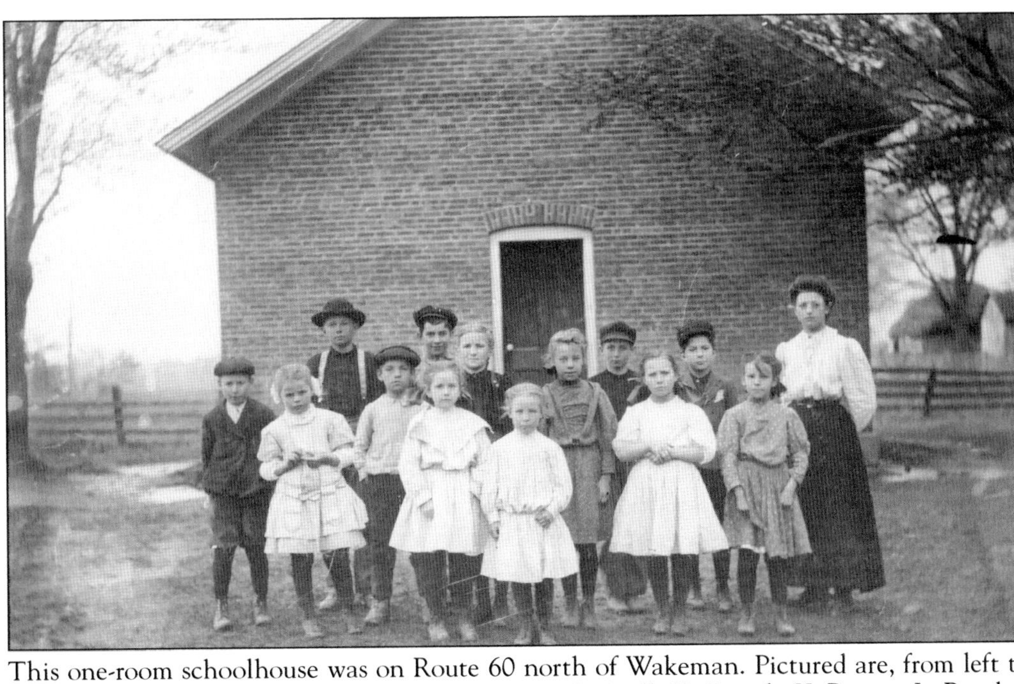

This one-room schoolhouse was on Route 60 north of Wakeman. Pictured are, from left to right, Harry Stoll, C. Parker, R. Barnes, M. Carter, B. Stoll, H. French, K. Barnes, L. Bentley, P. Parker, C. Soper, Minnie Carter, G. Gibson, Mildred Carter, and teacher Rosalia Schoettle (Rose Parsons).

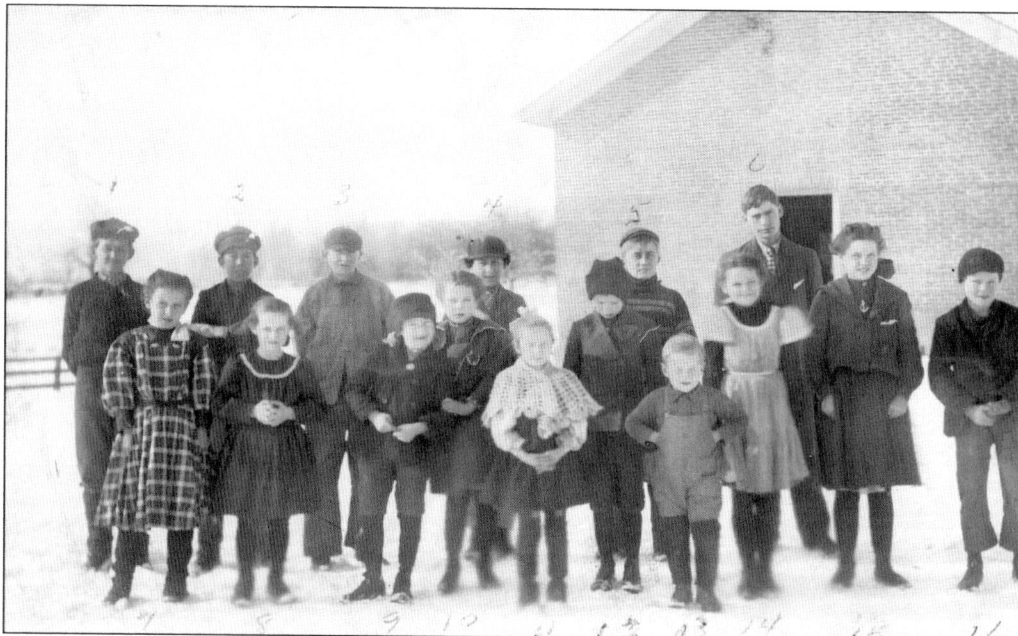

This school, operated by Platt Beecher, was east of Wakeman and is pictured in 1907. From left to right are (first row) Mary Ward, Mary Burke, John Dugan, Anna Dugan, Ethel Holden, unidentified, Leon Holden, and Mary Dugan; (second row) George Hill, Harry Murphy, Pat Buckley, Leonard Mason, Email Kassell, Platt Henry Beecher, Ester Murray, and John Burke.

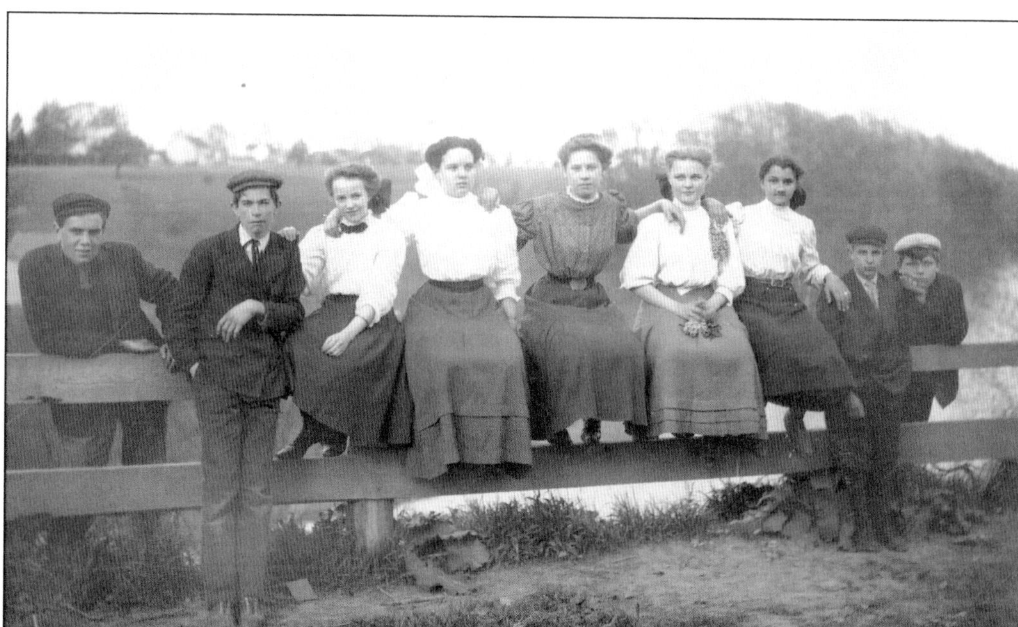

A group of classmates, possibly from the class of 1912, gather for a photograph. From left to right are Paul Cooley, Harold Reed, Florence Pierce, Violet Sayles, Blanche Sanford, Florence Davenport, Grace Elmes, and two unidentified boys.

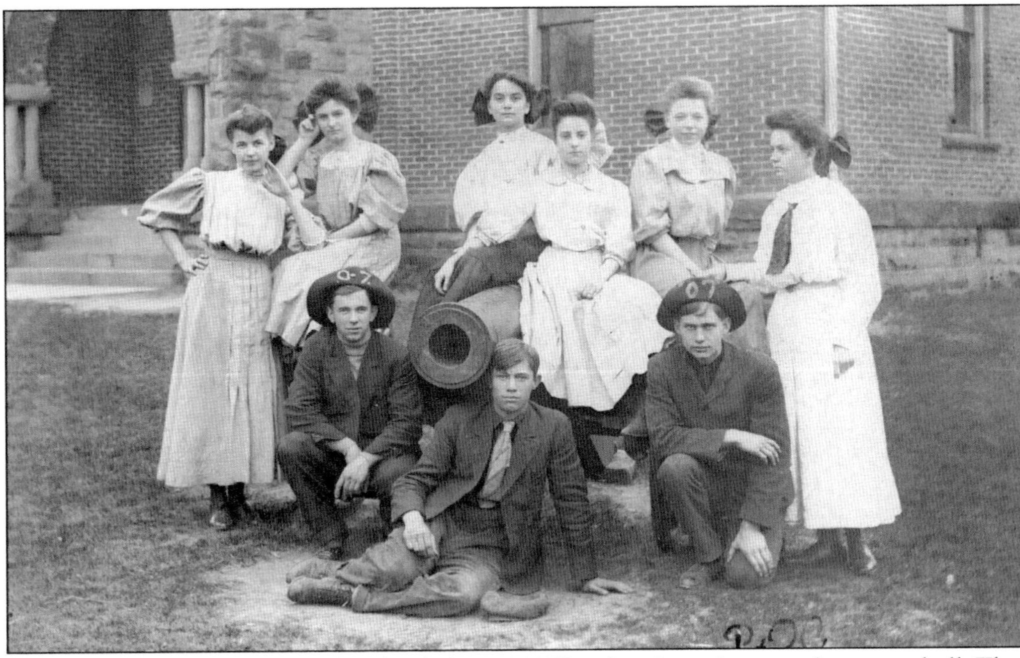

Students in the Wakeman High School class of 1907 gather for a photograph at town hall. They are posing on the Civil War cannon in the front yard.

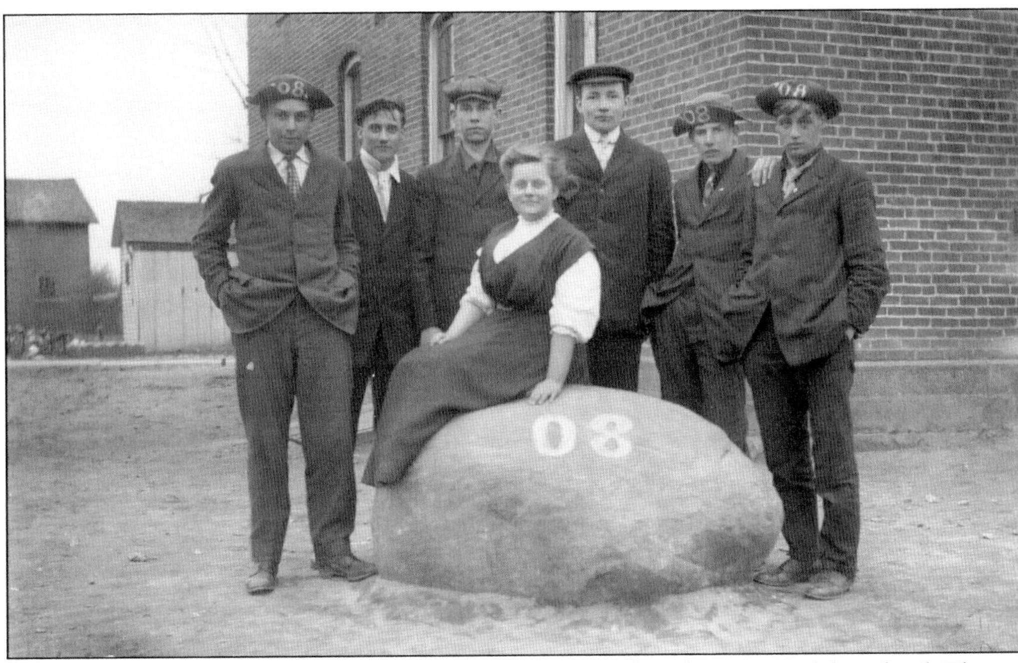

The Wakeman High School class of 1908 poses on the rock at the corner of the school. The girl on the rock is Mildred Beecher. Pictured behind her are, from left to right, Lawton French, Lyman Scott, Horace Hurst, Frank Parsons, Glen Beecher, and Claude Peabody.

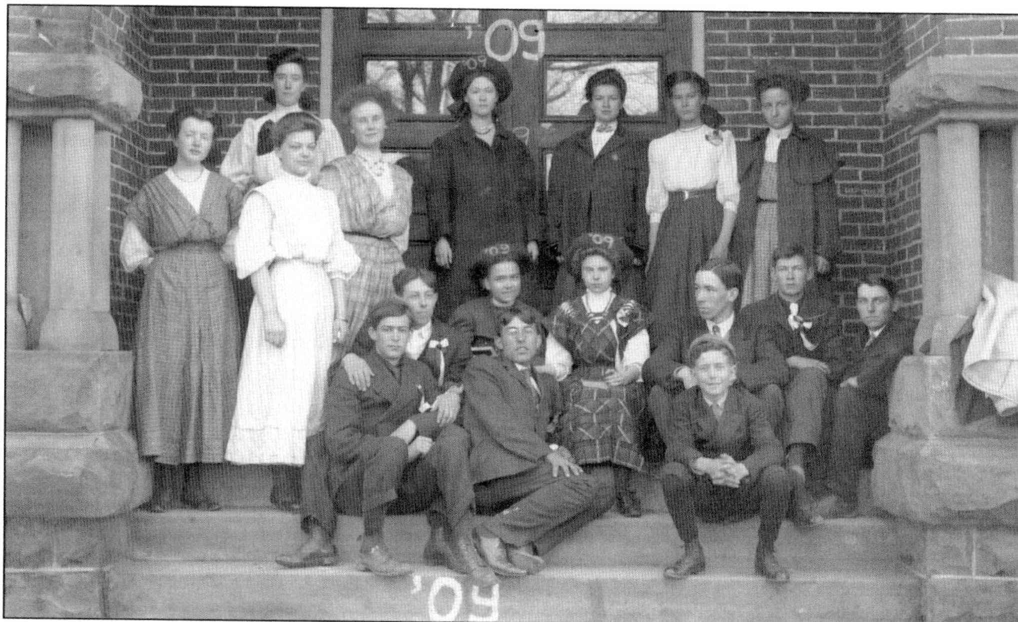

The Wakeman High School class of 1909 gathers in front of the town hall, where they probably held their graduation ceremony. They are from left to right (first row) Clarence Bailey, Louie Scutt, Mabel Downing, Lee Ross, Harriet Clark, Bernie Wood, Ralph Coon, Ed Croxford, and Don Byron; (second row) Ruth Shelton, Ina Sprague, Flora Pierce, Mildred Draper, Nina Gibson, Georgia Barnes, Edna Seeley, and Freda Didelius.

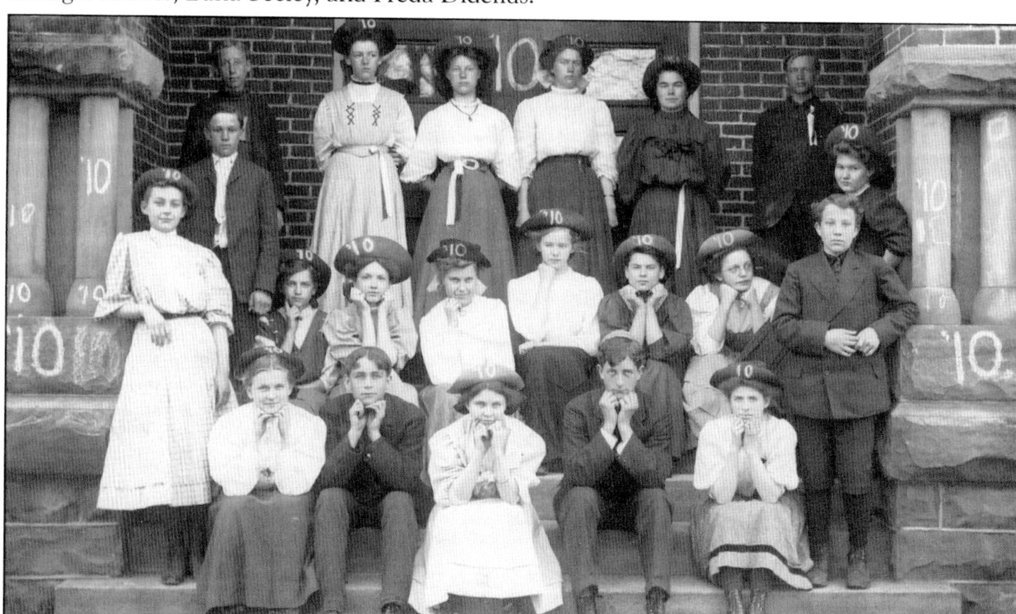

Members of the Wakeman High School class of 1910 pose on the front steps of town hall. From left to right are (first row) Elizabeth Beecher, George Birmingham, Eona Seeley, Robert Gamber, and Alma Whitney; (second row) Helen Denman, Lester Pierce, Margaret Stoll, Marion Peck, Bess Piere, Hazel Bristol, Mary Stoll, Vera Johns, Merton Campbell, and Eloise Loretz; (third row) Louie Scutt, Lillian Smith, Leona Squires, Elsie Beecher, Mabel Downing, and Earl Peabody.

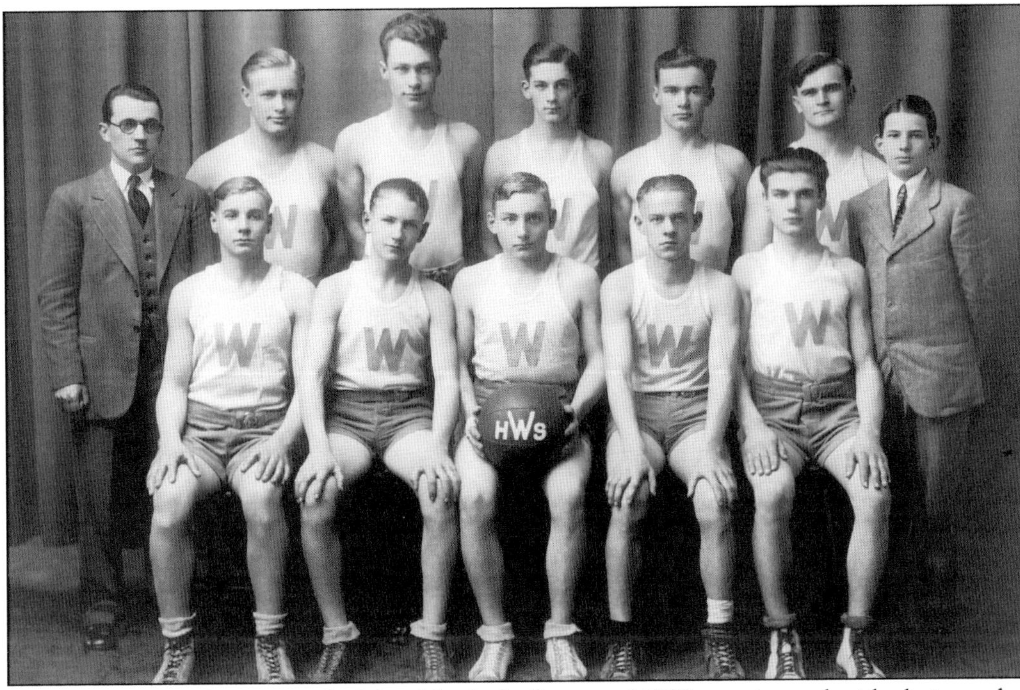

Players on the Wakeman High School basketball team of 1929 are pictured with their teacher and coach, W.H. Jones (left), who taught there for many years. From left to right are (first row) Charles Weeks, Paul Murray, Fremont Holmes, Bob Hoyt, and unidentified; (second row) W.H. Jones, Russell Caywood, Steve Pierce, Charles Bement, Werner Todd, James Felton, and Max Kellar (manager).

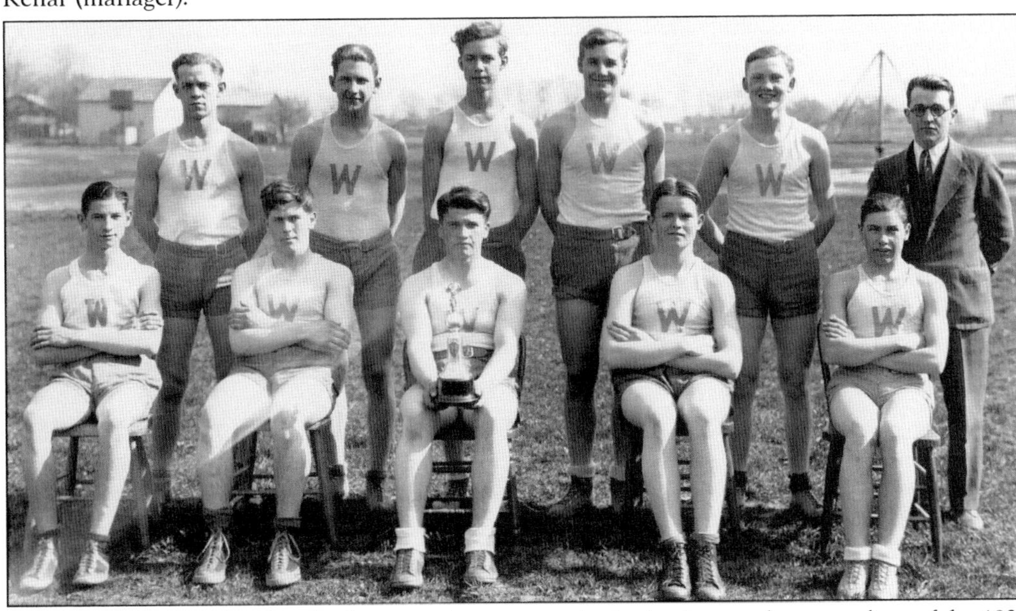

Seated outside the school with playground equipment in the background are members of the 1932 Wakeman High School basketball team. From left to right are (first row) Horace Martin, Ben Humm, Bill Parsons, J. Guthrie, and P. Gerber; (second row) Bob Hoyt, Paul Murray, Andrew Clark, Charles Weeks, Oliver Thomas, and W.H. Jones (coach).

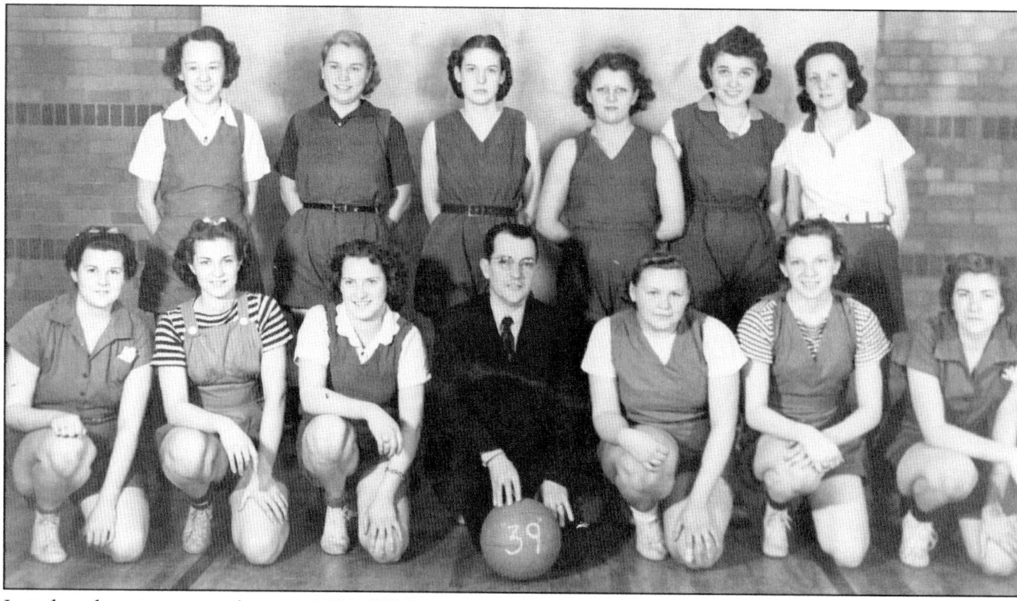

It is hard to imagine, but in 1939, Wakeman High School had a women's basketball team long before it was common to have women's sports in schools. The senior girls played the freshman girls at noon. Note that the coach is W.H. Jones, who also coached the men's teams for many years. From left to right are (first row) Betty Haskins, Laura Wesell, Mildred Mikloda, W.H. Jones, Gertrude Saik, Jean Foreman, and Wandabell Felton; (second row) Helen O'Brien, Betty Sheldon, Cecelia Daugherty, Alice Watson, Laura Erbs, and Inez Tousley.

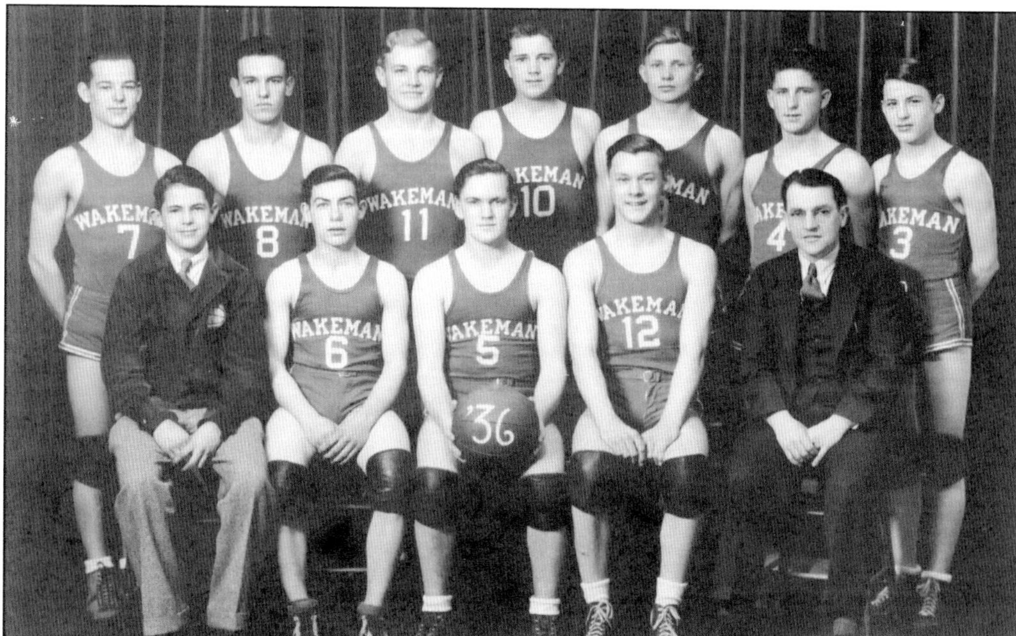

The 1936 Wakeman High School basketball team won 11 games and lost four under the direction of coach W.H. Jones. From left to right are (first row) manager Al Murray, J. Boyle, Dohr Thomas, Pierce McCready, and W.H. Jones; (second row) Brant Bailey, Gaius Campbell, Bill Johnson, Clinton Bement, ? Celeski, Leonard Bisgrove, and Louis Murray.

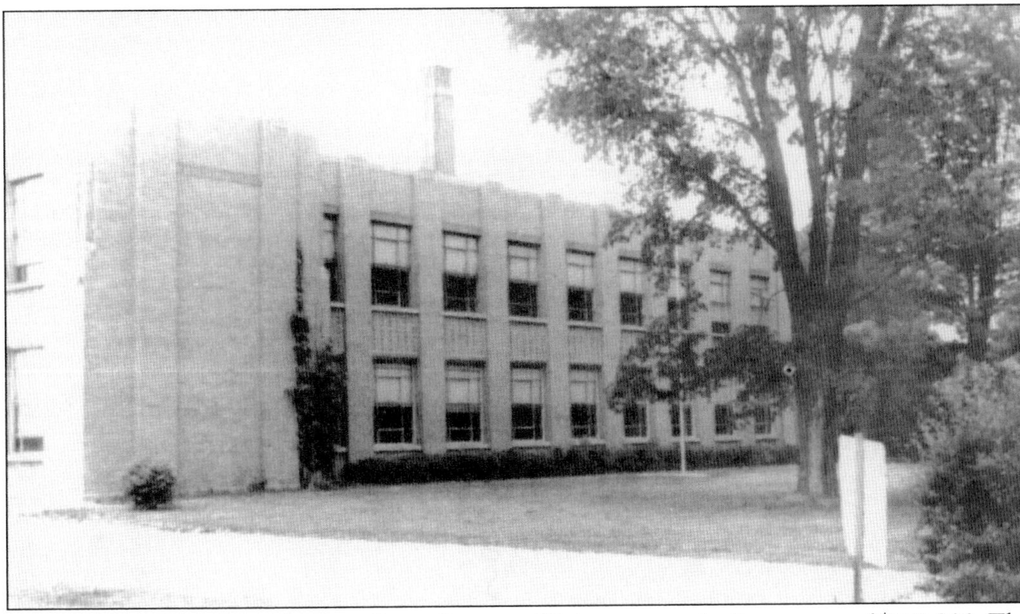

The 1937 WPA project school on River Street in Wakeman was built at a cost of $100,000. The same architect also designed a school for the nearby Village of Monroeville, and the buildings were mirror images of each other. The Monroeville building is still in use, but Wakeman's was torn down in the 1990s.

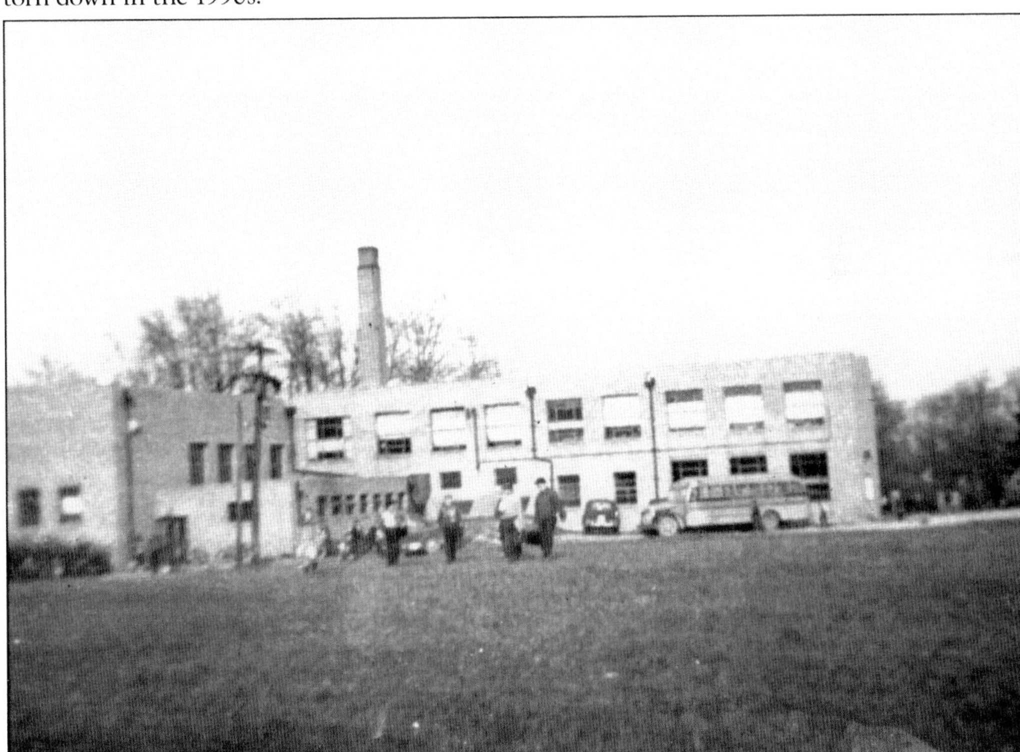

This 1950 photograph shows a rear view of the 1937 WPA school in Wakeman. Note the school bus in the photograph.

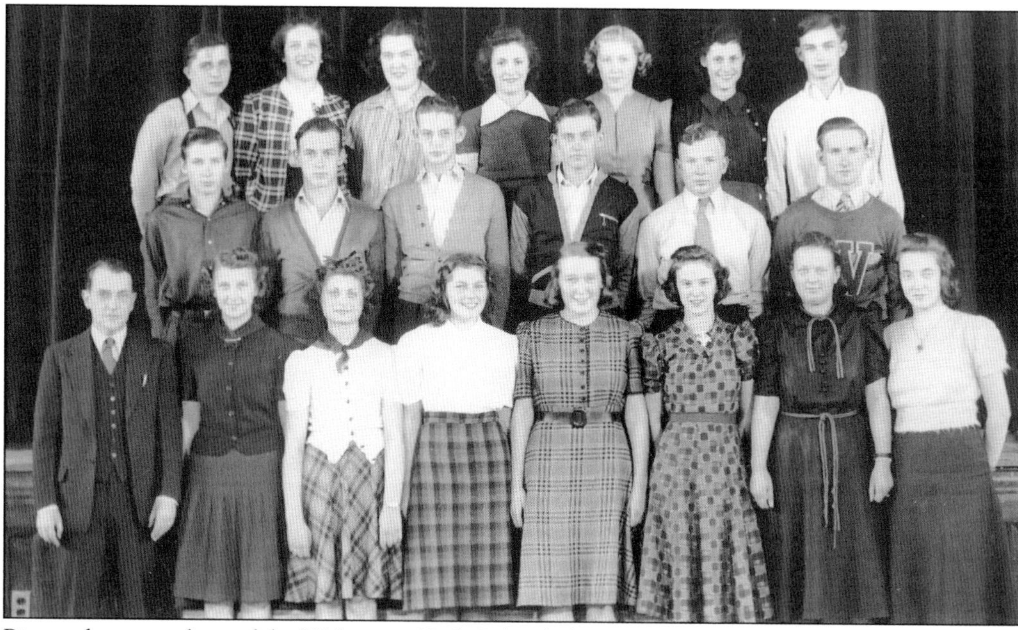

Pictured are members of the Wakeman High School class of 1941. From left to right are (first row) W.H. (Bill) Jones, Francis King, Doris Hurst, Christine Dalton, Jean Mockler, Margaret Miller, Thelma Timbs, and Gertrude Hurst; (second row) Jack Small, Billy Wasniak, Maynard Clark, Louie Morgan, Dale Wilson, and Richard Addison; (third row) Jerry Byron, Louise Daugherty, Mary Ruth Barnes, Bertha Davis, Betsy Bennett, Lois Bryden, and Dick Eastman.

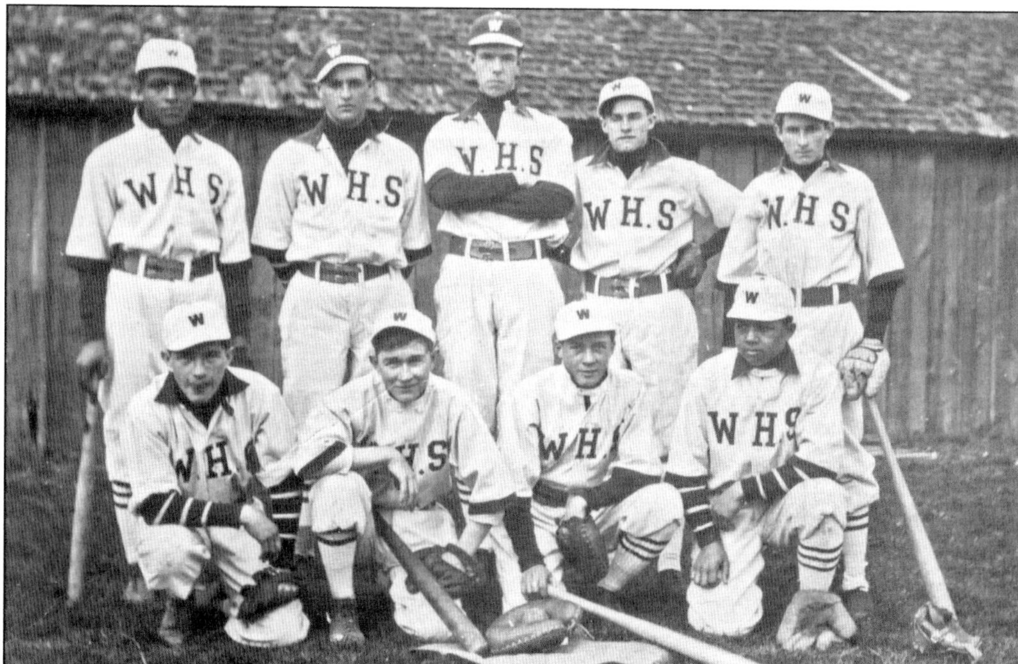

The 1943 Wakeman High School baseball team poses in this photograph. The very tall man, back row center, is Harold (General) Divers. The other men are unidentified. The horse barn of the Congregational church (which is near the school) is behind the team.

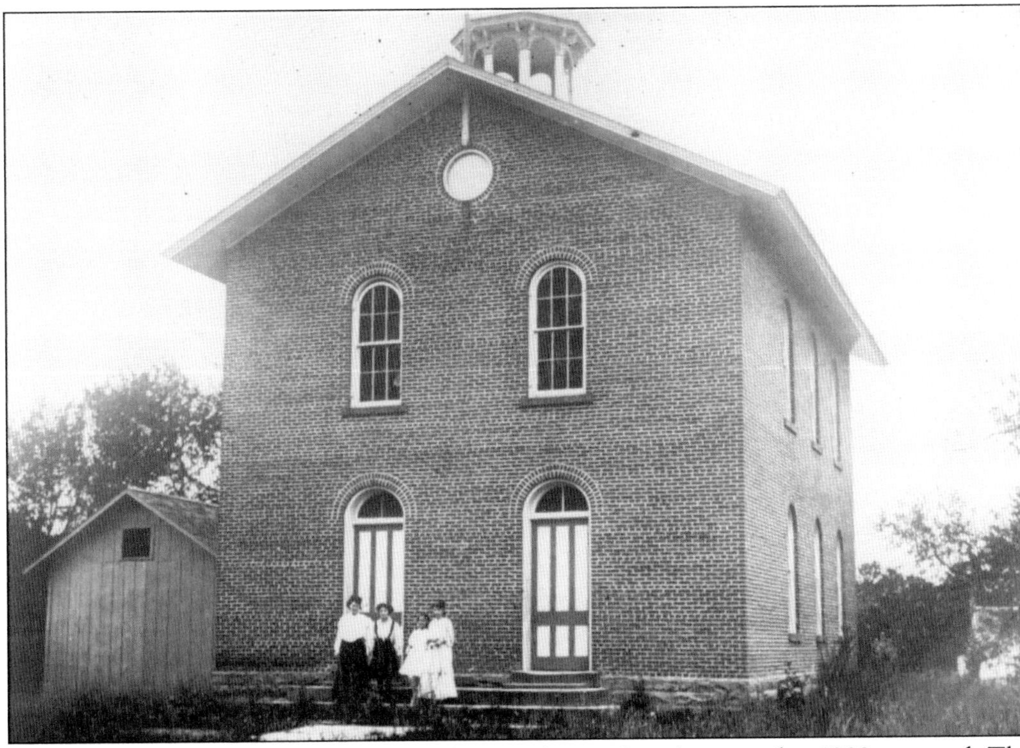

The Birmingham school is pictured with a teacher and students in this 1909 postcard. The school was built in 1889 and used until 1916, when the newer and larger school opened on Main Street in town. This building was later part of a mill until it burned down in 1929. (Courtesy of Jason Gargasz.)

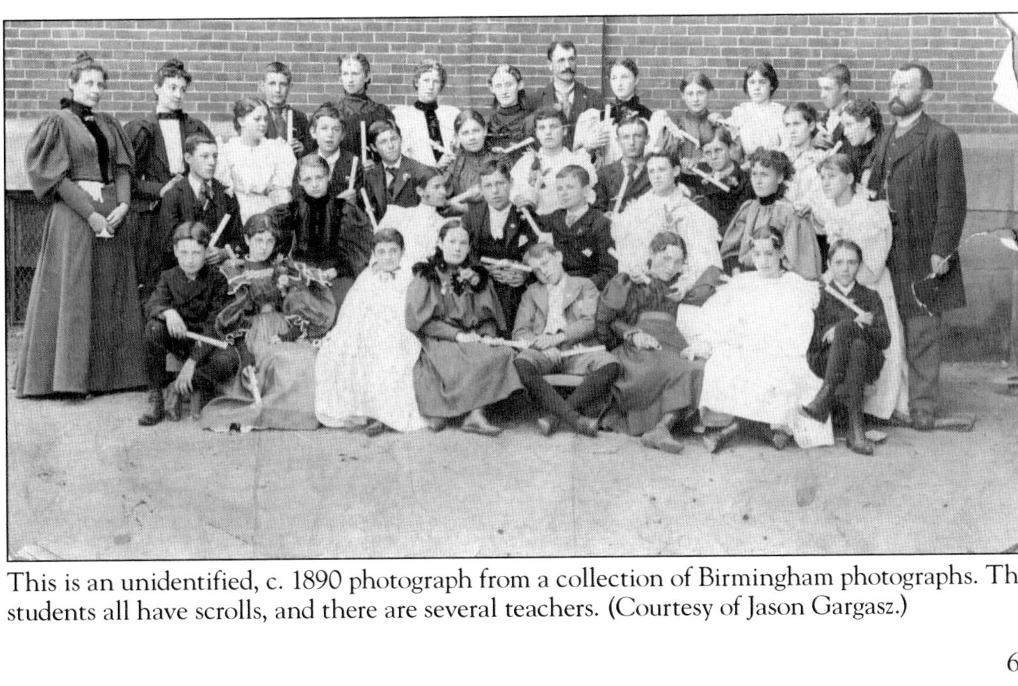

This is an unidentified, c. 1890 photograph from a collection of Birmingham photographs. The students all have scrolls, and there are several teachers. (Courtesy of Jason Gargasz.)

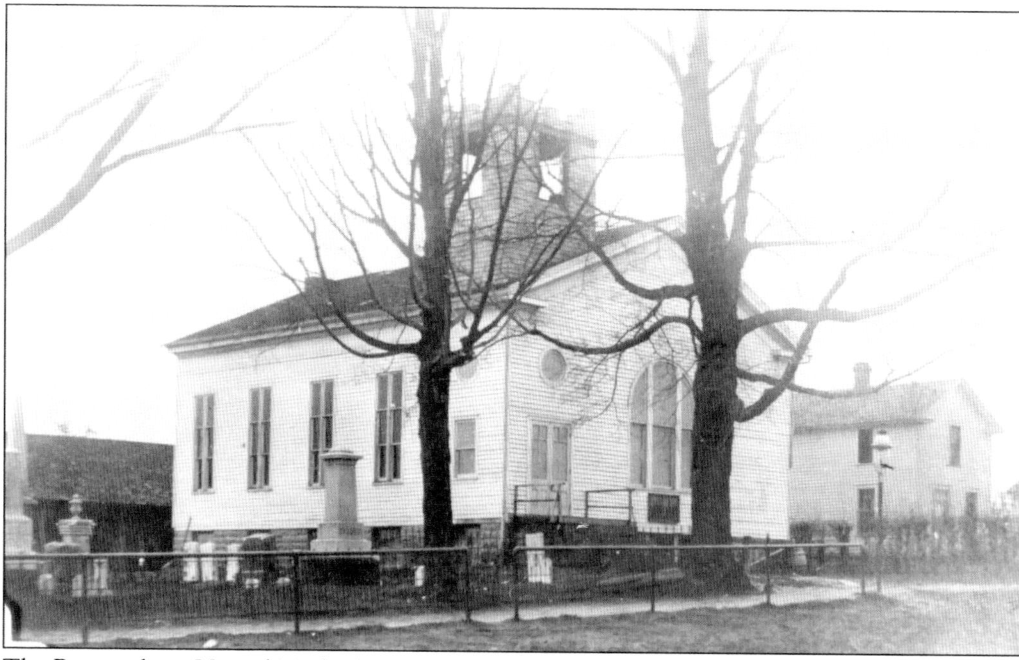

The Birmingham United Methodist Church was built in 1841. This 1910 photograph shows the building in its original design. It has since been renovated several times, but is still a thriving church in Birmingham. (Courtesy of Jason Gargasz.)

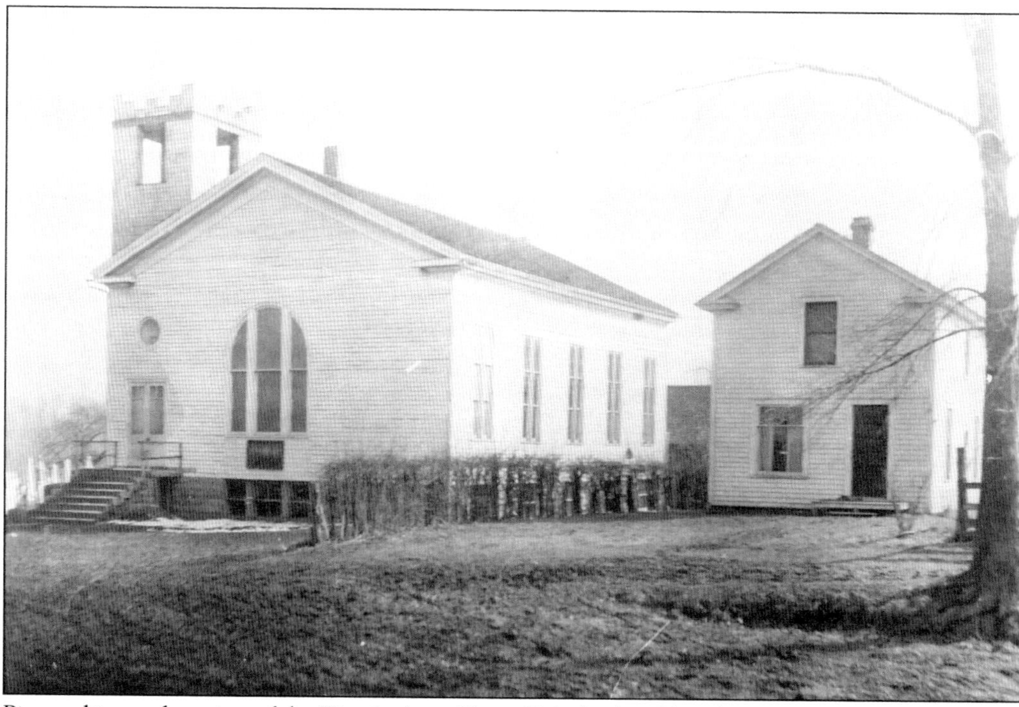

Pictured is another view of the Birmingham United Methodist Church. For many years, the church has sponsored a large fall craft festival, which draws thousands of people to the small Village of Birmingham. (Courtesy of Jason Gargasz.)

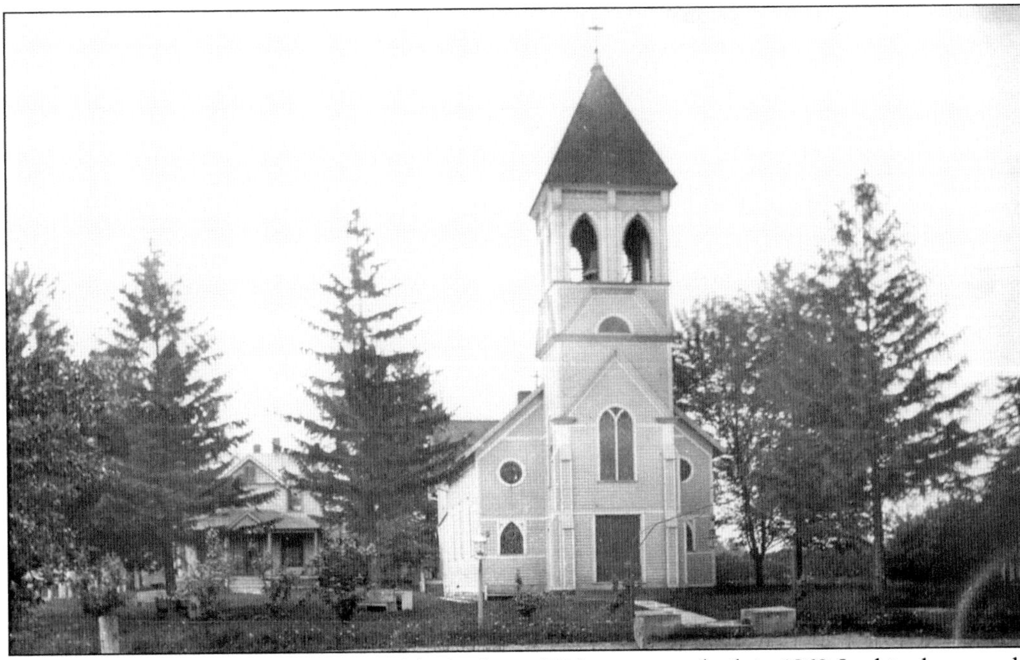

St. Mary's Catholic Church, just east of the bridge in Wakeman, was built in 1868. In this photograph, the front steps are almost level with the road. The road was lowered during bridge construction, and the church now has a set of steps leading down to it. The church was remodeled in 2010. The center part remains the same, but the sides are wider to accommodate a larger congregation.

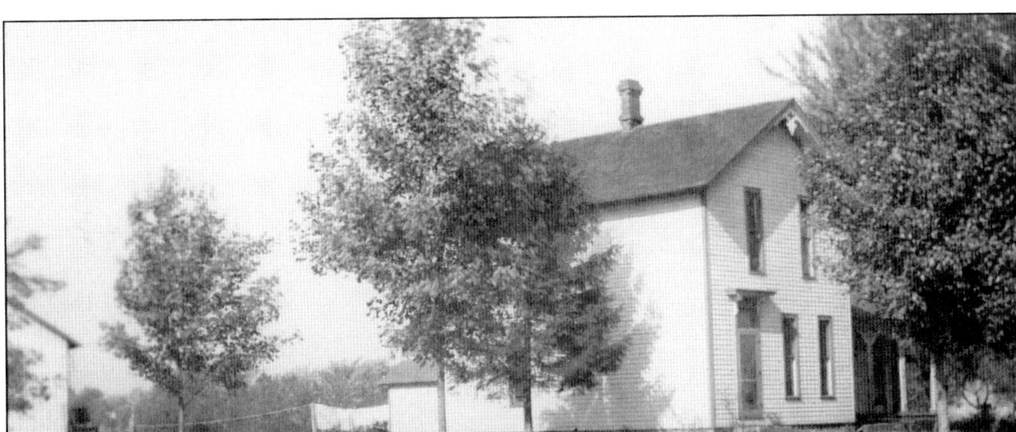

The parsonage for the Congregational church in Wakeman is pictured around 1900. The house still stands on River Street near the location of the former school.

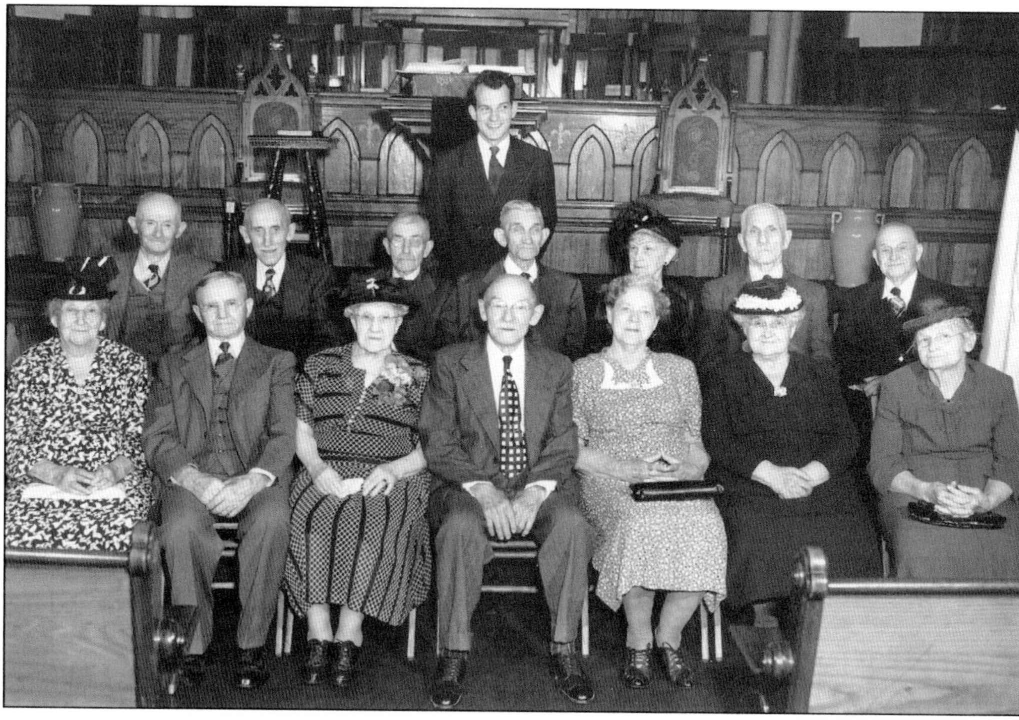

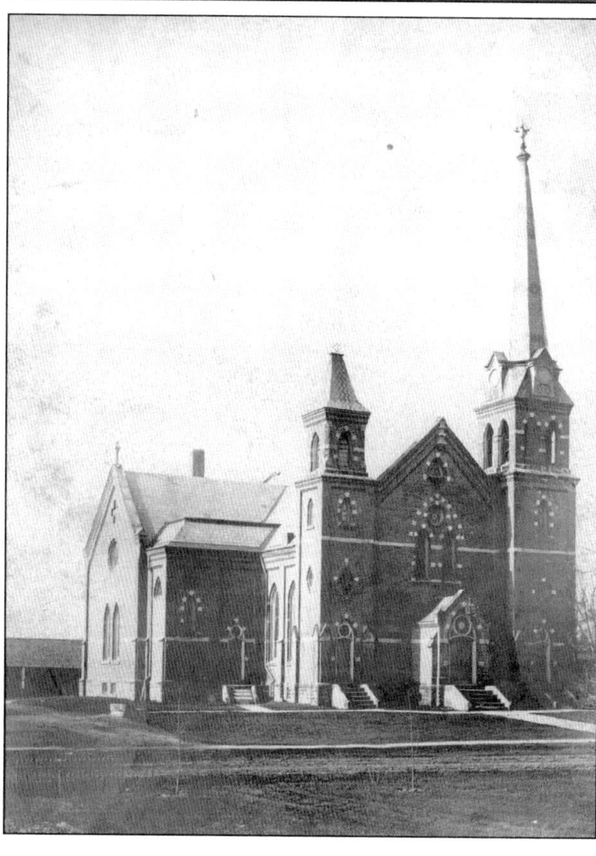

The Octogenarian Club of the Congregational church was a social group of Wakeman residents who had reached the age of 80. This photograph from the 1950s shows the group with the church's beautiful organ in the background. Pictured from left to right are (first row) Mrs. Frank Arnold, Fred Elms, Mrs. Elms, C.H. Pierce, Mrs. Pierce, Flora Pierce, and Delia Hatchenburg; (second row) C.A. Cooley, Charlie Todd, Art Twadle, F.A. Denman, Dottie Walters, Dennis Ross, and Sanford Stiles.

The Wakeman Second Congregational Church on Abbott Street was dedicated on January 1, 1879 with a sermon from Rev. James H. Fairchild, president of nearby Oberlin College. The church was built at a cost of $16,000 and has a seating capacity of 932.

Five

Business and Commerce

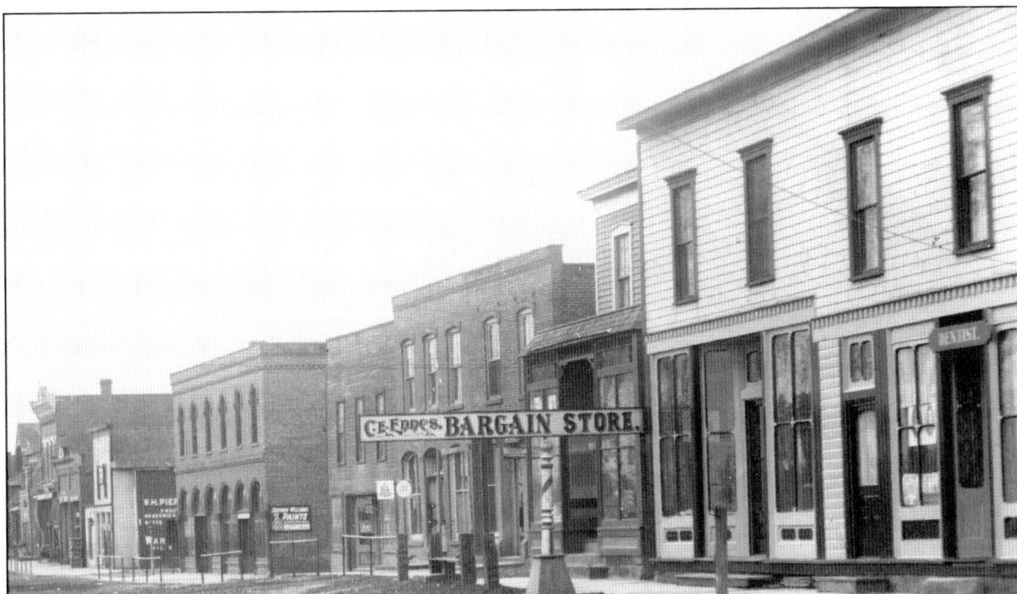

Downtown Wakeman is pictured prior to 1908. Visible businesses are a dentist, a bargain store, a barbershop, a building with a Sherwin Williams Paint sign, and Pierce's original grocery building. Hitching posts and dirt roads welcomed shoppers.

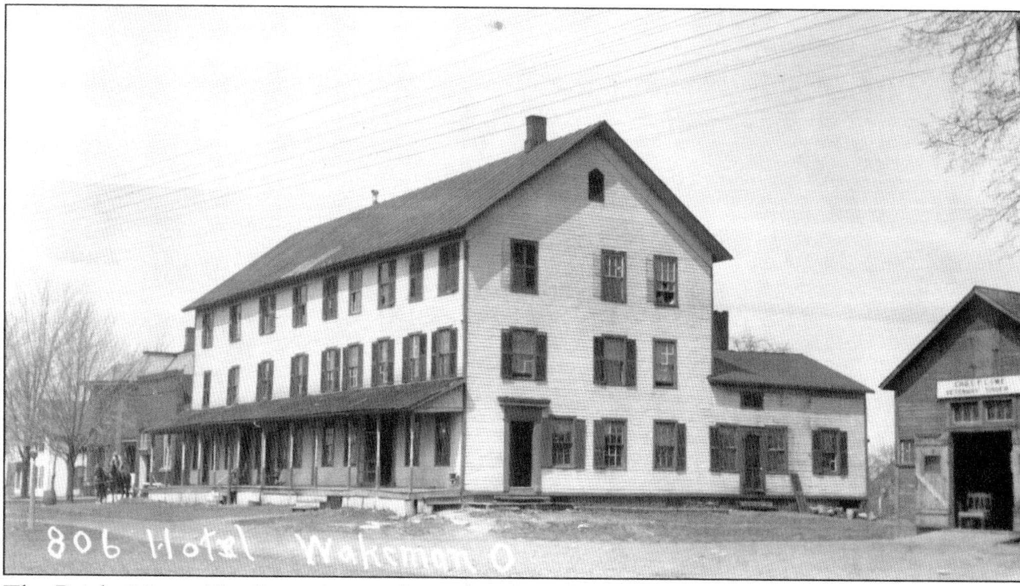

The Bright House Hotel stood near the railroad tracks in downtown Wakeman. Sally Bright, a conservative, unmarried woman, owned the hotel. The building was torn down in the early 1920s, and the materials were used to build a grain elevator in downtown Wakeman.

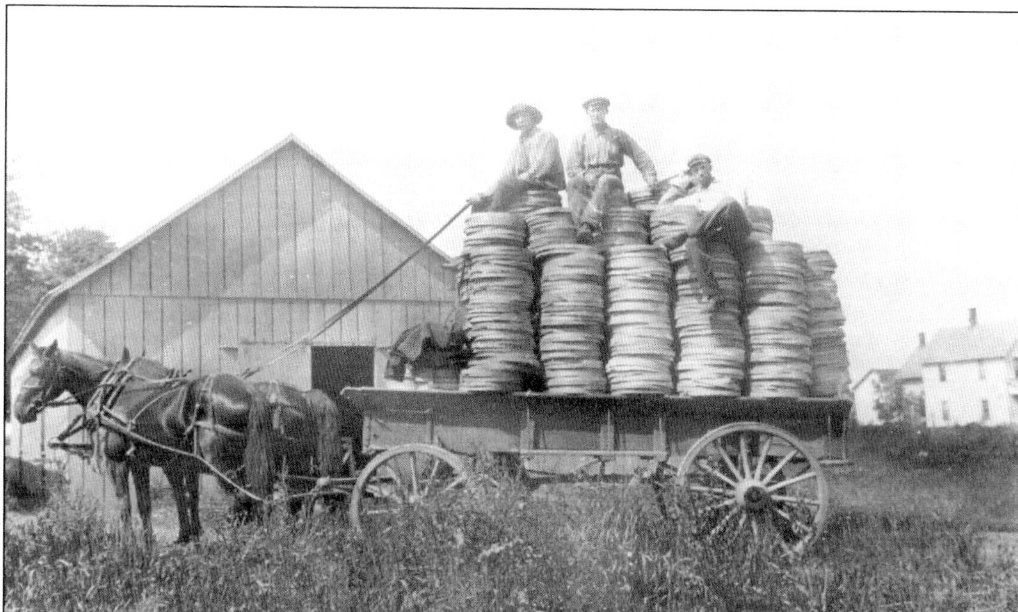

Clarence Carey's cooper shop, located near the railroad tracks in Wakeman, made barrels. Clarence Carey is pictured in this c. 1900 photograph wearing the white shirt and resting on top of the barrel rims.

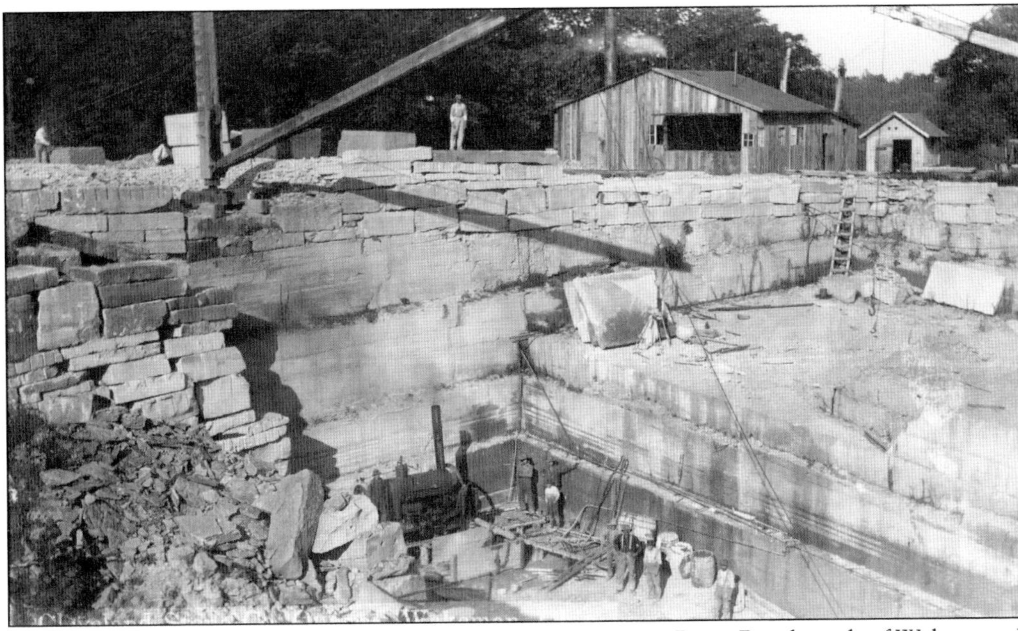

This c. 1900 photograph shows the Robinson Quarry on West River Road north of Wakeman. It was later owned by the Cleveland Cliffs Quarry and was one of the reasons for the large amount of rail siding in town.

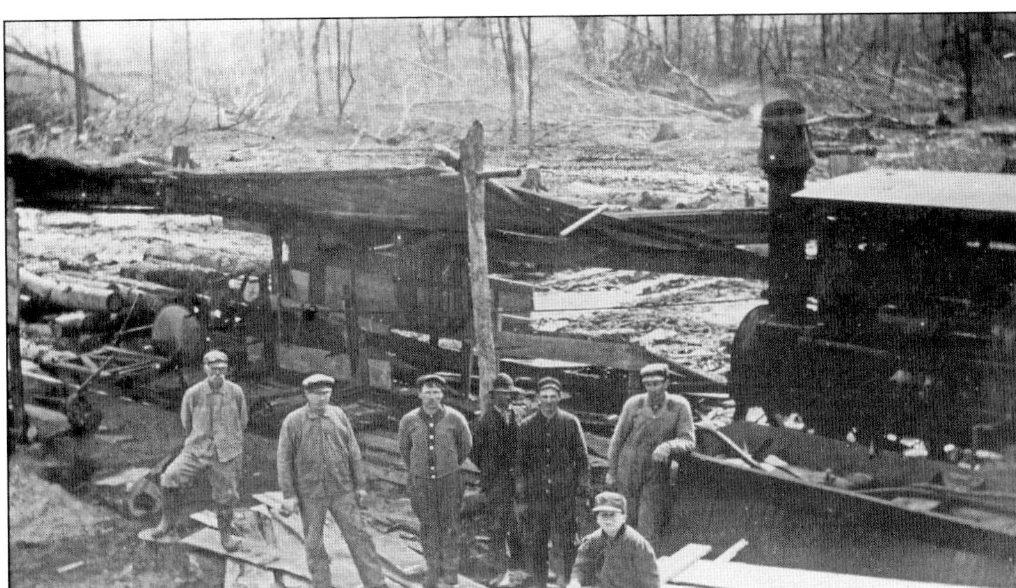

Workers pose for this photograph at Hyde's Sawmill, which was located at the end of Clark Street in Wakeman. The steam engine was used to power the sawmill.

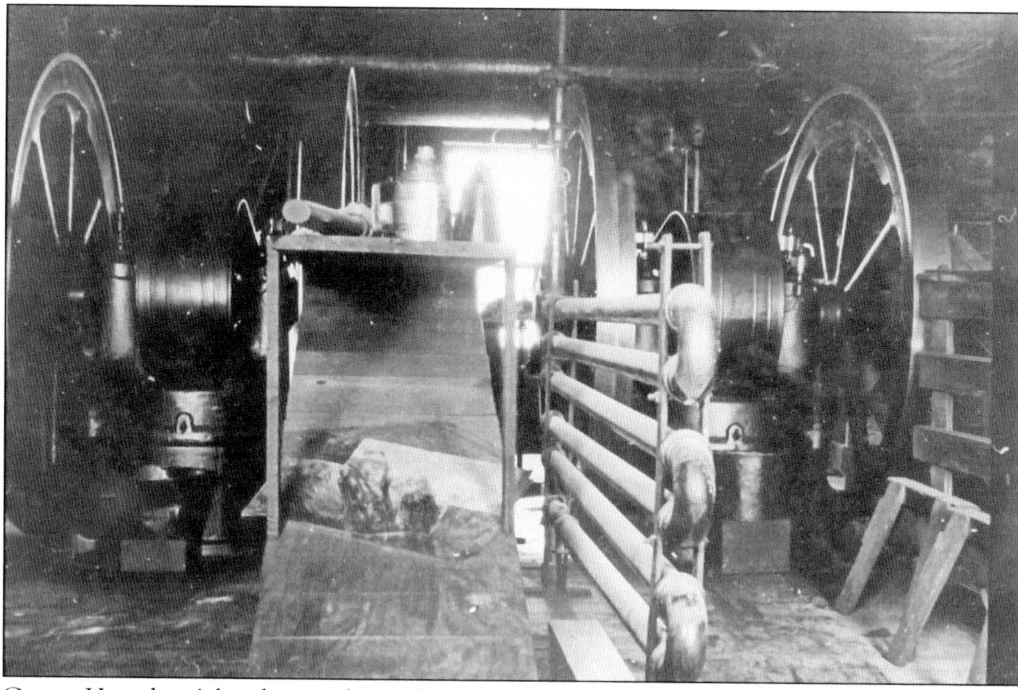

George Humphrey's bending works used this steam engine to make stays for barrels. This building in downtown Wakeman was sold to F.A. Denman in 1900 to be converted into a mill.

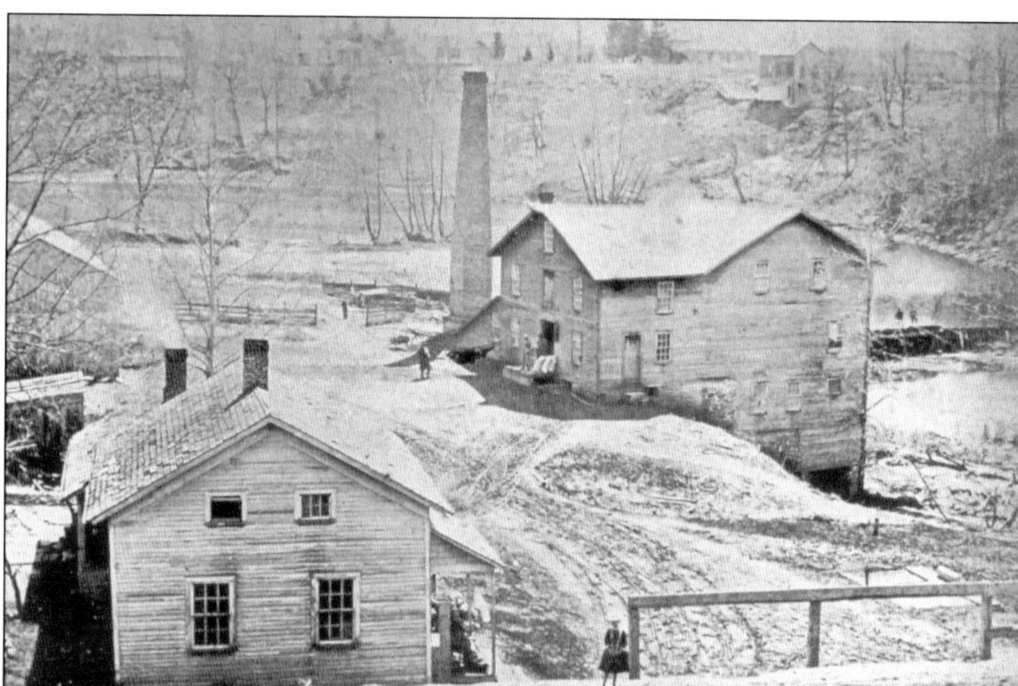

This flour mill, formerly located on the Vermilion River in Wakeman, used hydraulic power. In 1901, the mill burned mysteriously the same night its owner disappeared.

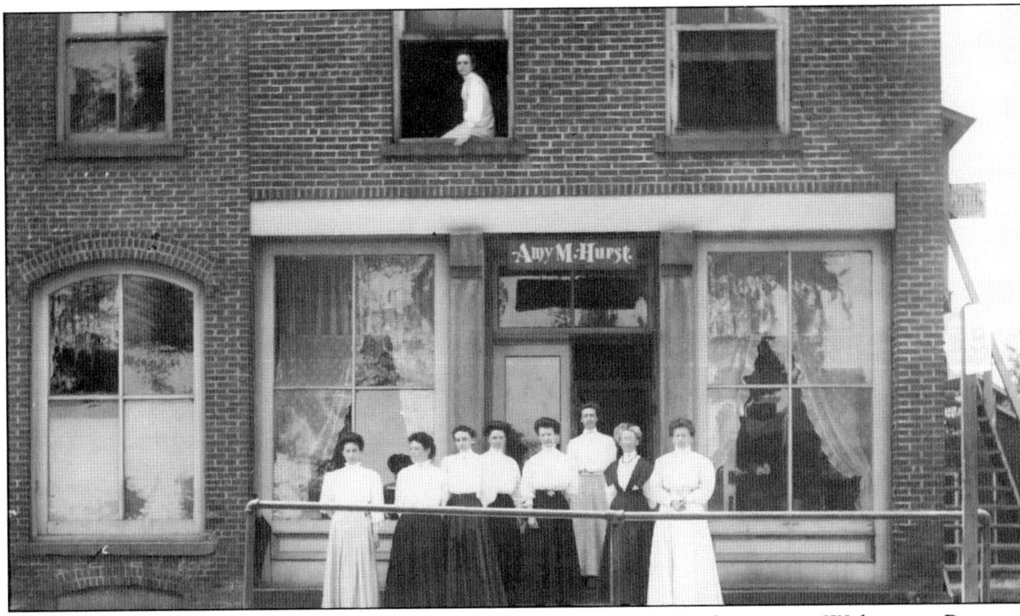

This c. 1900 photograph shows the storefront of Amy M. Hurst in downtown Wakeman. Pictured from left to right are Beulah Eastwood, Maude Munger, Malthy Bumenstul, Nellie Krebs, Marion Hurst Peck, Madge Sherman, Miss Swift, and Amy Hurst. The person in the upper window is unidentified. Amy Hurst's shop was a millinery with an emphasis on fine dressmaking. (Courtesy of the Wakeman Community Library.)

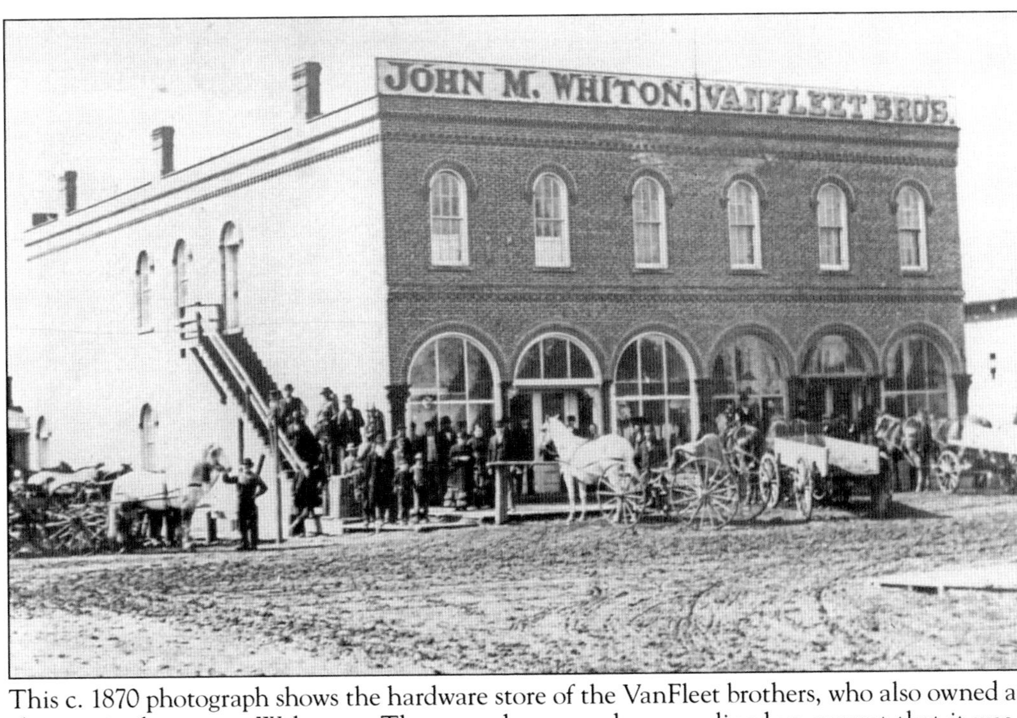

This c. 1870 photograph shows the hardware store of the VanFleet brothers, who also owned an elevator in downtown Wakeman. The many horses and wagons lined up suggest that it was a busy place. A bank currently occupies this corner in Wakeman.

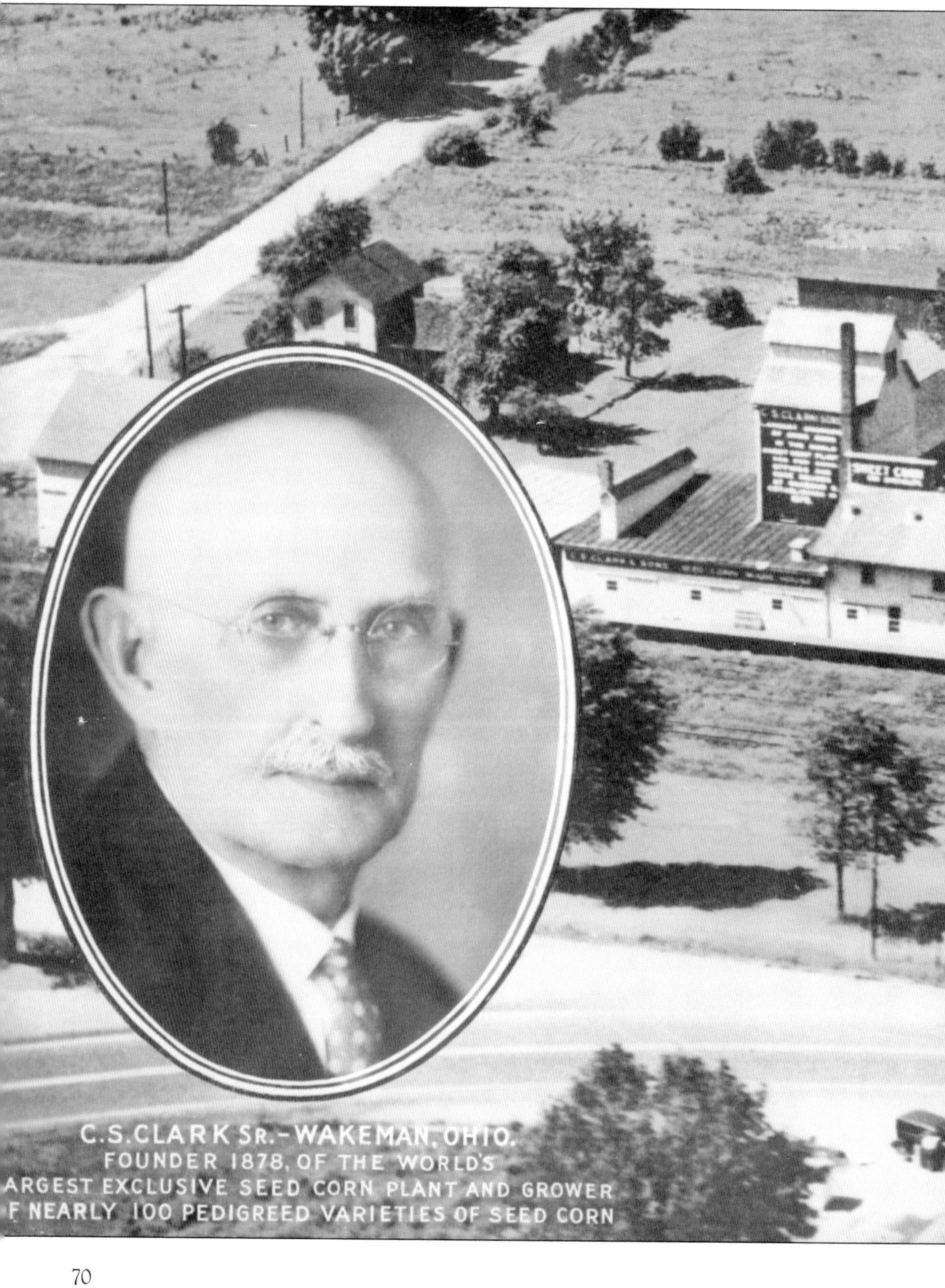
C.S.CLARK SR.-WAKEMAN, OHIO.
FOUNDER 1878, OF THE WORLD'S
ARGEST EXCLUSIVE SEED CORN PLANT AND GROWER
F NEARLY 100 PEDIGREED VARIETIES OF SEED CORN

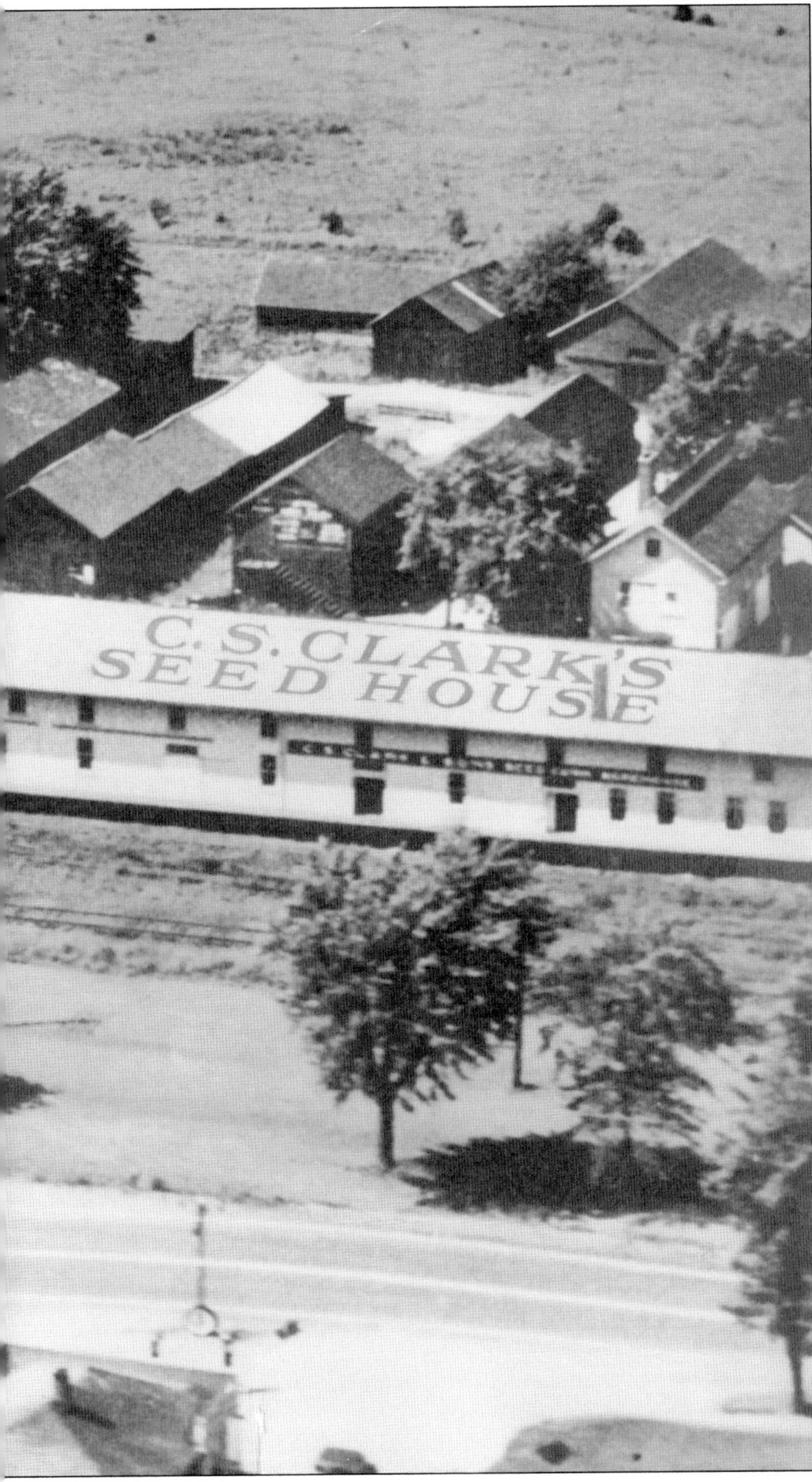

C.S. Clark himself probably took this photograph, from either the 1920s or 1930s, from his private airplane. He founded C.S. Clark's Seed House in 1878 and was one of the largest exporters of seed corn in the United States. He produced nearly 100 pedigreed varieties of seed corn. The seed house still stands in downtown Wakeman along the railroad tracks, and his name is still partially visible on the roof. In the foreground, a gas station is visible. The buildings of J.J. McMann's lumberyard are also visible behind the long white seed house. (Courtesy of the Wakeman Community Library.)

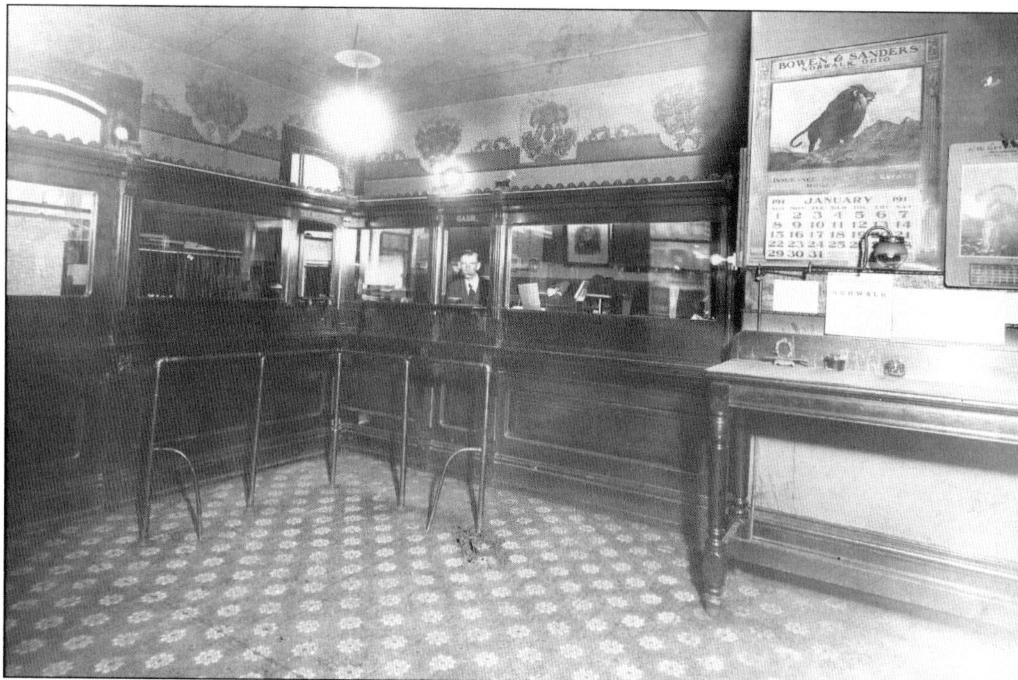

This interior photograph of the Wakeman Bank shows Gale White at the teller's window. The calendar on the wall reads January 1911. The bank was located on Main Street in downtown Wakeman east of its current location. (Courtesy of the Wakeman Community Library.)

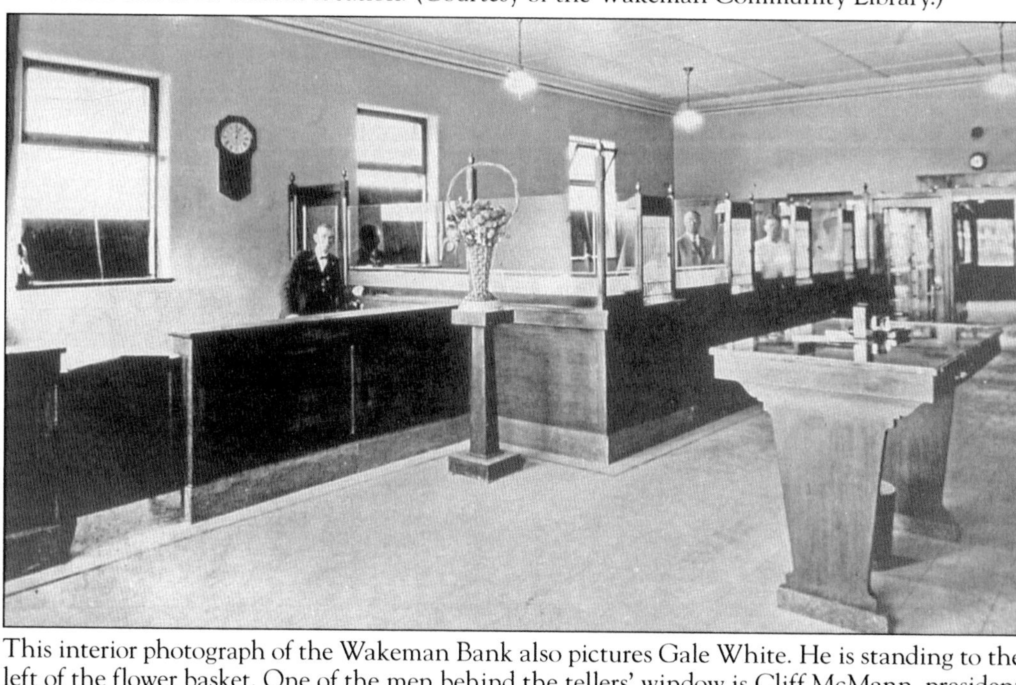

This interior photograph of the Wakeman Bank also pictures Gale White. He is standing to the left of the flower basket. One of the men behind the tellers' window is Cliff McMann, president of the bank for many years. This photograph is from about 1930, after the bank moved to its current location on the corner of Main and Pleasant Streets. White was a longtime executive of the Wakeman Bank.

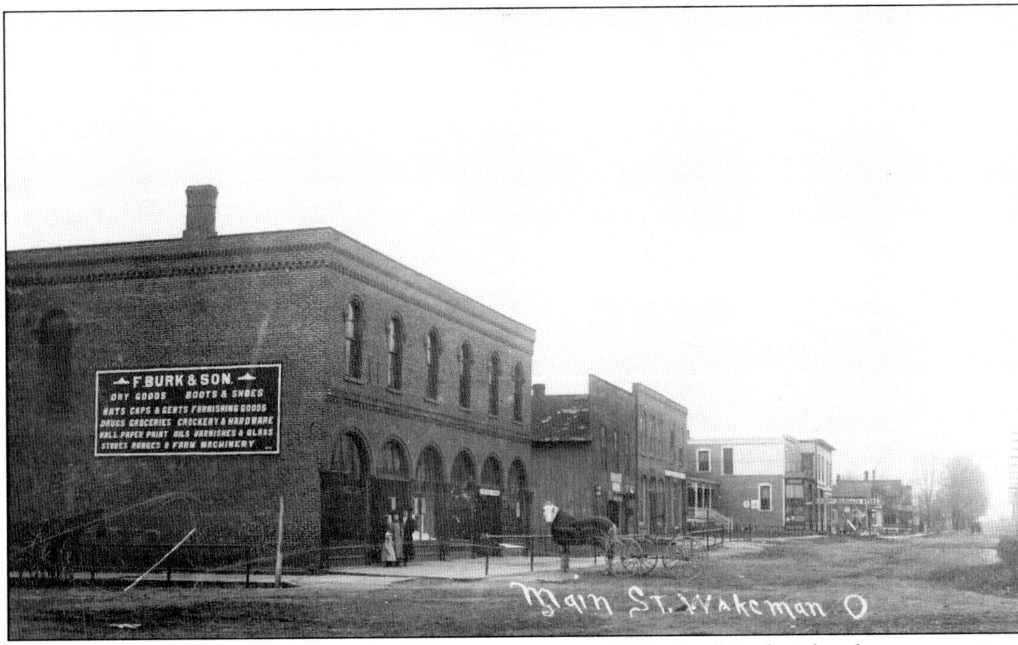

This photograph shows downtown Wakeman prior to 1908. Fred Burke's hardware store is on the corner in the former VanFleet Bros. store. The horse looking at the camera is blanketed for winter.

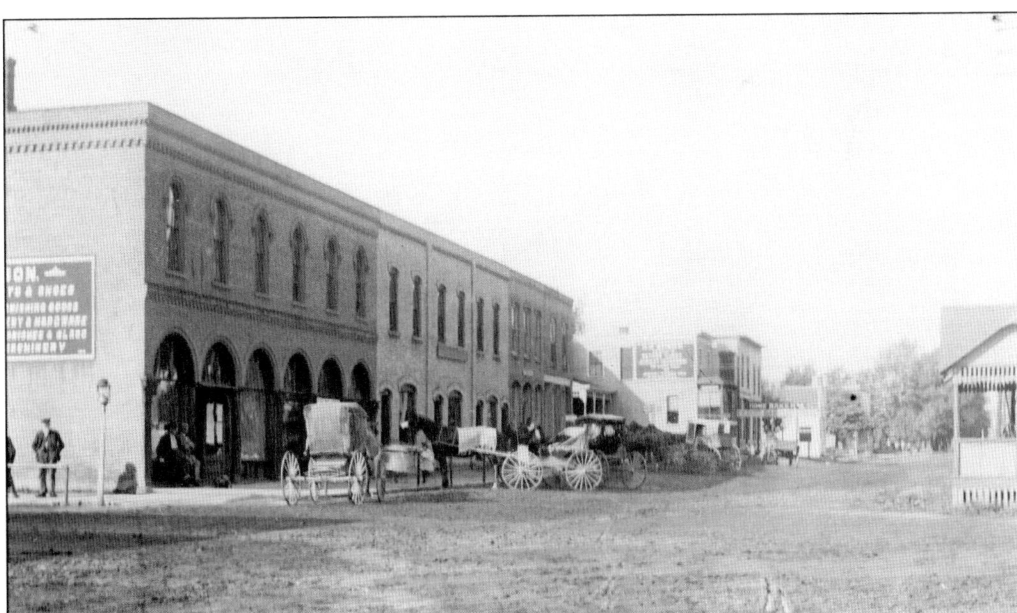

This photograph was taken around 1910 after part of the block was constructed, as seen by the lighter-colored brick. The village bandstand is visible on the far right of the photograph.

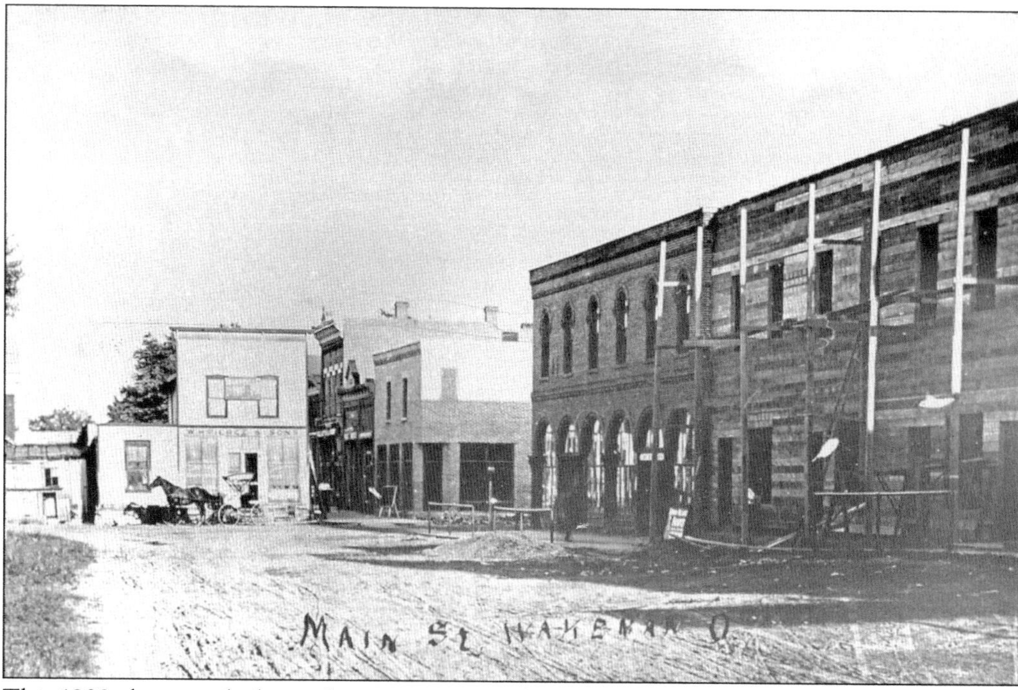

This 1908 photograph shows the construction of a new corner grocery store in the center. The existing grocery store had been moved to the middle of the street and was in business. Construction was also ongoing on the "Gibson block" on the far right of the picture.

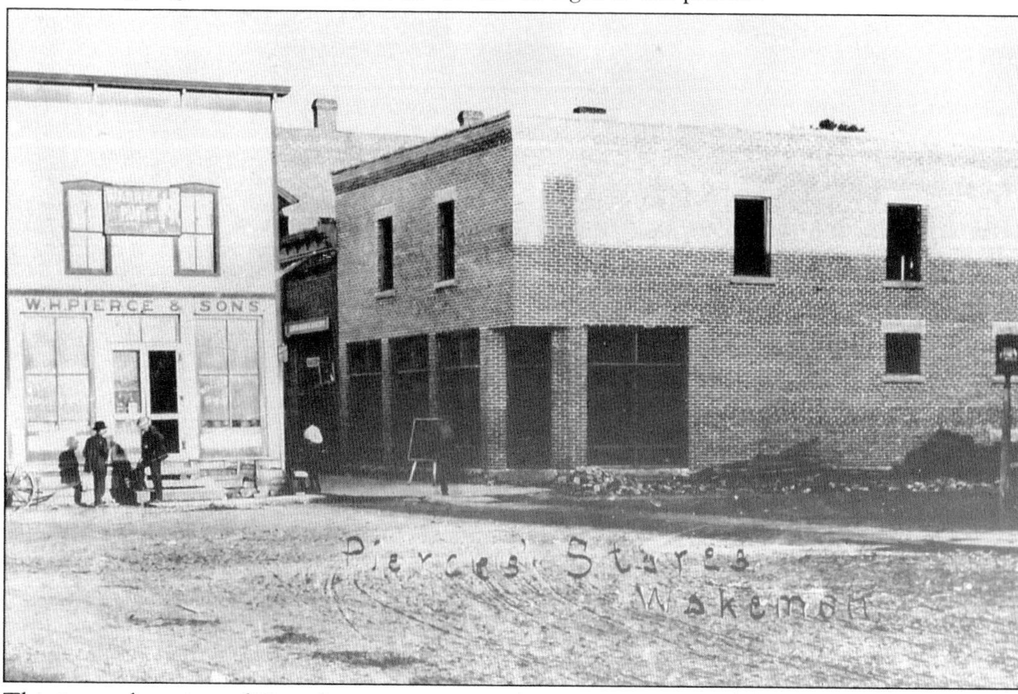

This is another view of Pierce's grocery store under construction and the former building out in the street. The newer grocery store on the corner continued to operate through many generations and owners until it finally closed in 2010.

Clifford "Pete" Campbell is pictured here in 1937 or 1938 in front of his restaurant that stood for many years in downtown Wakeman. The dog in the photograph, Duke, is Clyde Walton's.

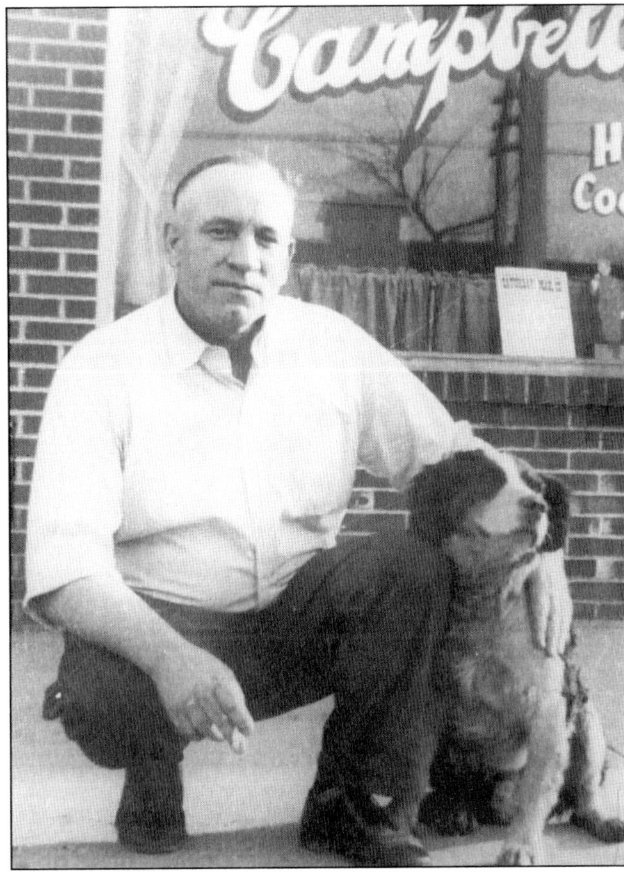

This 1930s photograph shows Cooley's Corner, a restaurant and gas station that stood on the corner of Route 20 and Butler Road east of Wakeman. (Courtesy of Ben Brookover.)

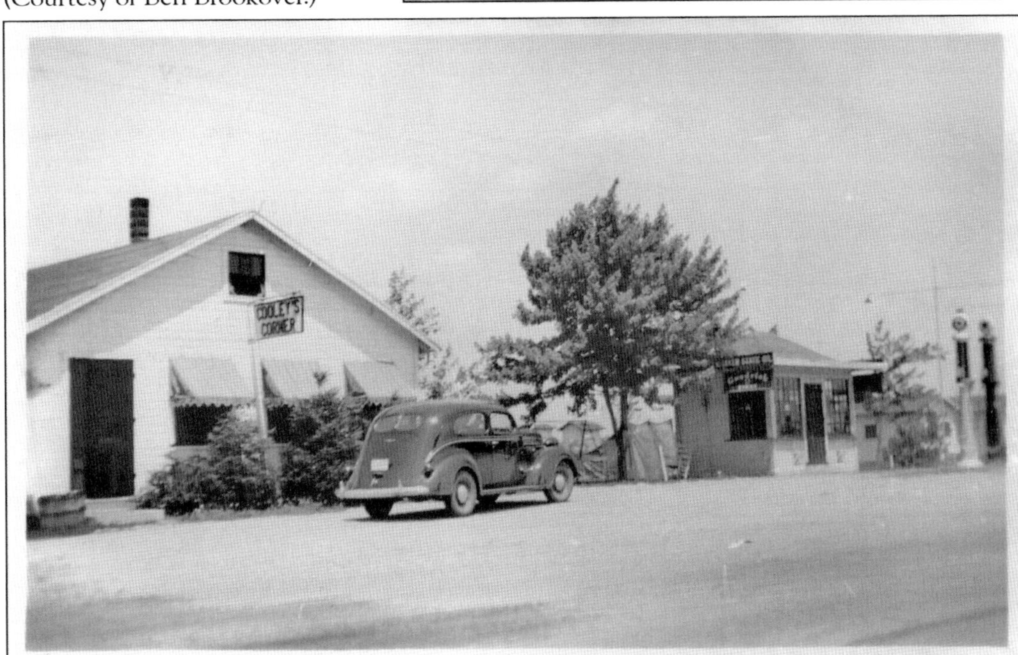

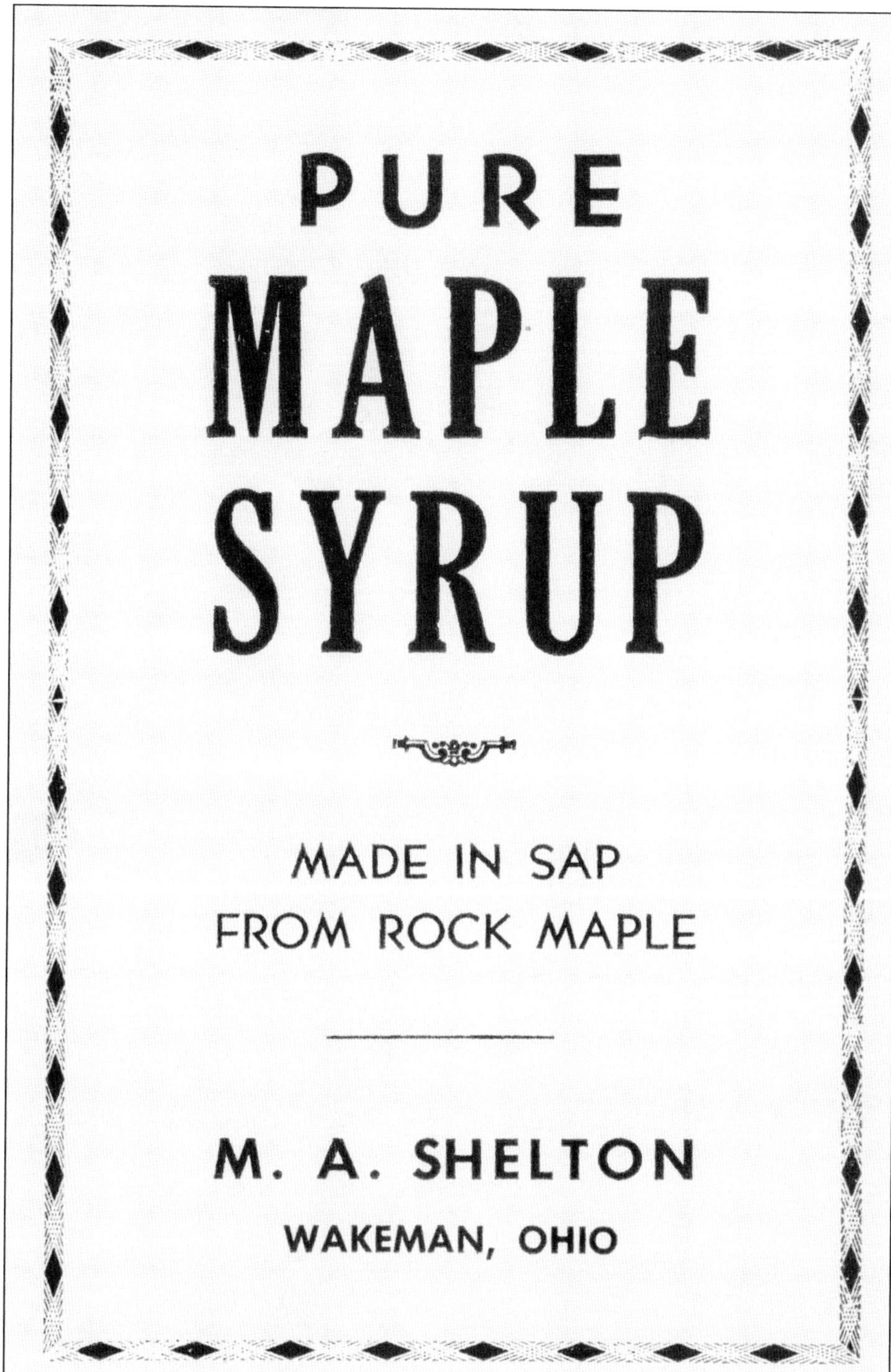

Shelton's sugar bush was located on Route 60 south of Wakeman. Myron Shelton owned the business, which made pure maple syrup. Tapping the maple trees in the winter and boiling down the sap in sugar shanties to make maple syrup is a time-consuming process. Many local residents recall growing up eating the sweet syrup on their pancakes.

Myron Shelton (left), who owned a business harvesting and selling pure maple syrup, talks to his friend Fred E. Graves, who owned the International Harvester Dealership. The abundant maple trees in the area made owning a "sugar bush" a profitable enterprise. They are pictured here behind Graves's house in the 1950s.

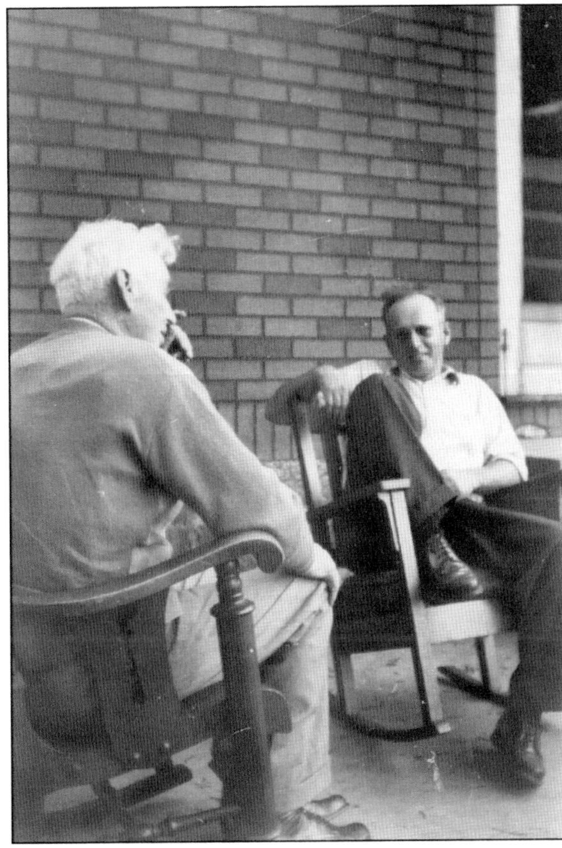

Graves Implement on 45 Pleasant Street in Wakeman is pictured in 1953. The business, which has operated since 1936, sells, services, and restores tractors. Amy Potter, standing in doorway, did part-time bookkeeping for Fred and Doris Graves. The 1952 Dodge in the photograph belonged to the Graves family.

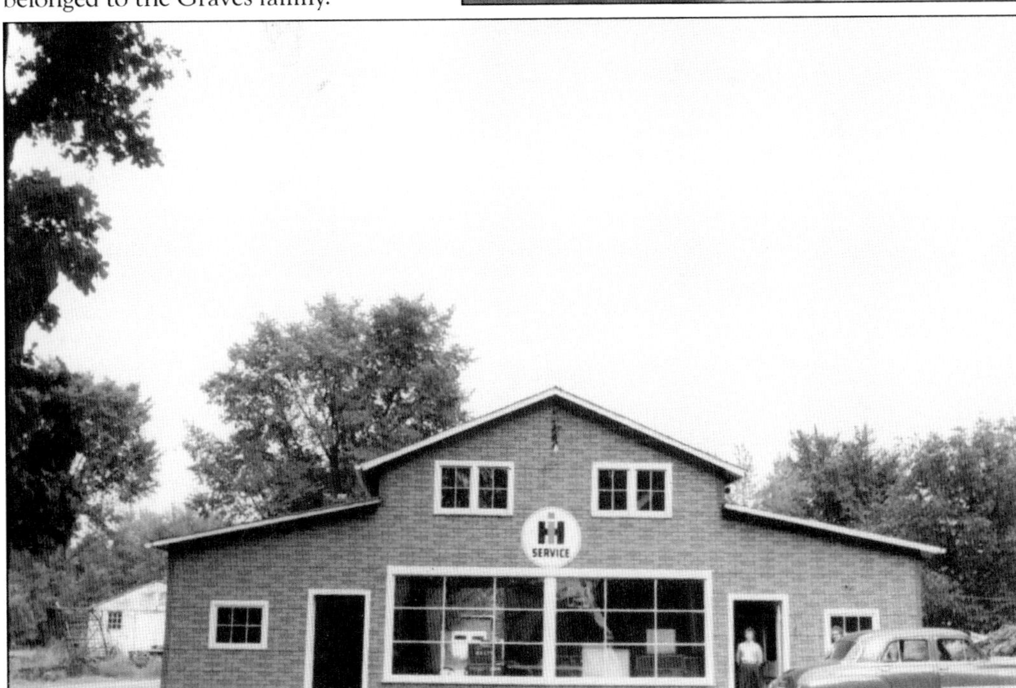

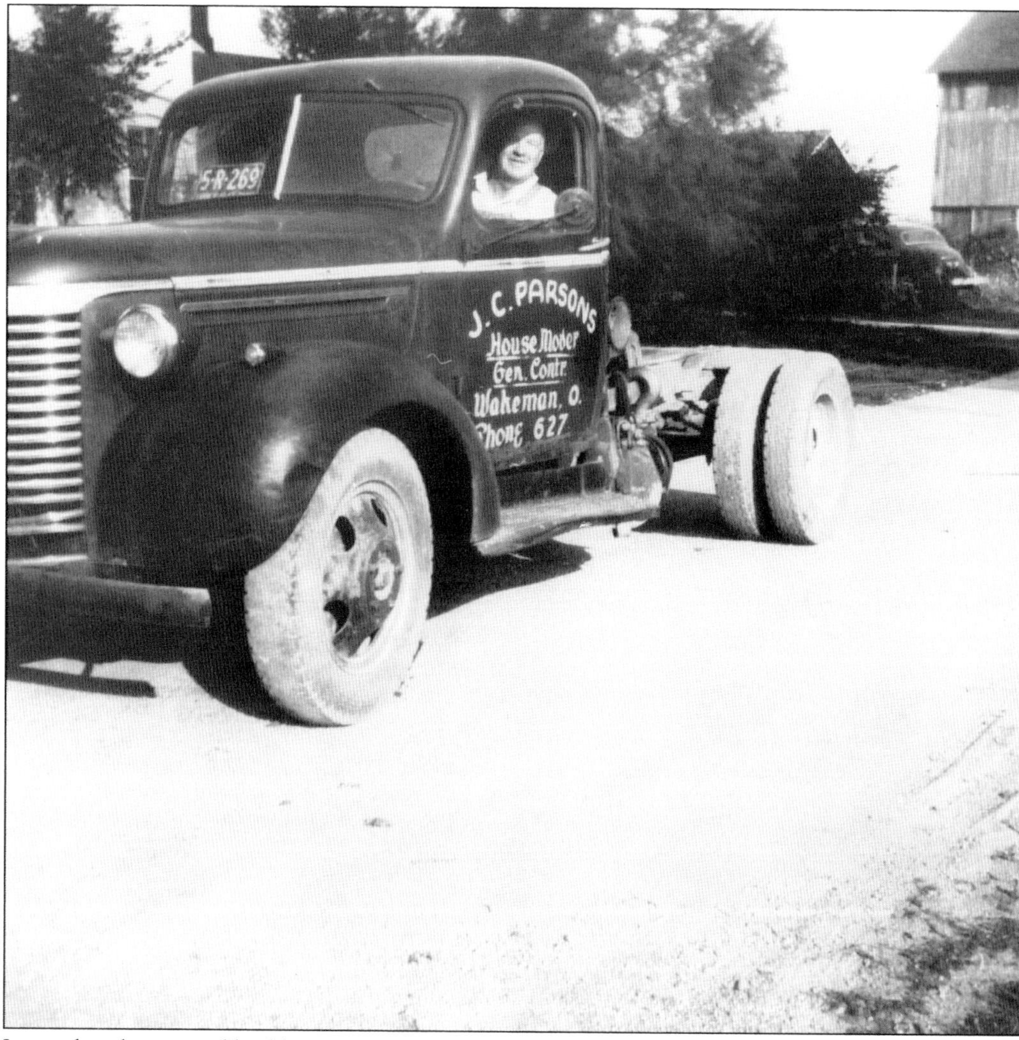

Legendary house and building mover James Parsons is shown in his 1941 GMC truck. The truck had a winch on the back for moving the variety of buildings that were all in a day's work for him. He was missing one finger, but liked to hook his fingers in his overalls in front and twiddle them; it made people look twice. His son Richard also helped with the family businesses of farming, moving, and serving the community.

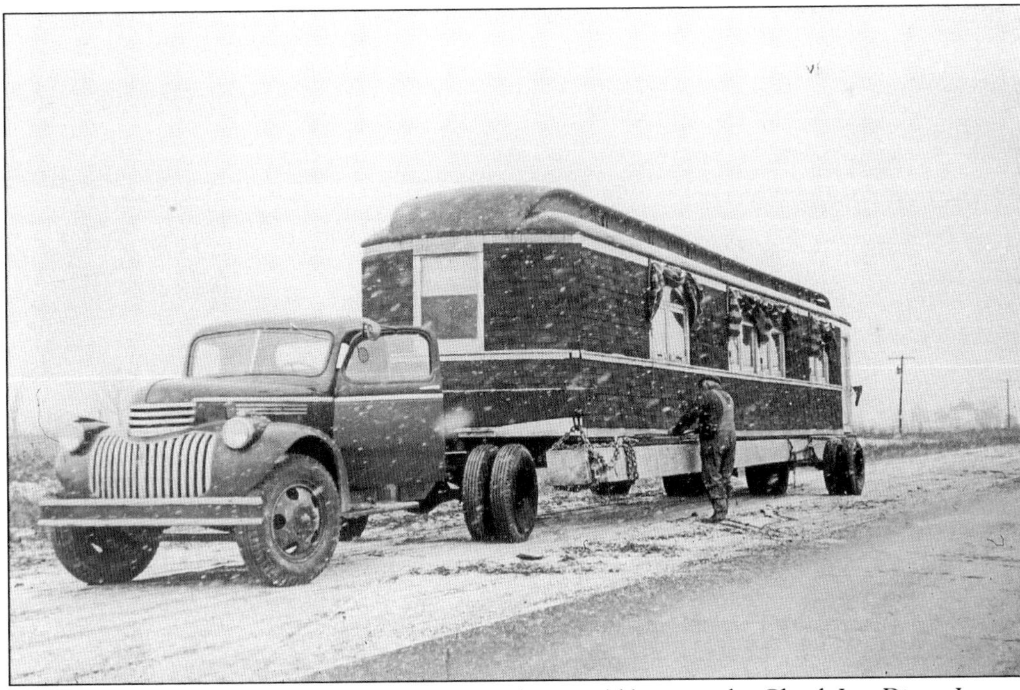

James Parsons is pictured moving the train car that would become the Check-Inn Diner. It was a snowy day at the diner's location west of Wakeman, where Townline Road meets Route 20.

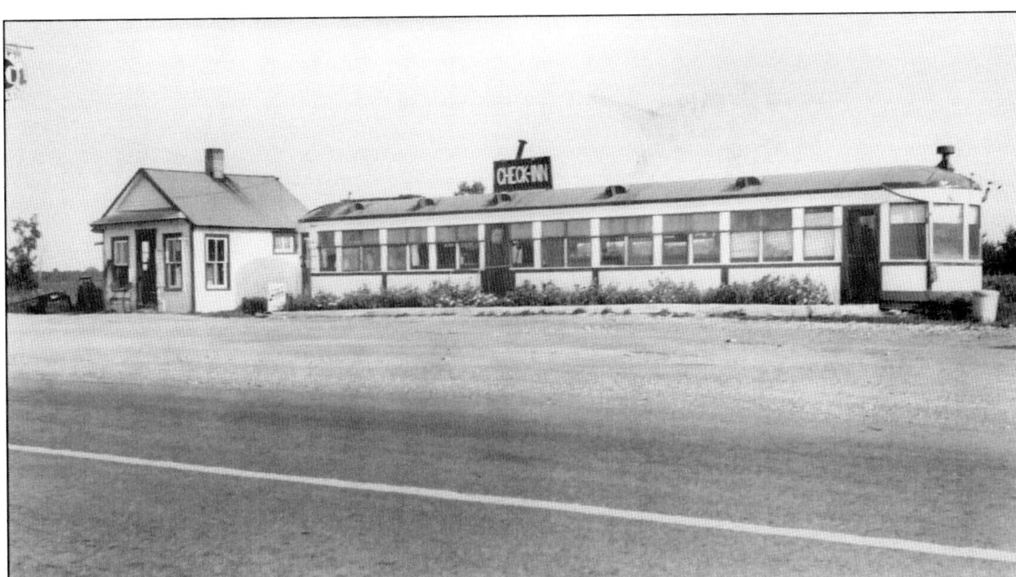

The Check-Inn Diner was opened in December 1937 by Ruth (Crabbs) Todd, Madge (Crabbs) Freeman, Freda (last name unknown), who was a friend of the Crabbs family, and Ruby (last name unknown), who was an older woman from Townsend. Helen (Crabbs) Nielsen Sowers joined her sisters at the diner when she graduated from high school. Ruby made pies while the others cooked and waited tables. Truck drivers were the largest groups of customers, with additional tourist trade on Sundays. The ladies sold the diner in the spring of 1941, and it remained open until the late 1950s. (Courtesy of Sue Palmer.)

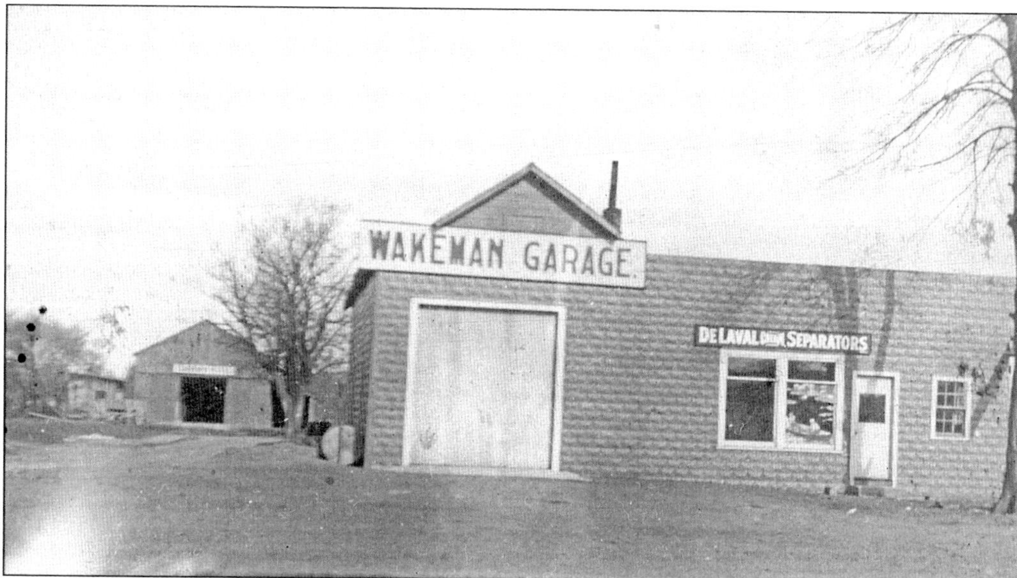

This photograph from the 1930s shows the Wakeman Garage, operated by Rollie Barnes. It later became Kenny Hurst Motor Sales (a Chevrolet dealer). The sign over the windows advertises DeLaval Cream Separators, which were not used after the 1940s. Barnes's brother, Louie, sold Ford vehicles down the street.

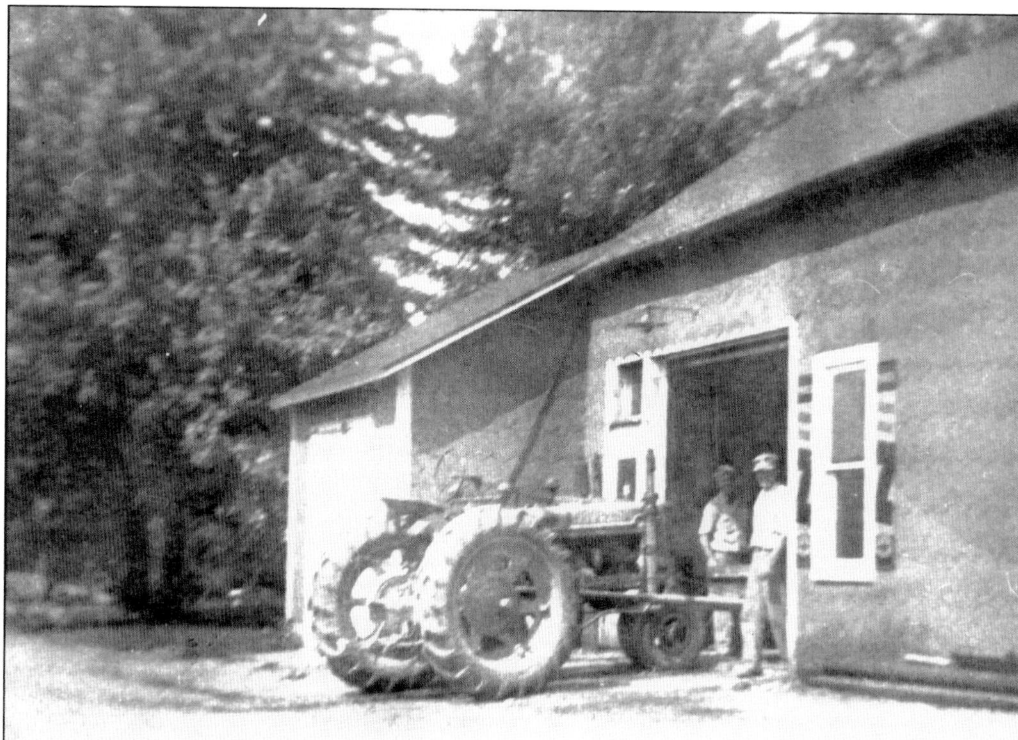

Kenny Hurst's Chevrolet Dealership is pictured, along with the 1941 International H tractor being repaired. The tractor belonged to his brother, John Hurst, also pictured.

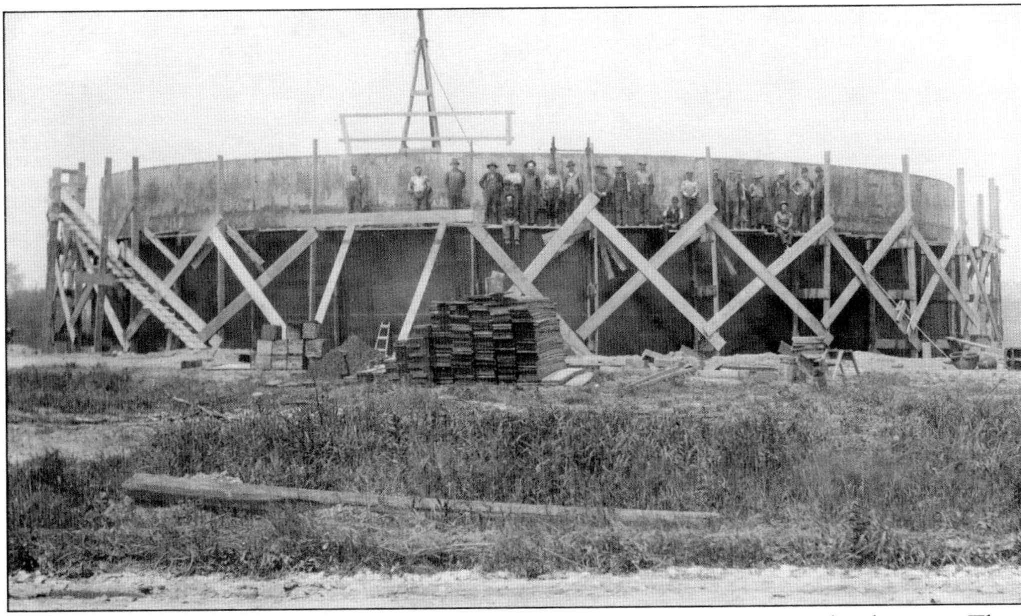

Workers construct storage tanks at the Buckeye Pipe Line pumping station by the river. There were four such tanks that were constructed with metal sides and tar-paper roofs and were large enough to drive a truck into. The plant was built in 1895 by the Standard Oil Company, which was owned by John Rockefeller.

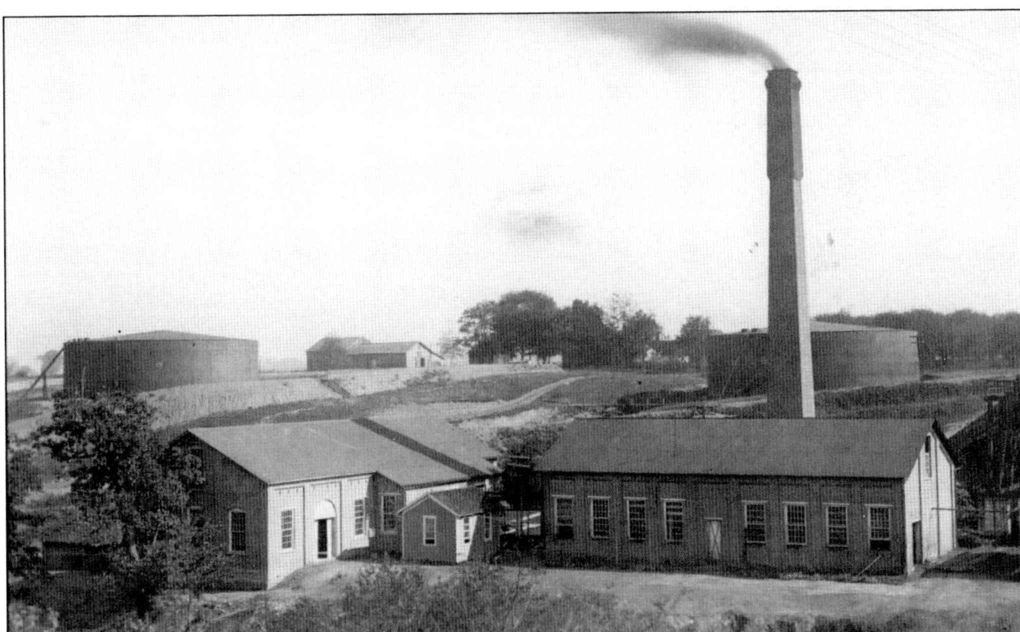

A view of the Buckeye pumping station shows two of the large round storage tanks and the tall smokestack. The tanks were believed to be necessary because they did not think oil could be pumped all the way from Cygnet, Ohio to Manaway, Ohio without stopping. They discovered otherwise, however, and the storage tanks became obsolete.

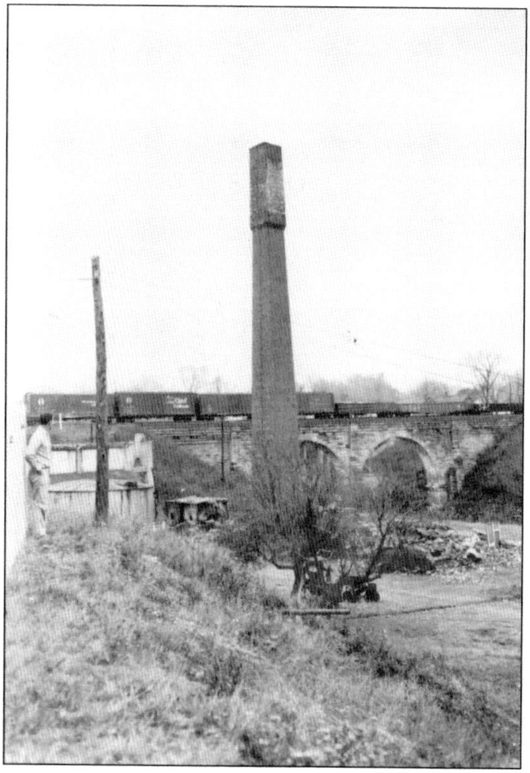

This 1948 photograph shows local resident Harry Swinehart, who worked for the Buckeye Pipe Line, on the far left. The large smoke stack was scheduled for demolition on this day.

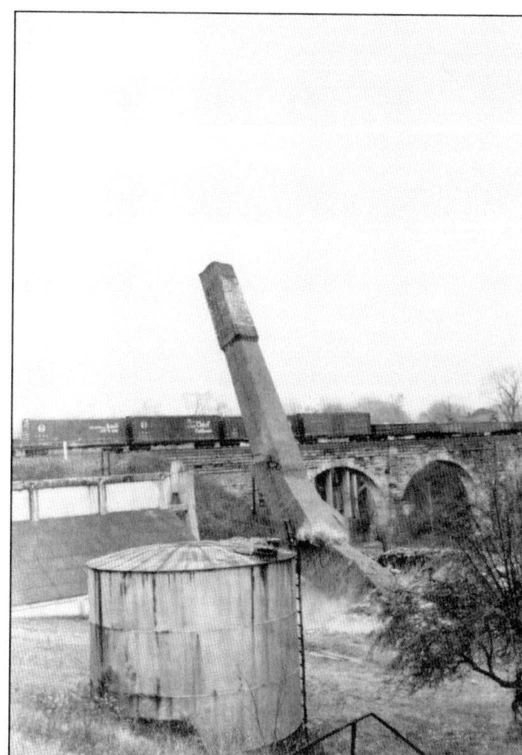

This photograph captures the smokestack in mid-demolition. Reportedly, 27 sticks of dynamite were used to destroy the unused smokestack.

This last photograph in the series of three shows the smokestack completely on the ground. Note the same train peacefully crossing the track on the railroad bridge behind the action. It gives one a good idea of how quickly the stack came down, but makes one wonder what the train engineer might have been thinking.

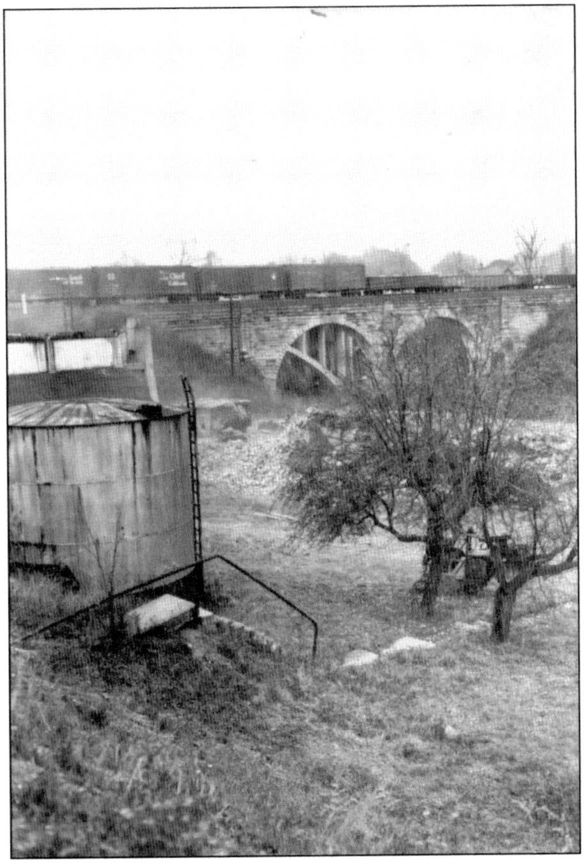

A rear view of the Buckeye Pipe Line property shows the coal tipple on the right. Railroad cars full of coal would back out on top of the structure and open on the bottom to dump the coal. Large amounts of coal were needed to feed the furnaces that ran the steam pumps.

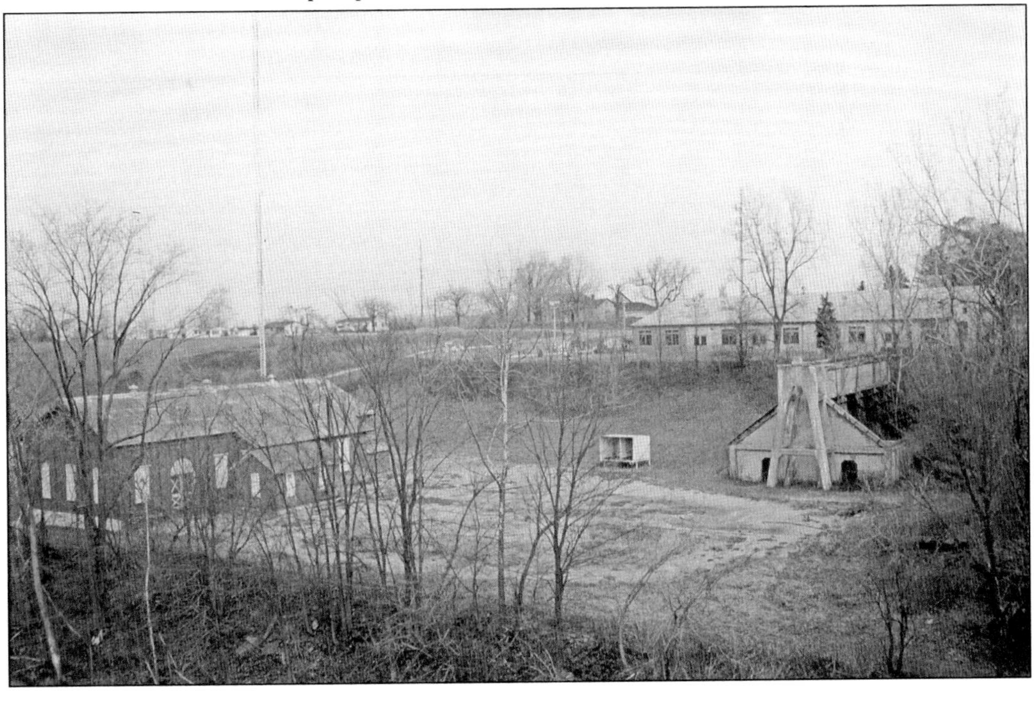

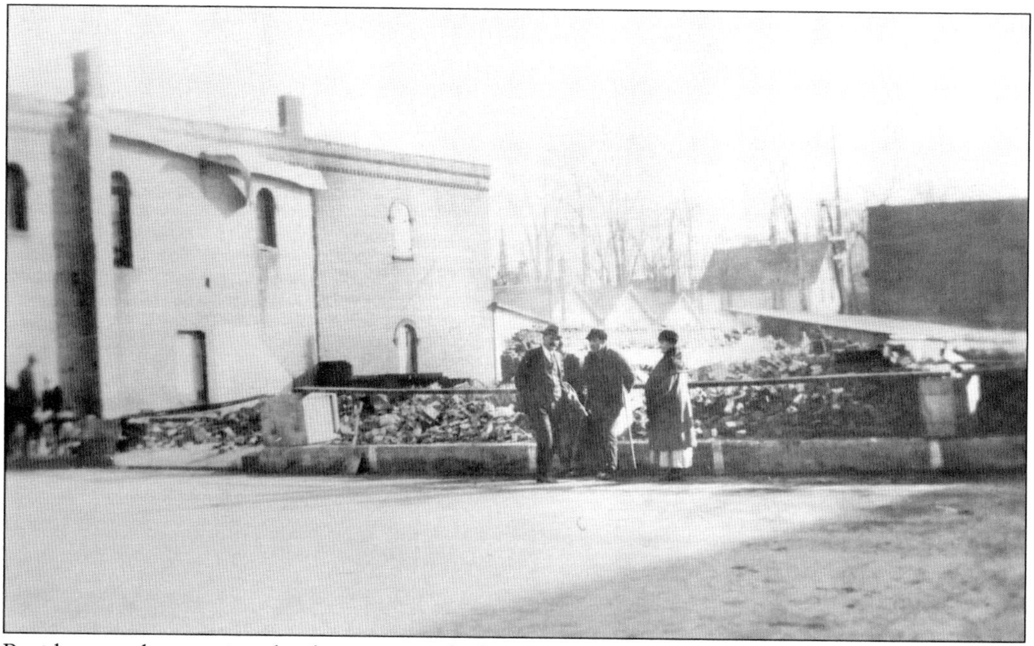

Residents gather to view the destruction of a fire that occurred on November 28, 1927. A portion of the business district in downtown Wakeman burned, including Campbell's Restaurant and the telephone office. Mrs. Benson was manning the switchboard at the time and stayed at her post long enough to alert the fire department in Norwalk, 12 miles away. The telephone office was quickly moved to the ladies' sitting room at the passenger depot across the street.

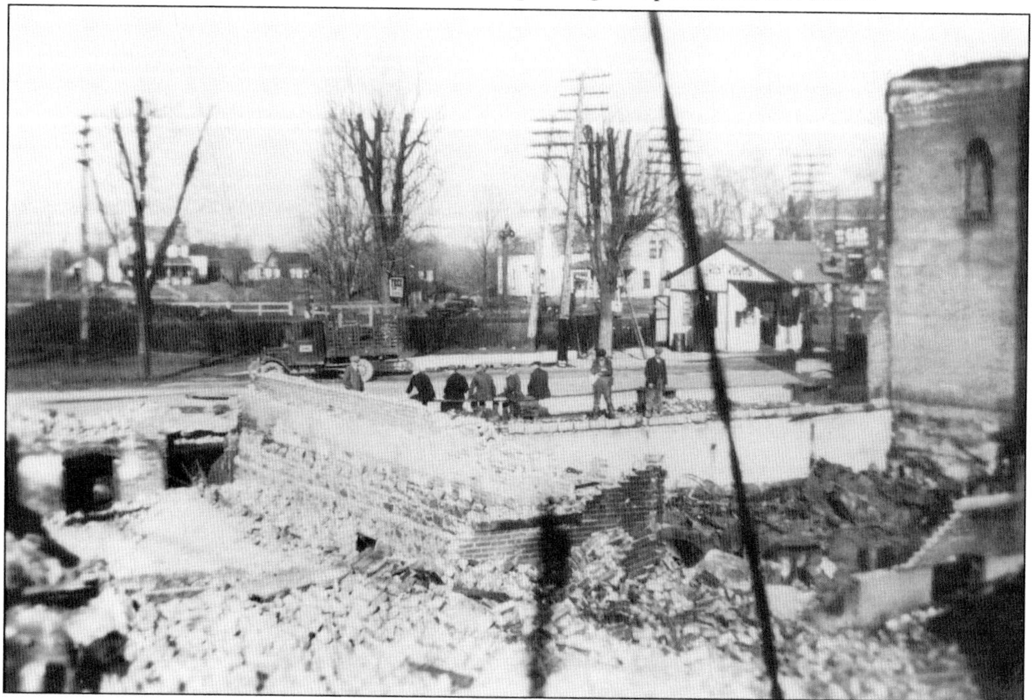

Cleanup begins after the fire of November 28, 1927. Wakeman owned a Model T fire truck at the time of the fire, but did not have an organized fire department to fight the blaze.

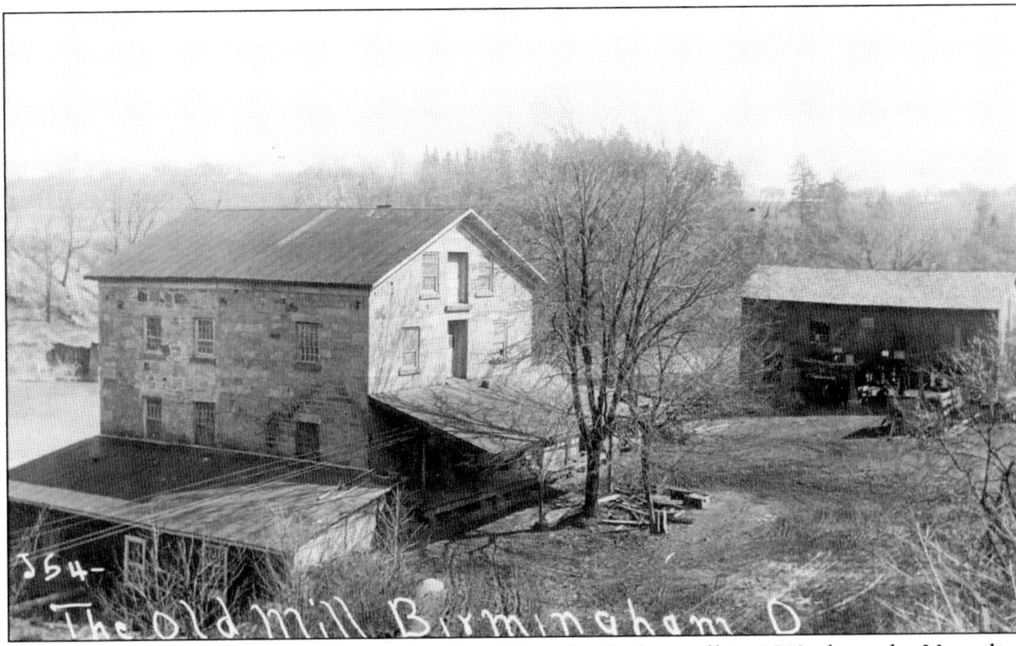

Perez Starr, one of the first citizens of Birmingham, built this mill in 1819 along the Vermilion River in Birmingham. The mill used a large wooden dam to harness the river's power. (Courtesy of Jason Gargasz.)

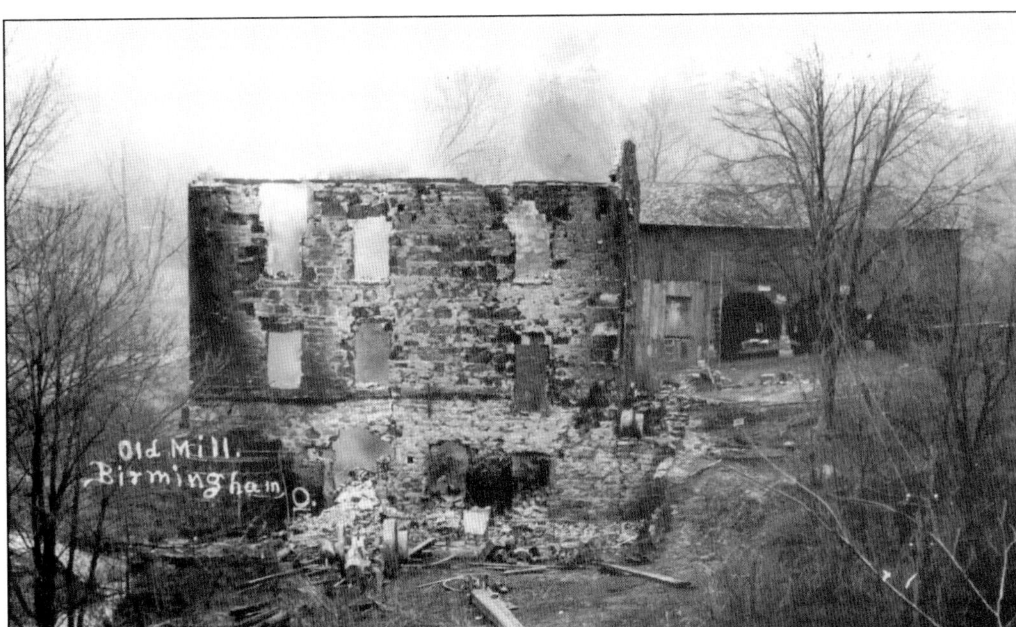

The mill was never rebuilt after it burned in 1906, and in 1913 the wooden dam washed out in a large flood. The foundations of the mill can still be seen on the Schoepfle Gardens property in Birmingham. (Courtesy of Jason Gargasz.)

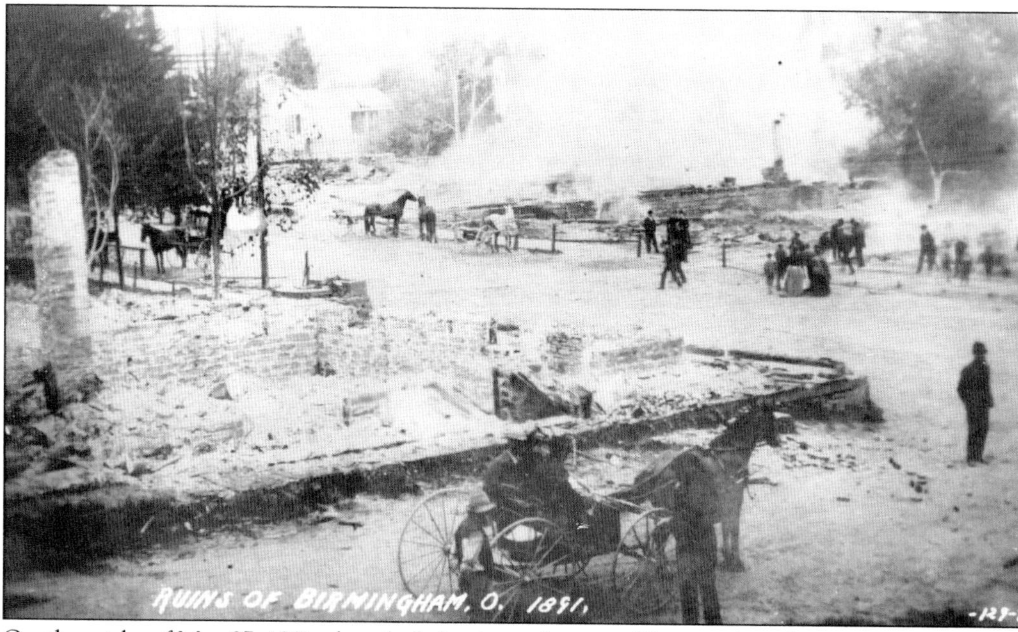

On the night of May 27, 1891, the whole business district of Birmingham burned to the ground. There was no fire protection available, and 10 buildings including a hardware, tin shop, general store, post office, dry goods store, barbershop, blacksmith shop, meat market, and hotel burned completely. A few houses burned, too. (Courtesy of Jason Gargasz.)

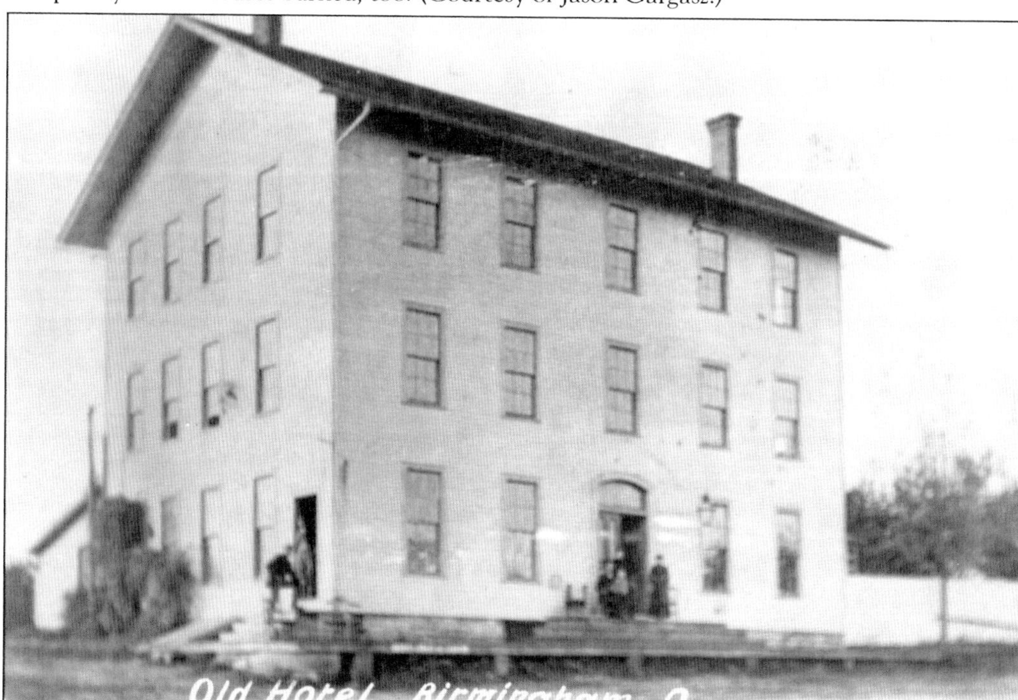

This photograph of the Shoff House, a hotel in Birmingham, was taken prior to the 1891 fire that destroyed the downtown. The Shoff House was known for social gatherings and elegant New Year's Eve parties. It was also destroyed in the fire. (Courtesy of Jason Gargasz.)

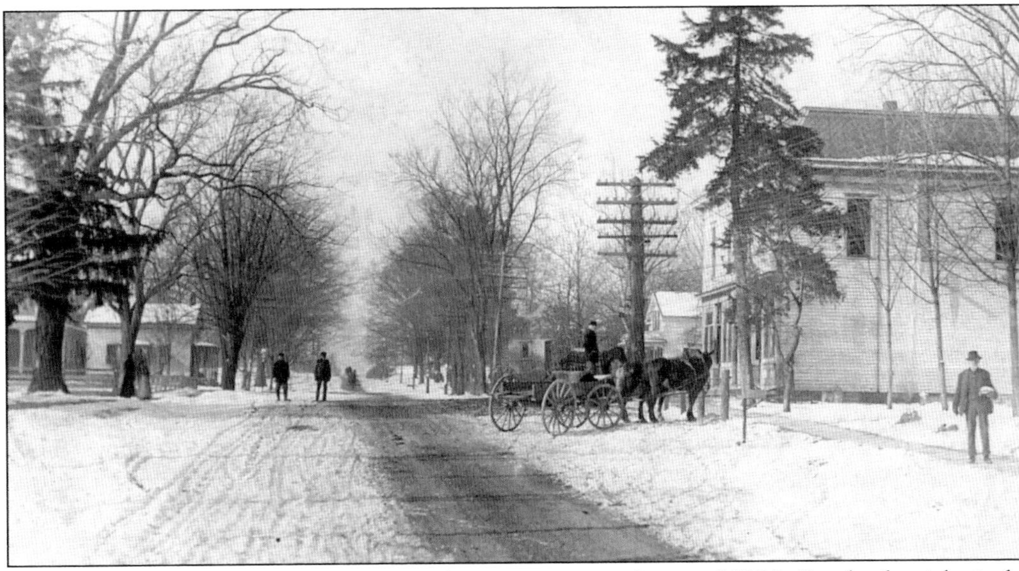

This wintry scene in downtown Birmingham was captured around 1900. On the far right is the Schisler and Gary Store. The upstairs of the building housed meeting rooms for the Masonic Lodge and also for the telephone exchange. (Courtesy of Jason Gargasz.)

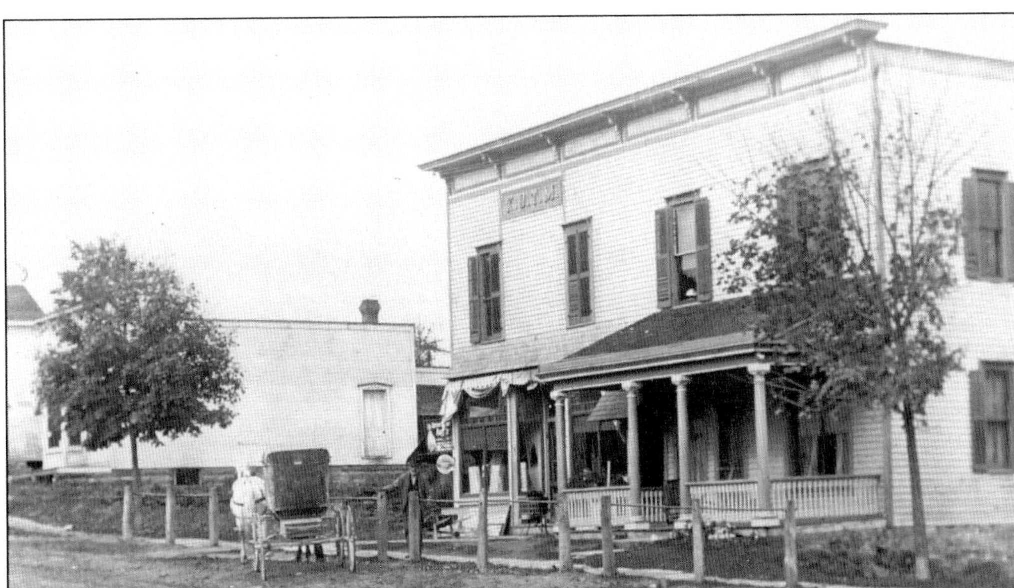

A general store labeled as W.P. Funk's Store is pictured here before 1900. At this time, Birmingham was a thriving town, rivaling nearby Wakeman and Kipton in business trade. (Courtesy of Jason Gargasz.)

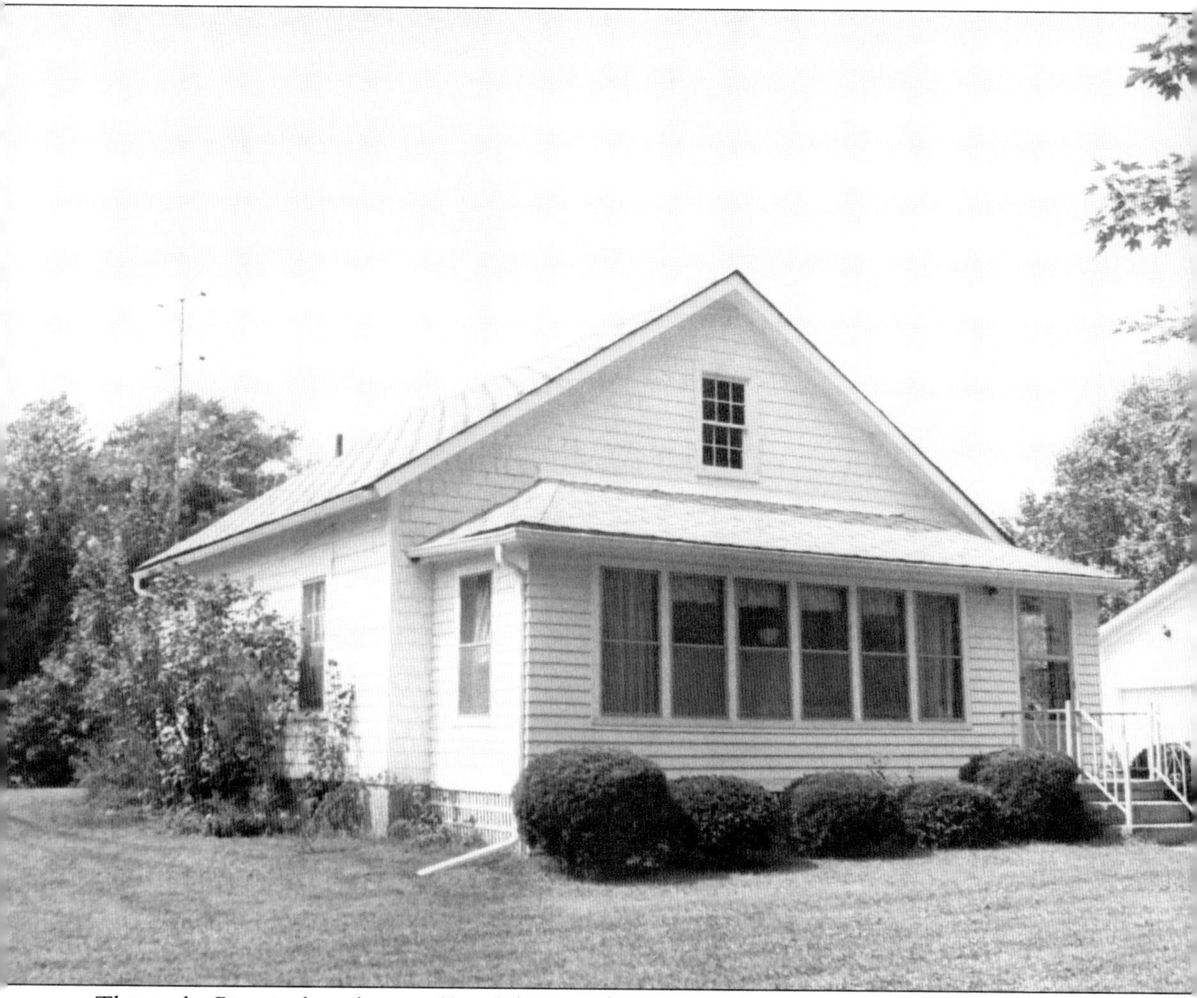

This is the Birmingham home of local doctor Edwin Eugene Beeman, who lived here from 1864 to 1876. He was not just a local doctor, but also a researcher and experimenter. He pioneered the use of pepsin in chewing gum and founded the Beeman Chemical Company. Beeman eventually sold his gum to the American Chicle Company in Chicago, and Beeman chewing gum continued to be manufactured until 1978. Dr. Beeman also had a home and practiced medicine in Wakeman, but he spent his later life in Cleveland, where he died in 1906. (Courtesy of Jason Gargasz.)

Six

Recreation and Entertainment

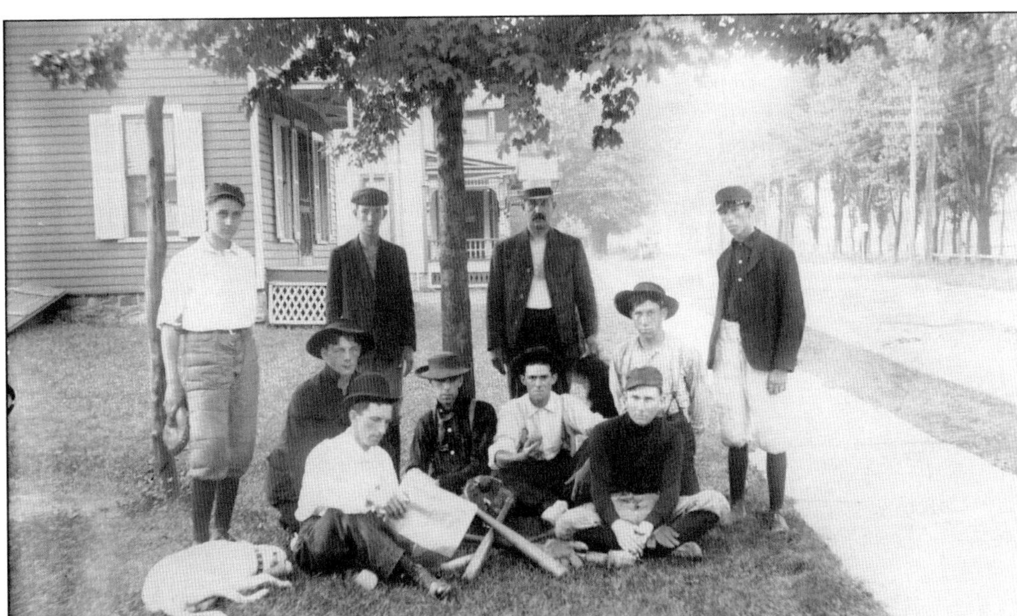

Members of the Wakeman baseball team pose with bats and a pet dog on Main Street. This photograph was taken on July 21, 1906, after an 18-6 win over the team from Birmingham. The names of the players and their positions are written on the back of the picture, though their order is unknown. They are Campbell, right field; Scutt, center field; Croxford, left field; Haskins, third base; Briggs, short stop; McMann, second base; Scott, first base; Mattiford, pitcher and captain; Bellamy, catcher; and Boehner, manager. (Courtesy of the Wakeman Community Library.)

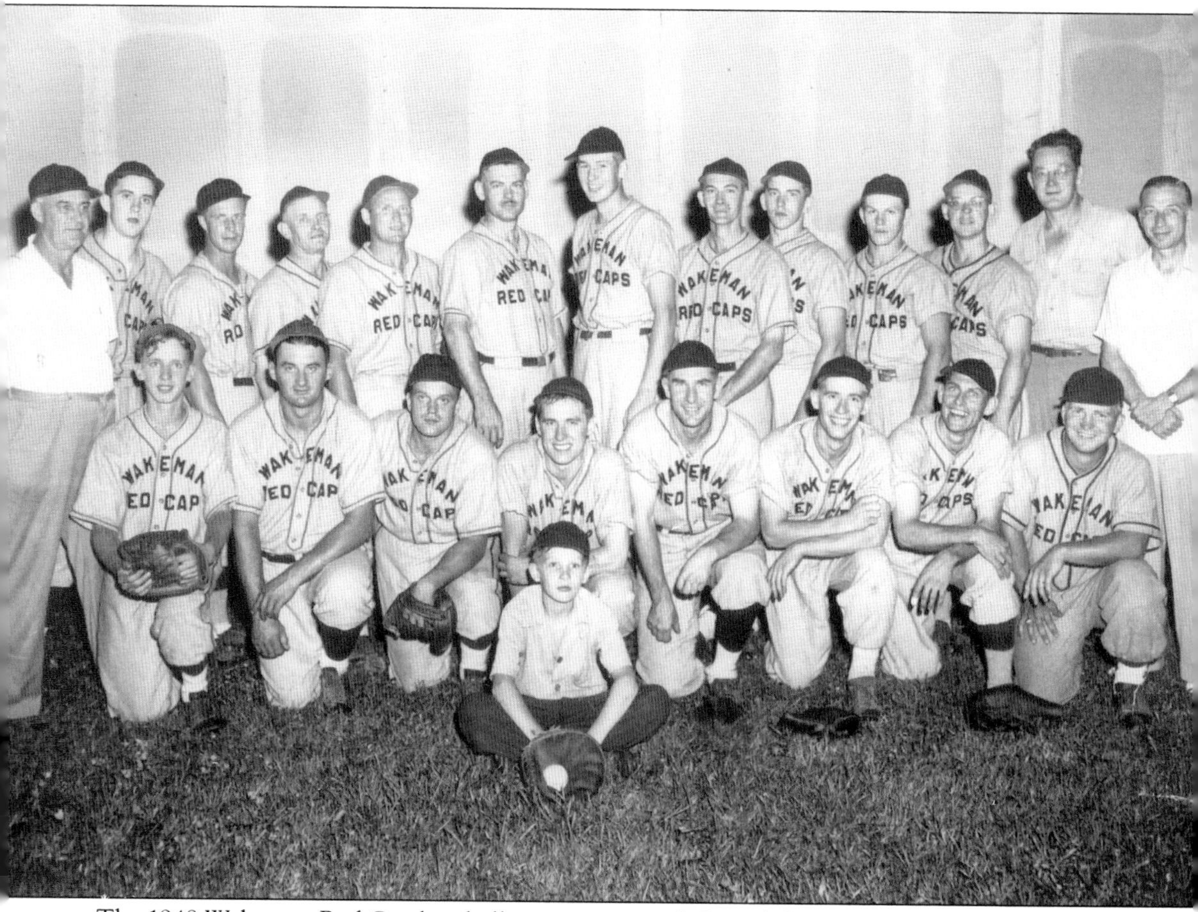

The 1948 Wakeman Red Cap baseball team is pictured. From left to right are (first row) Batboy Roger Howe; (second row) ? Long, ? Zukowski, ? Molnar, Eugene Buckley, Dick Daniels, Lloyd Buckley Jr., Fritz Gerber, and Bob Roe; (third row) Clarence Bailey, Jack Burke, Scortchie Cooper, Lloyd Buckley Sr., Don Wasem, Len Gerber, Tommy Mockler, Charlie Bement, Hayden Buckley, Ed Matus, ? Hoyt, Stan Ketchum, and Gaius Scutt.

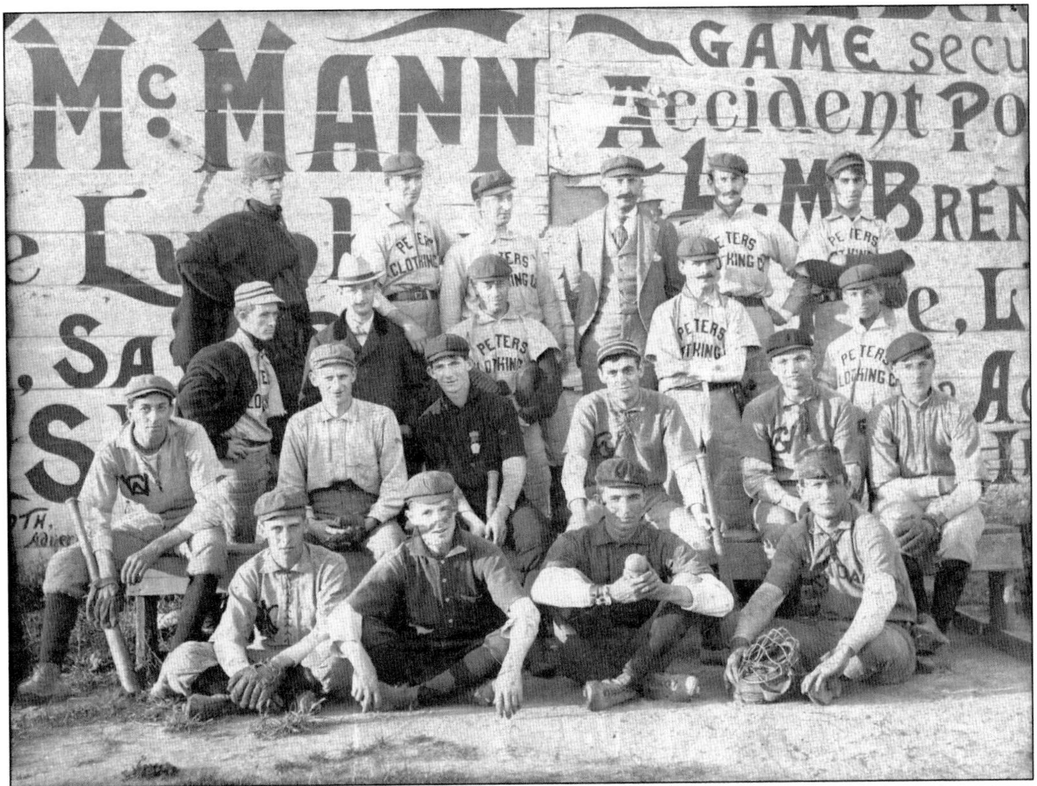

The Wakeman Red Cap baseball team is pictured around 1920. C.S. Clark, the founder of the seed company and a sponsor of the team, is wearing a suit and tie in the back row. The name "McMann Lumber Company" is also visible behind the team, as that company was a sponsor of the local sport.

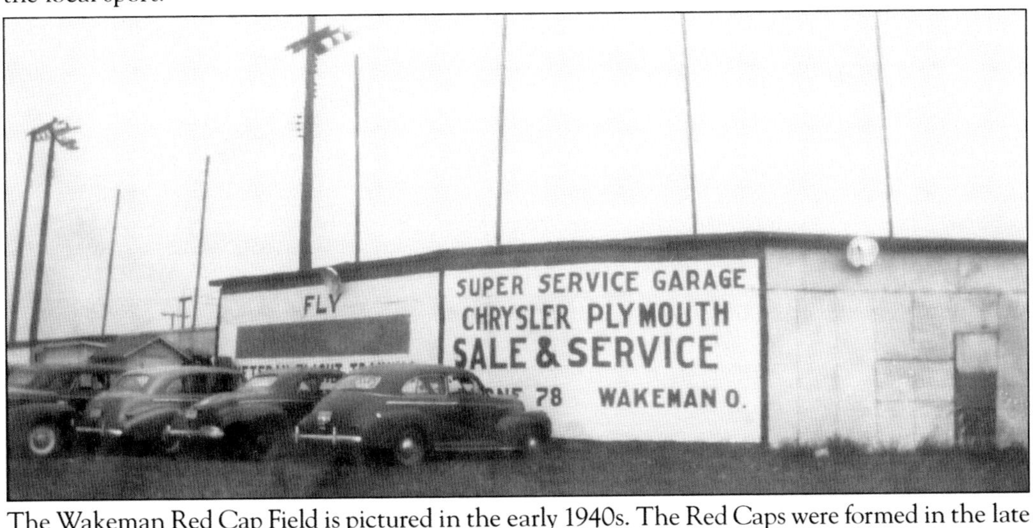

The Wakeman Red Cap Field is pictured in the early 1940s. The Red Caps were formed in the late 1800s and played until 1948, when they disbanded and the stadium was torn down. The stadium stood along Route 20 on the west side of Wakeman. In 1935, it was one of only two fields in Ohio to have lights installed for night games. Crowds of 1,000 were common, and an occasional crowd of 2,000 could be seated in the large stadium.

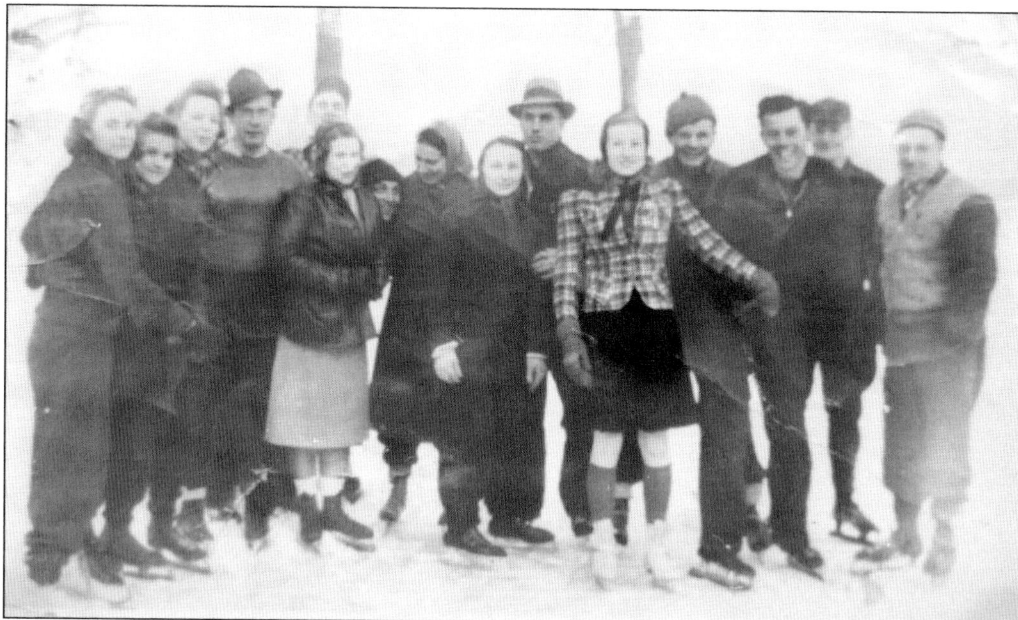

A skating party gathered on the frozen Vermilion River, Wakeman, for this c. 1905 photograph. From left to right are Lorie Seringer, Janet Tinker, Ruby Peabody, Art Licht, Peg Fay Martin, Mike Polchey, Monica Fay Grady, Helen Eastman, Bob Martin, Eleanor Breisch, Hawk Erbs, Bob Brucker, and ? Hotchy.

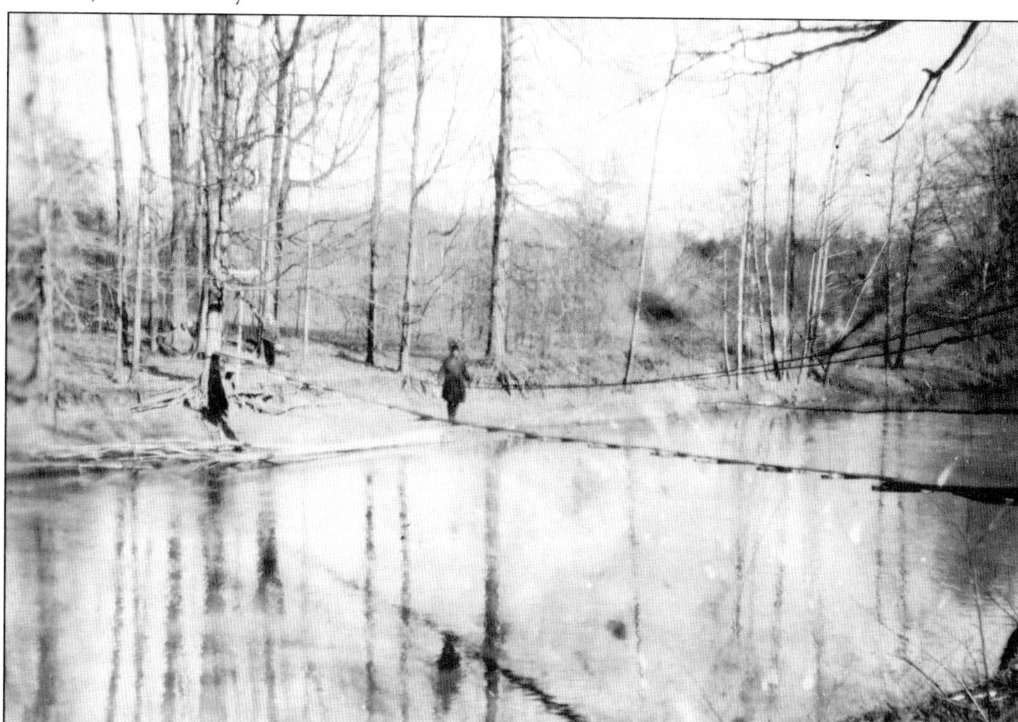

A swinging bridge led across the river to Myron Shelton's sugar bush. The bridge was a useful way to cross the river, but it was also a fun temptation for children.

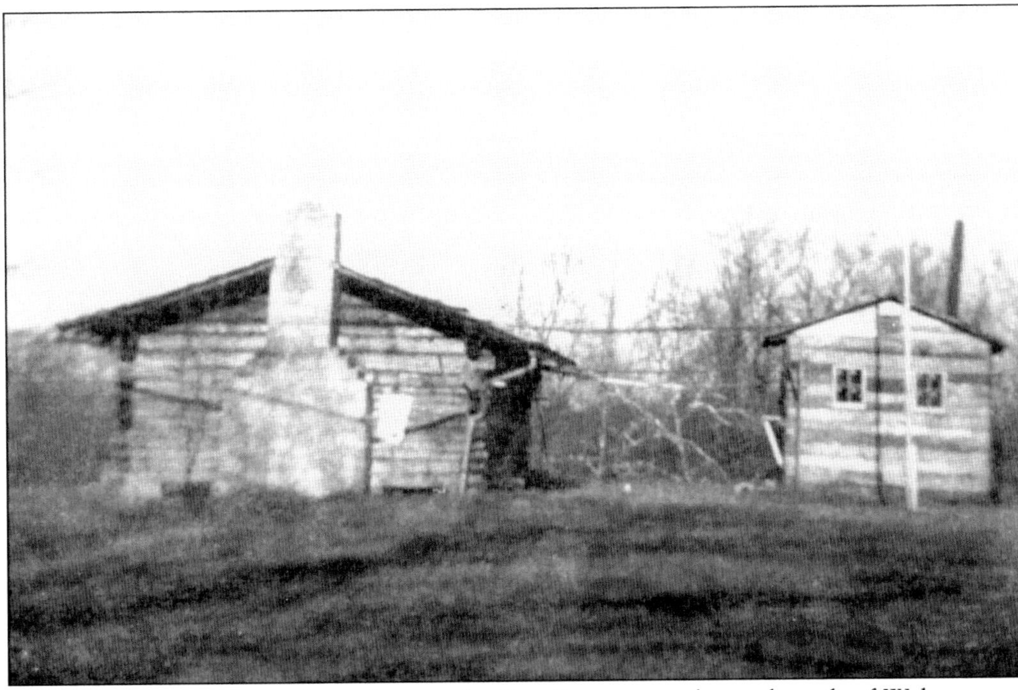

This photograph shows a few cabins at the Boy Scout camp located south of Wakeman on Chenango Road. Many local boys spent time at the camp along the river during the summer, learning to light fires, fish, and enjoy the wilderness.

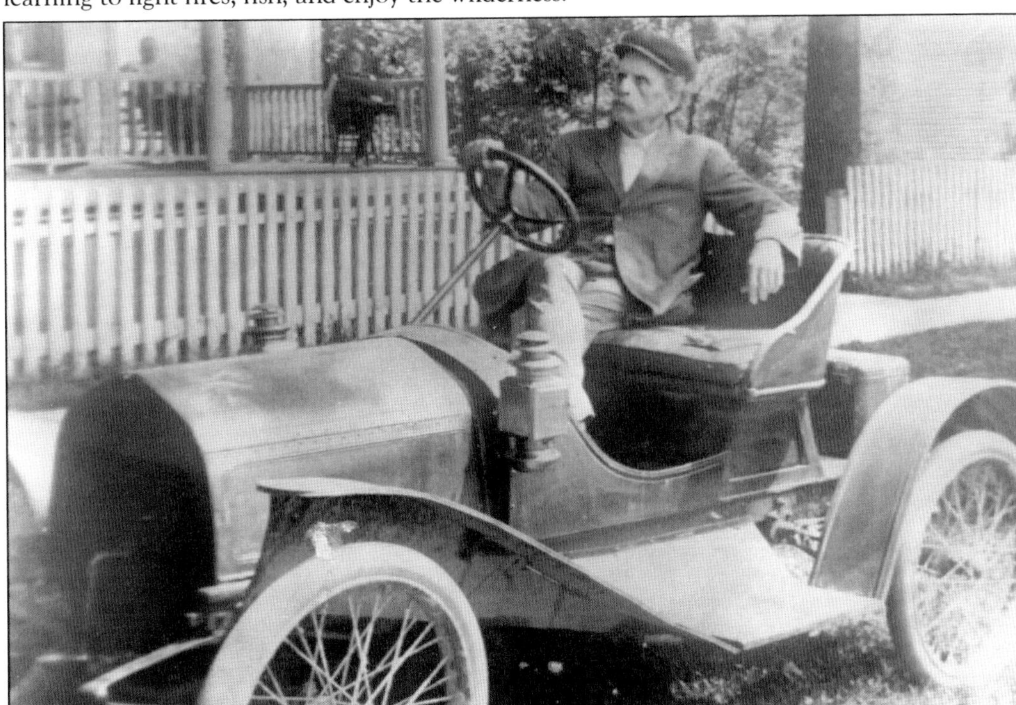

The first car in Birmingham, owned by Oscar Hayes, created quite a stir in this c. 1905 photograph. (Courtesy of Jason Gargasz.)

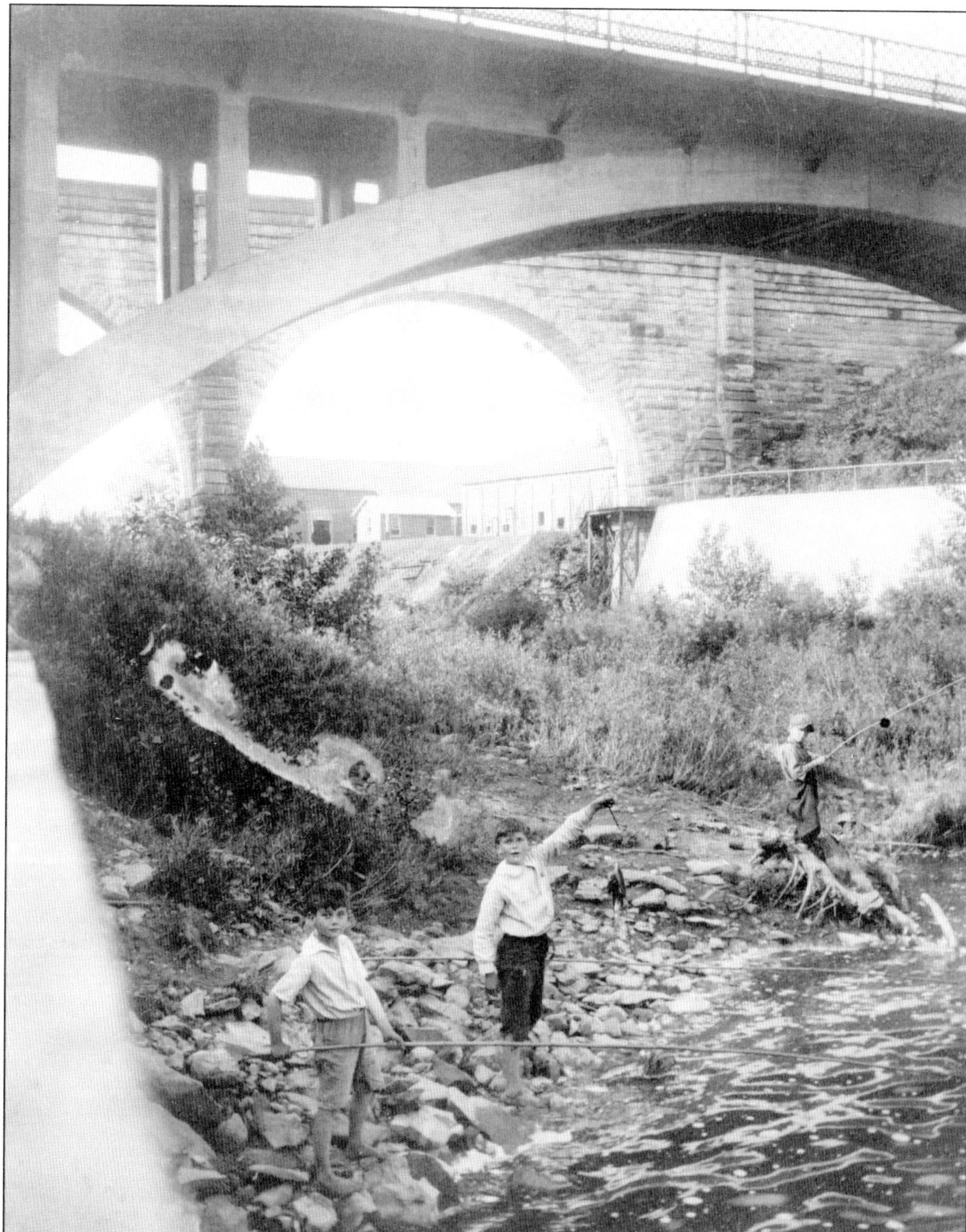

Three boys enjoy fishing along the banks of the Vermilion River in Wakeman in this c. 1910 photograph. Over their heads is the road bridge built in 1908. The railroad bridge, featuring stone from a local quarry, is behind the road bridge. Seen through the arches of both bridges are the buildings of the Buckeye Pipe Line, built in 1895.

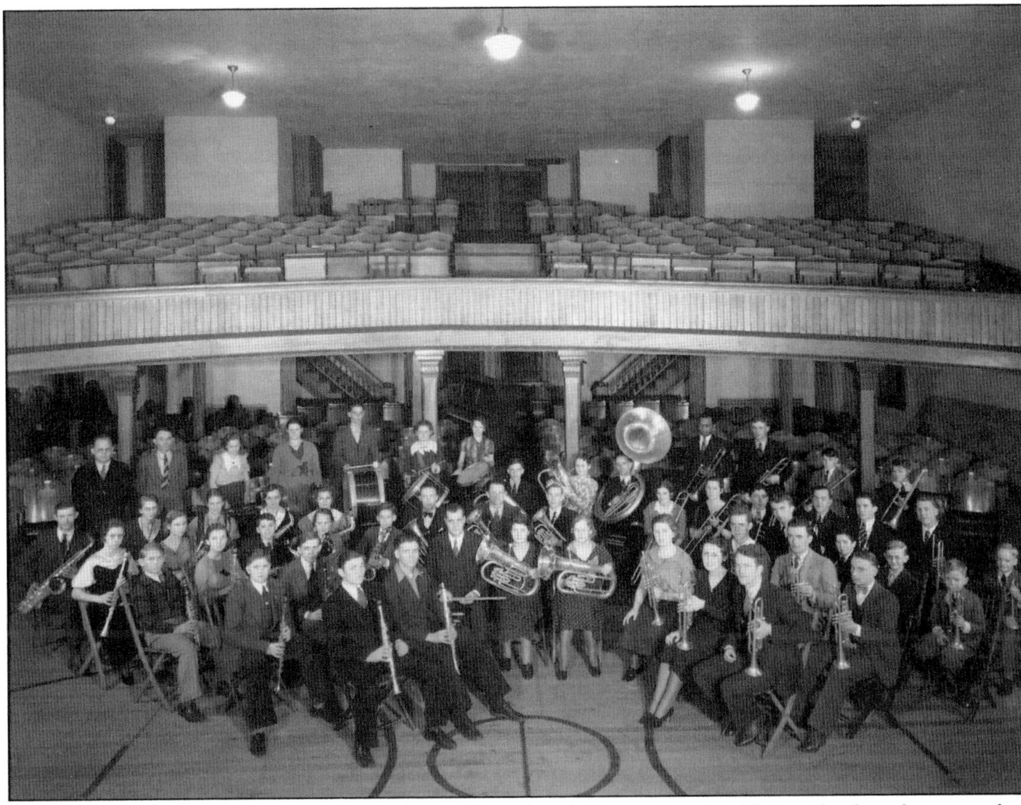

This photograph, labeled "Wakeman Band," is dated December 14, 1933. The band is seated in the town hall, also known as the opera house or the Masonic Temple, and is probably preparing for a Christmas concert. All ages are represented in the photograph, so it must have been a true community effort. (Courtesy of the Wakeman Community Library.)

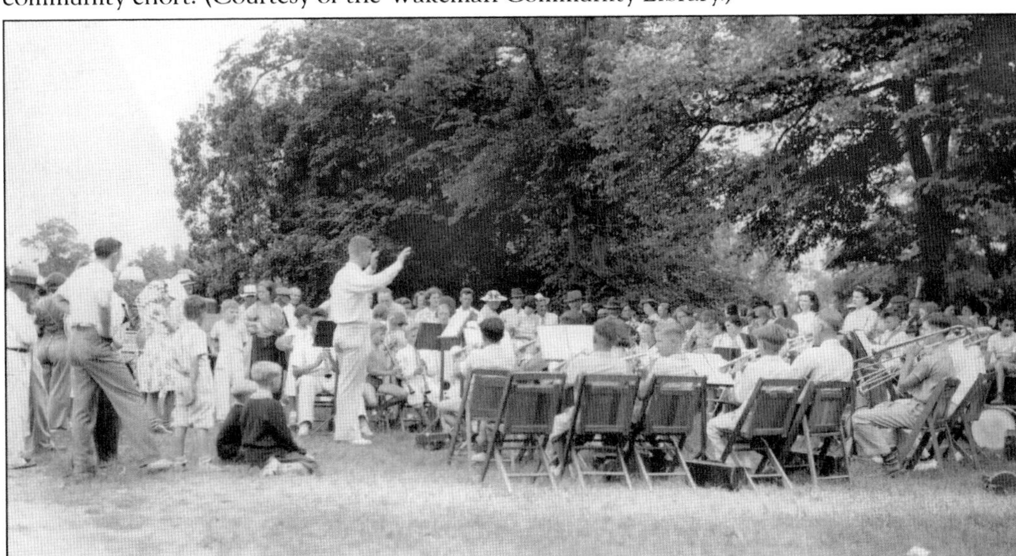

On a beautiful day on Dunn's Flats along the river south of Wakeman, a community orchestra gathered to play. Although it was an annual event, this photograph is from either 1939 or 1940.

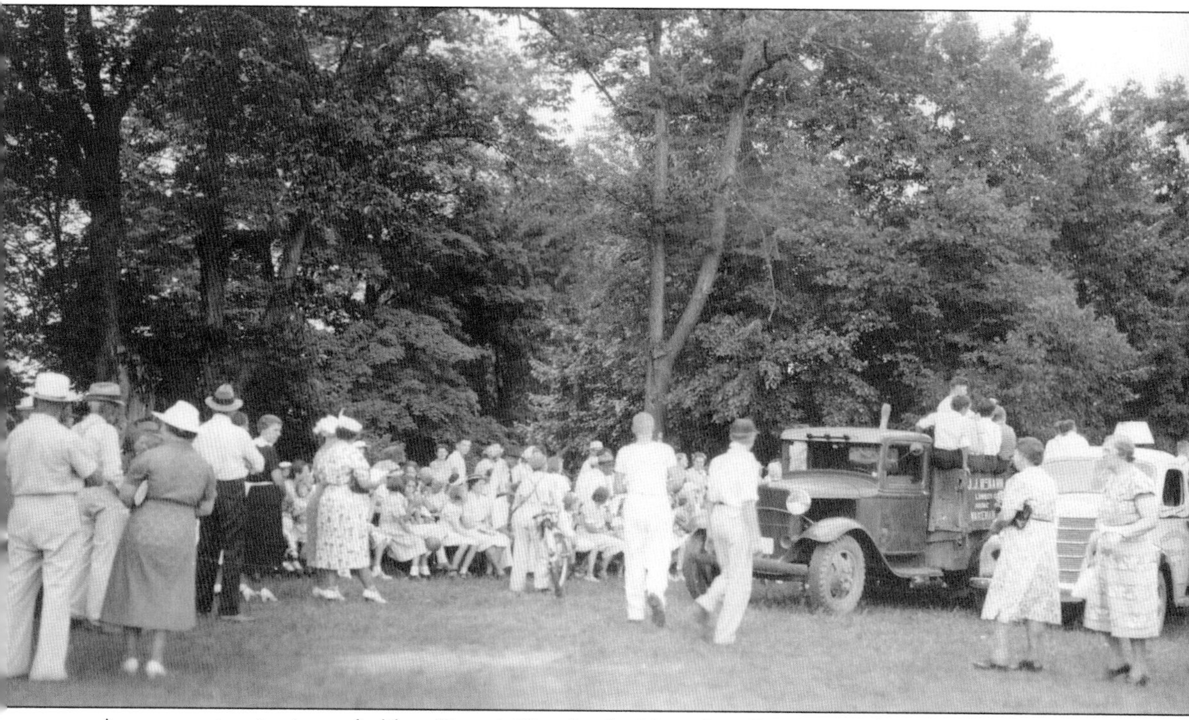

A community picnic was held on Dunn's Flats by the Vermilion River in Wakeman. The black truck pictured belonged to J. J. McMann, who owned the lumber company. The other truck is a 1939 yellow International with red fenders belonging to Fred E. Graves, who owned the International tractor dealership. The trucks are probably delivering tables and chairs for the picnic.

Seven

Homes

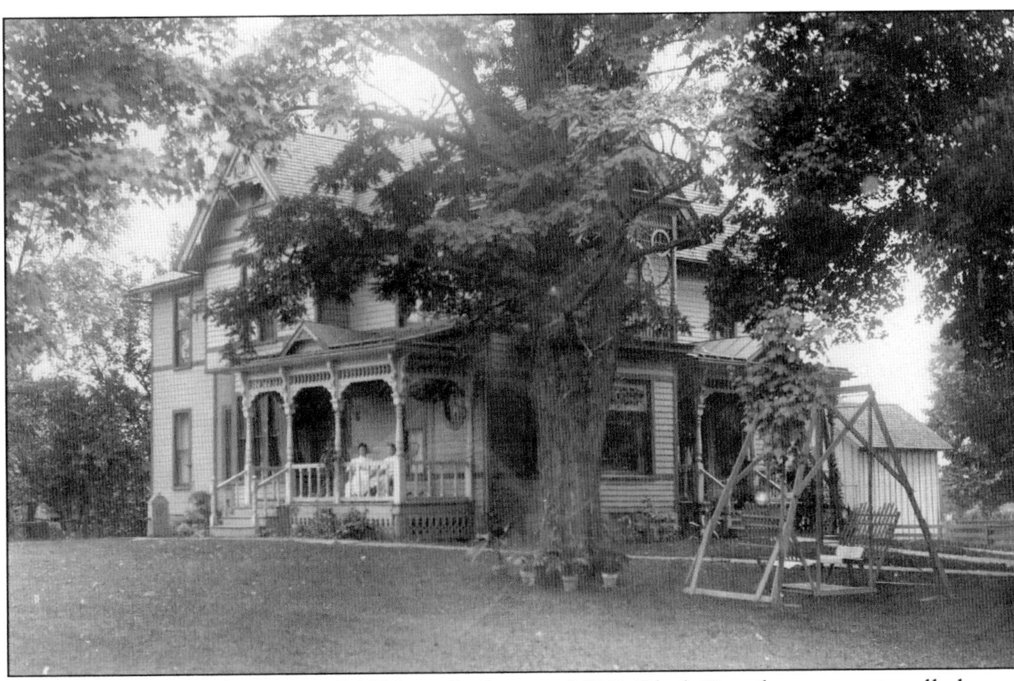

This photograph, taken around 1900, is the home of C.S. Clark Sr., who was nationally known as the "seed corn king." In addition to having a large and prosperous seed house in Wakeman, Clark owned many tracts of land in town. His elaborate house was built c. 1880. He had two daughters and one son. The women sitting on the porch are unidentified, but they are probably family members. The "old" Congregational church built in 1845 was originally at this location, but it was moved nearby. His son, C.S. Clark Jr., built an elegant home next door in 1924. Both houses remain.

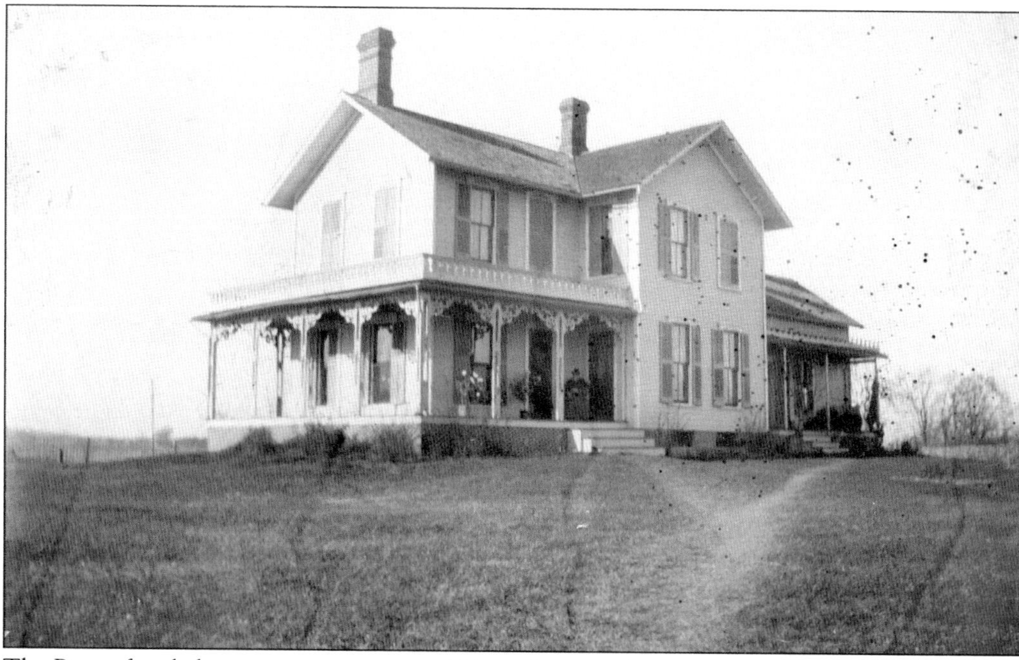

The Pierce family home sits on a corner of Pierce Street right across from the downtown district in Wakeman. The Pierce family owned a grocery store, and the location made it a convenient walk. The dwelling was originally built by Joseph Haskins in 1886 or 1887 but was then purchased by Mr. and Mrs. Clarence Pierce. The house still stands in the same location.

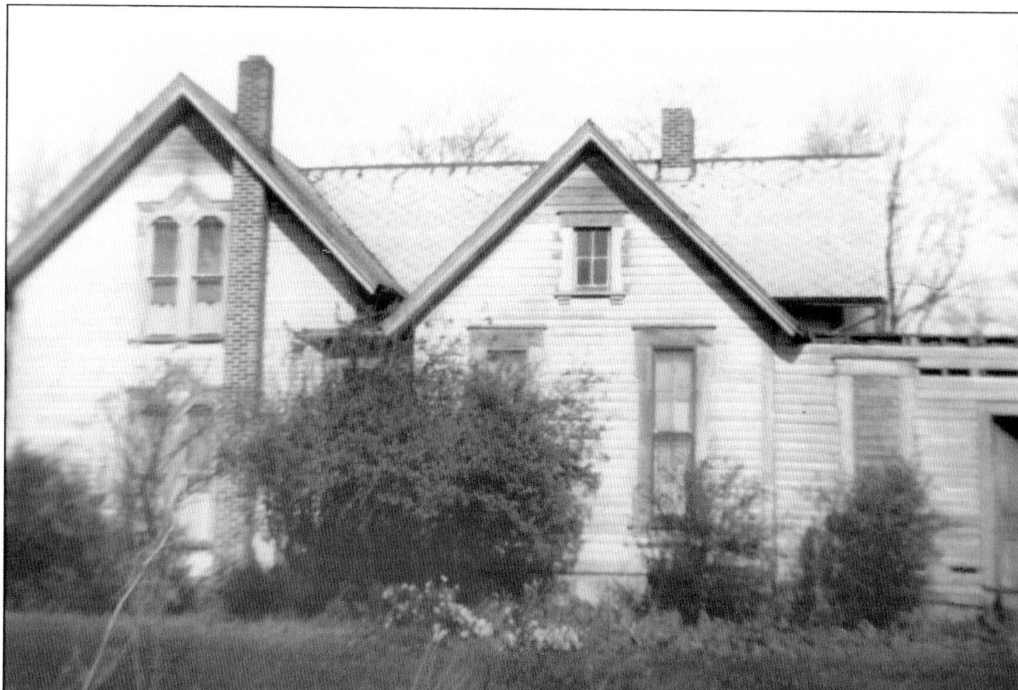

This house on the corner of Farmers and Pleasant Streets was originally built by Charles R. Shelton around 1870. For many years, Charles Cooley and his daughter Ann lived here.

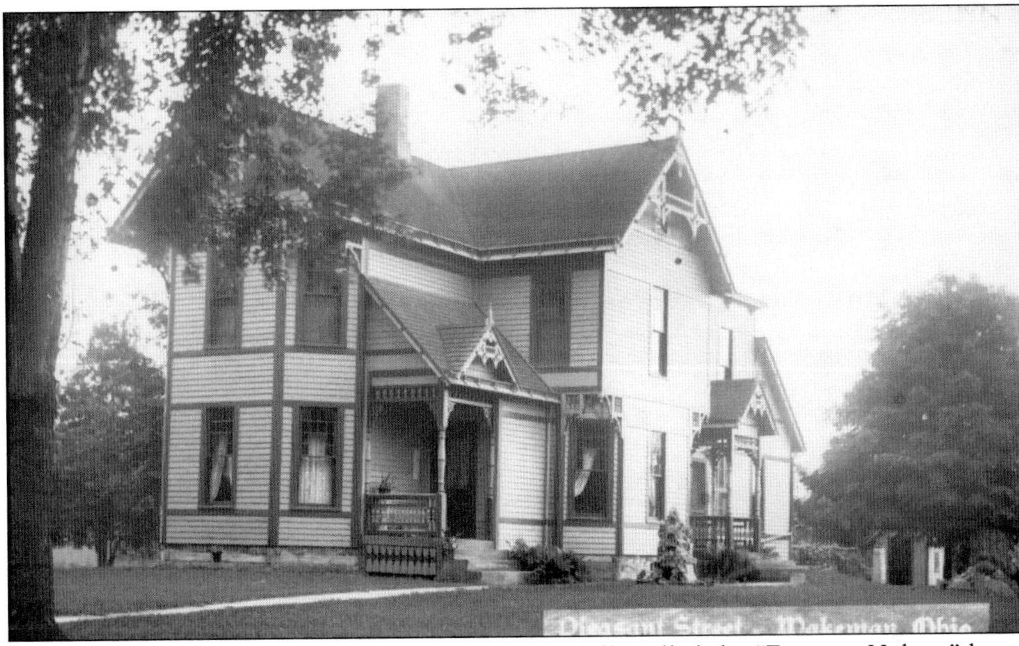

This home on Pleasant Street in Wakeman is generally called the "Fremont Holmes" house because he lived there for many years. John Whiton, an owner of a downtown hardware, built the house in 1886. Whiton lived there until his death in 1916.

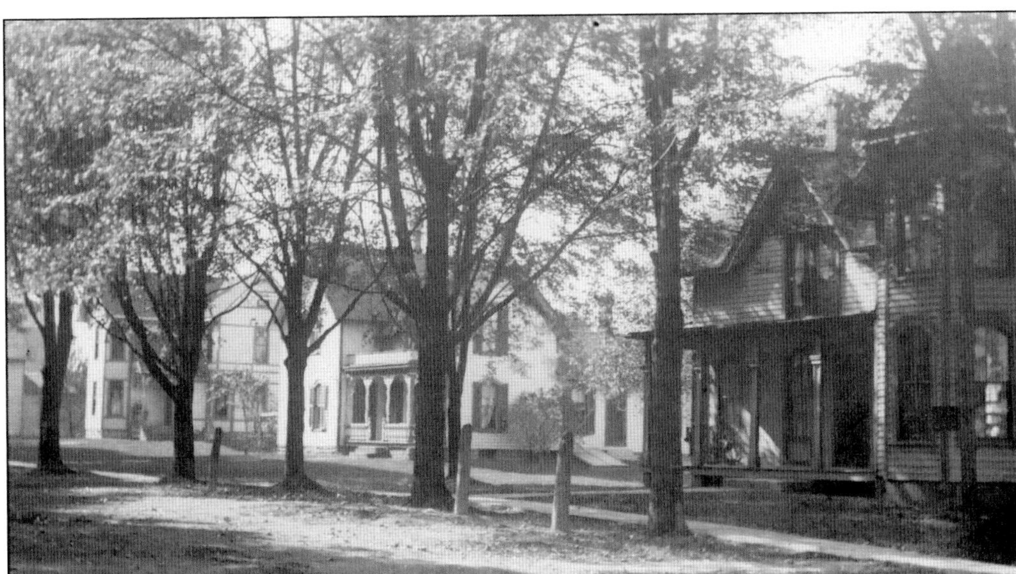

A view of Pleasant Street near downtown shows hitching posts for horses, dirt streets, and the shade trees that made the street match its name.

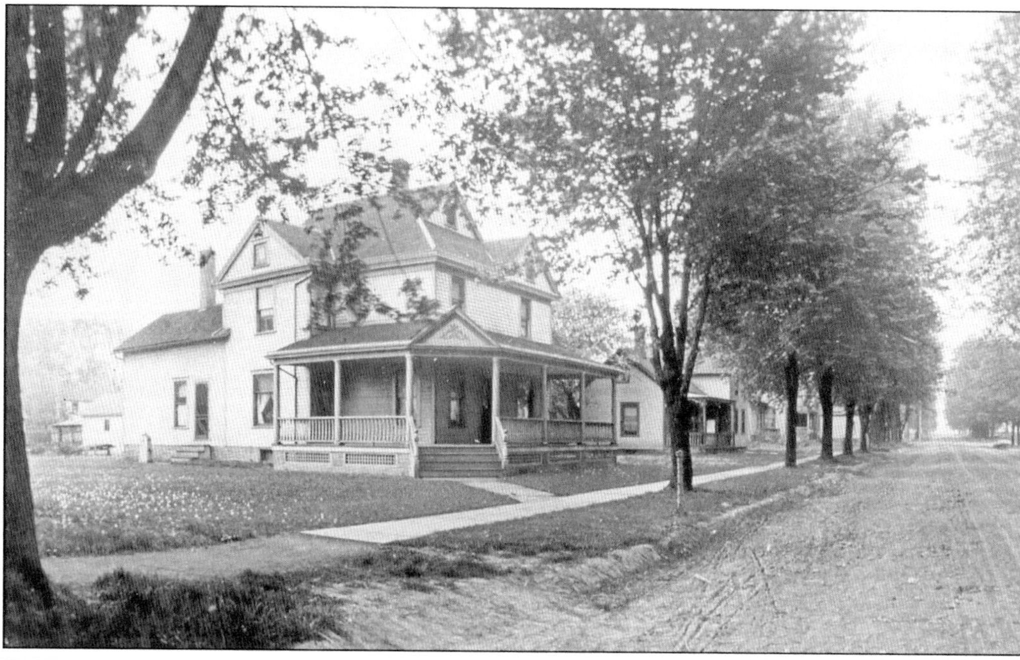

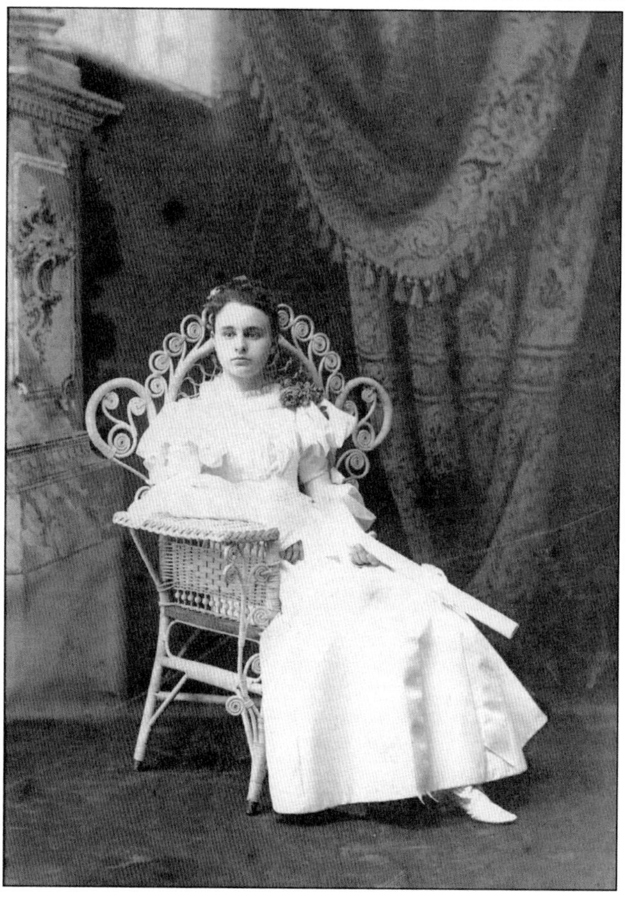

This stately home on Pleasant Street near downtown was the home of Mae Bacon and her sister Sarah Haskins for many years. P. O'Leary, who was a night foreman at the Buckeye Pipeline Company in Wakeman, built the home in 1902.

This c. 1900 portrait shows a young Mae Bacon.

The home of Tim and Alice Schaus was the location of the first store in Wakeman. It was on the corner of Farmers and River Streets.

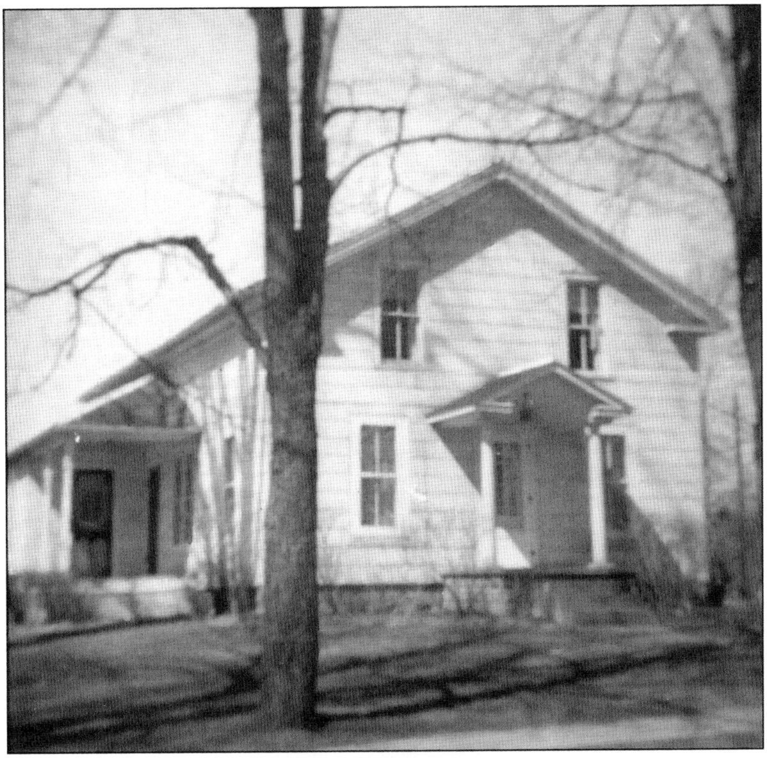

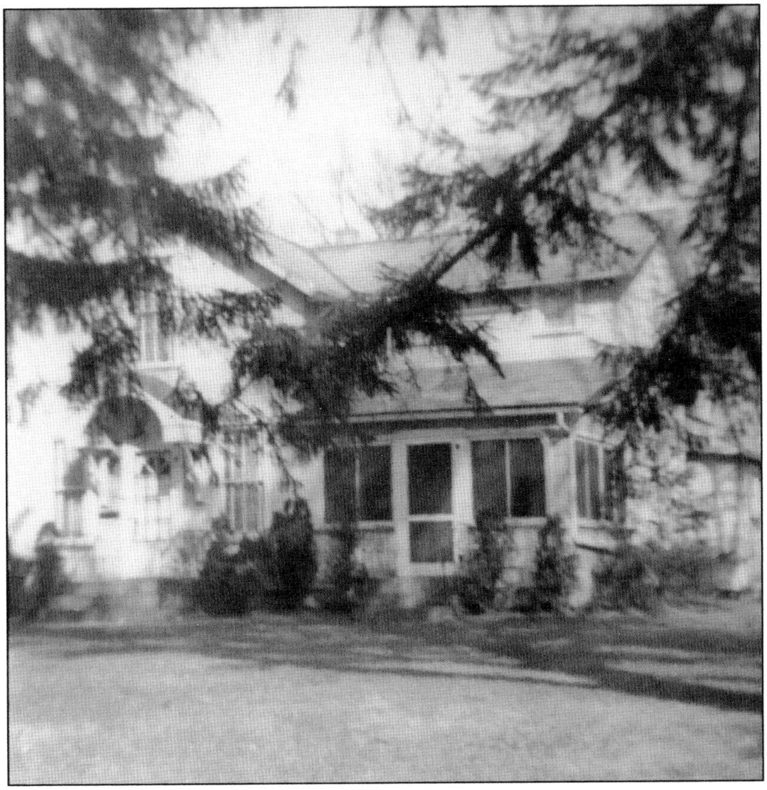

This structure on the corner of Abbott and Cooper Streets in Wakeman housed the telephone office and switchboard for the town. It has since been renovated and made into apartments.

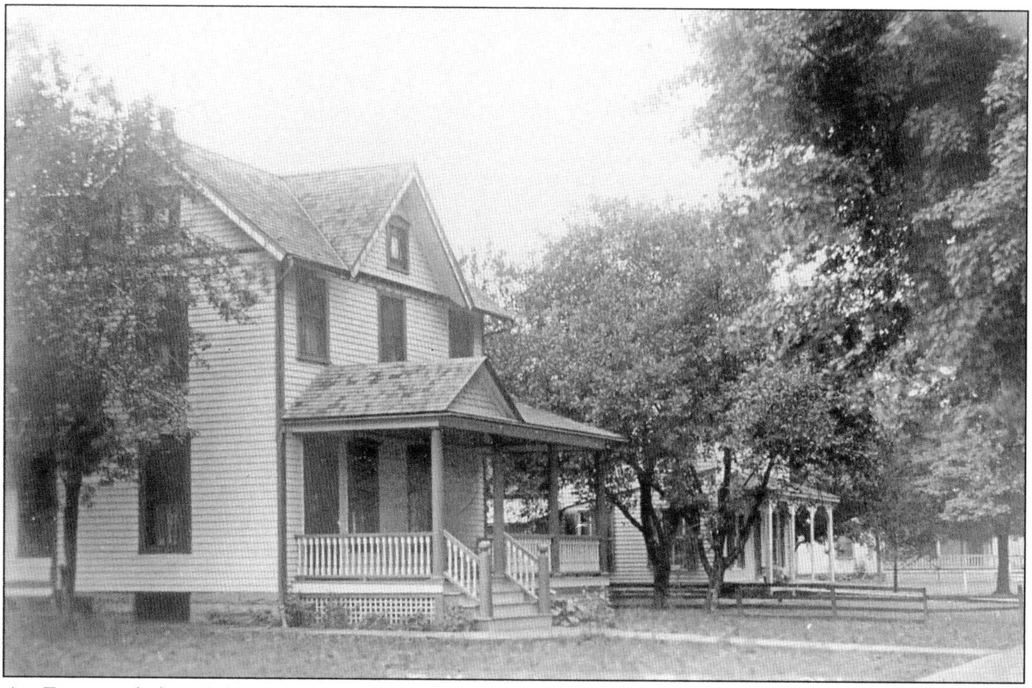

An Episcopal church built in the 1840s once stood on this property, but John Kirschner bought the lot in 1905 and tore it down. He built the house pictured with the help of carpenter Rastus Wolvin. Carl Ketchum, the station agent for the railroad passenger depot, lived here for many years.

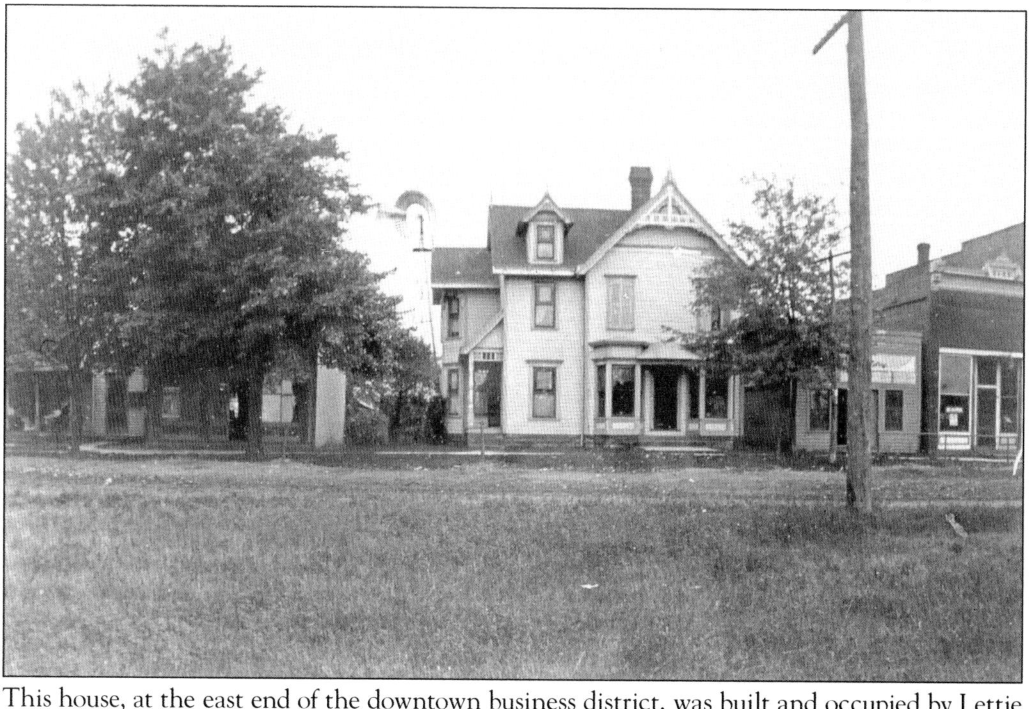

This house, at the east end of the downtown business district, was built and occupied by Lettie Bright prior to 1900. She operated a millinery shop and lived in the home. Later, it was the home of well-known local resident Bill Pease. Note the large windmill next to the house.

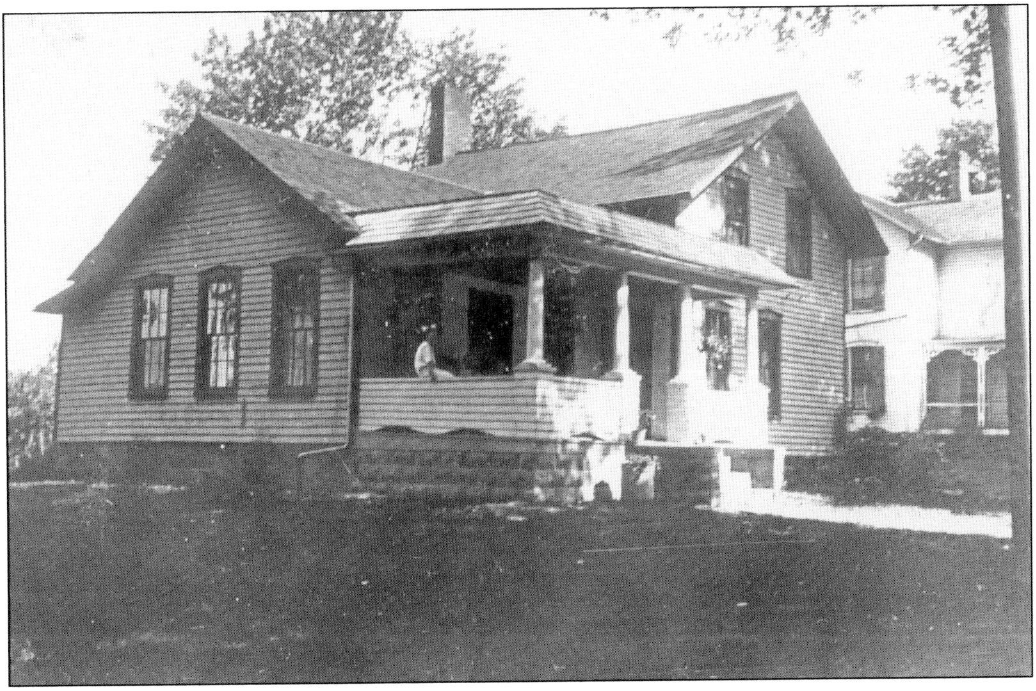

This house, built before 1860, was purchased by F.A. and Mamie Denman in 1907. It was sold in 1938 to their daughter and son-in-law, Doris and Fred Graves. Doris (Denman) Graves is pictured on the front porch around 1915. The home was eventually torn down in the 1990s.

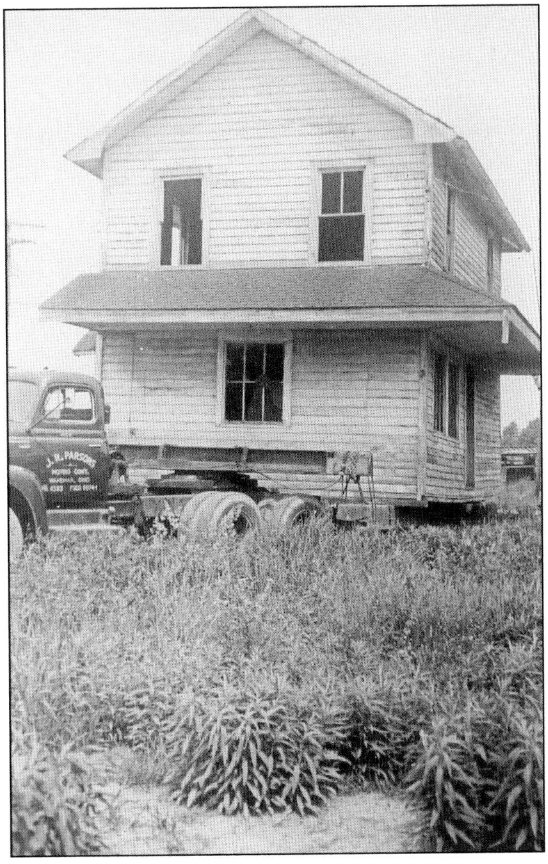

The truck of J.R. (Dick) Parsons, son of J.C. (Jim) Parsons, moves a home from the curve on Route 20 to a quieter location on Clark Street in Wakeman. The house burned in 1951. Its shell was moved a few years later, as pictured.

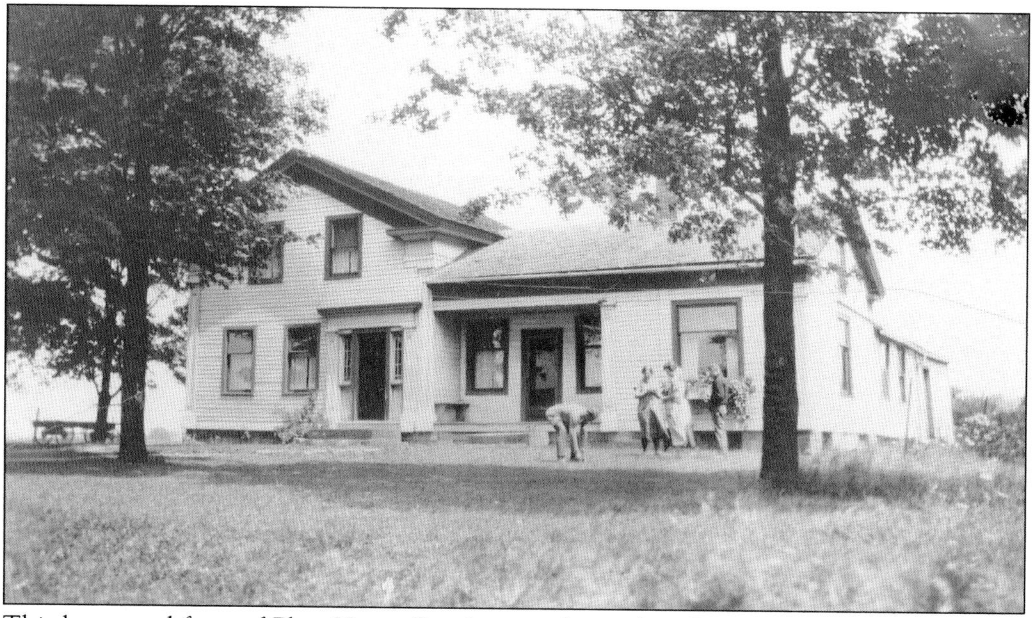

This home and farm of Platt Henry Beecher was located on Route 60 north of Wakeman. The home still stands. The four people, pictured around 1920, are probably members of the Beecher family.

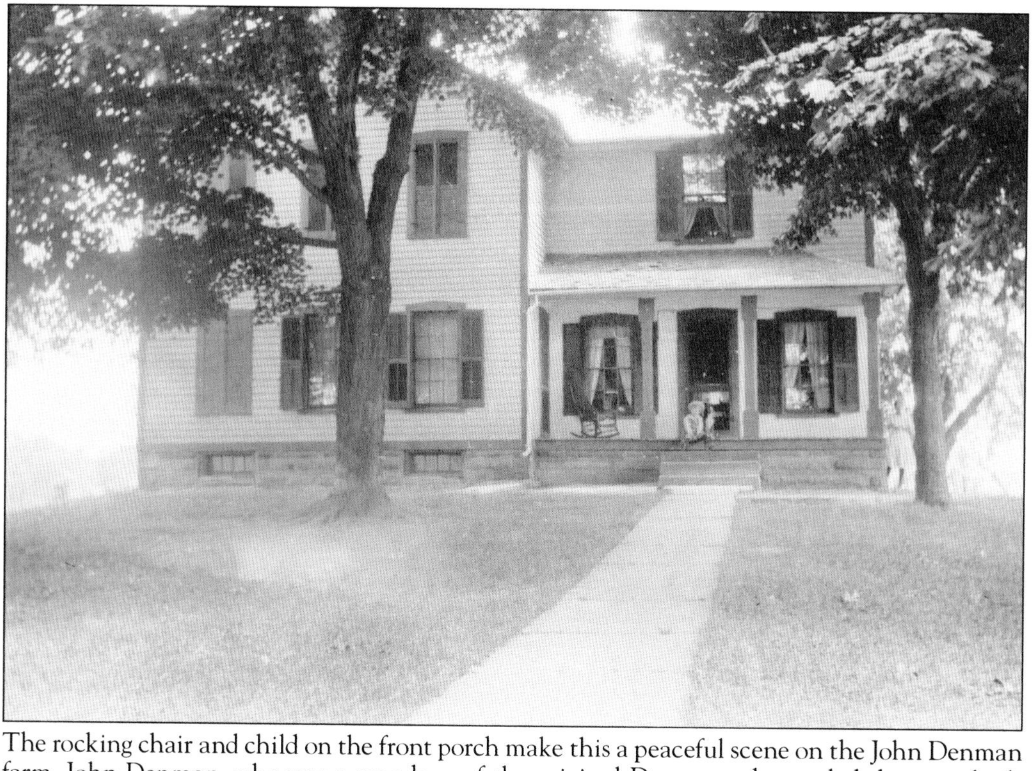

The rocking chair and child on the front porch make this a peaceful scene on the John Denman farm. John Denman, who was a grandson of the original Denman who settled the area, built the house in 1868 and then had 14 children. The house still stands in its location on Route 60 between Wakeman and Birmingham.

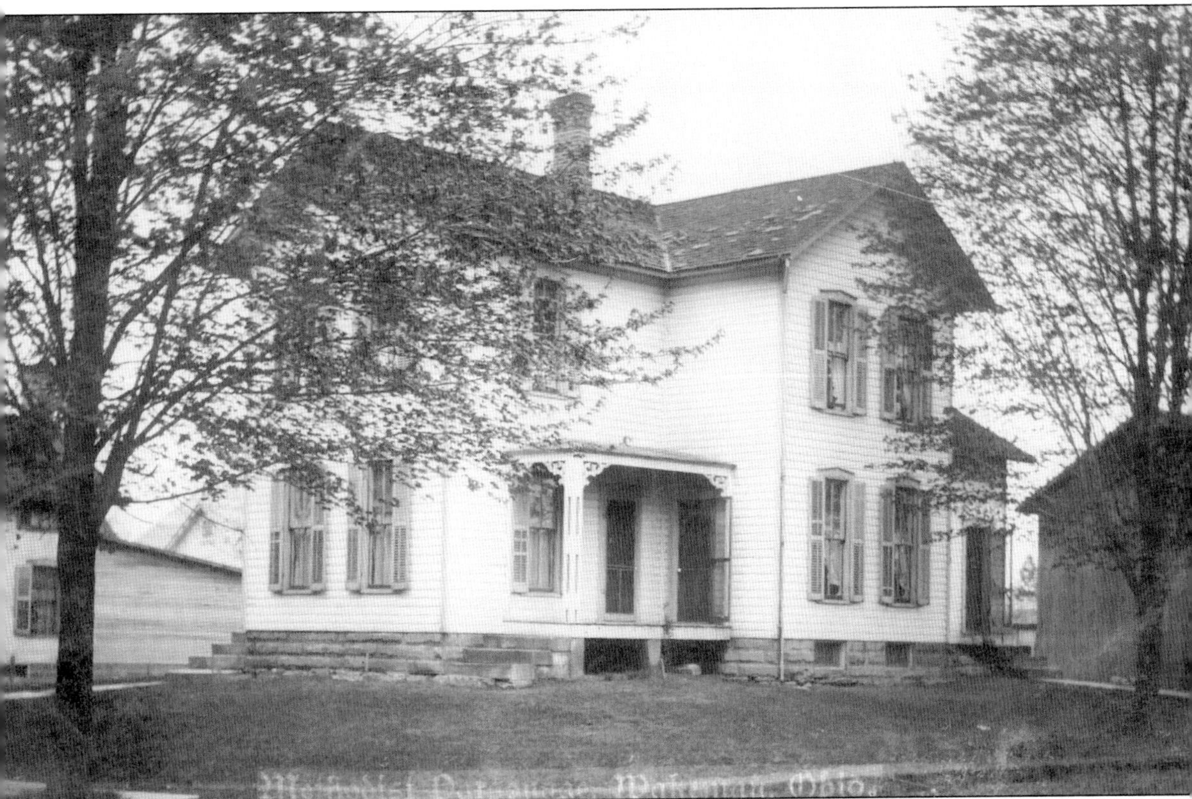

This house on the corner of Pleasant and Maple Streets in Wakeman was used as the parsonage for the Methodist Church, which was located just up the street. The house was built by the Methodist congregation before 1885. In 1952, it was purchased by John Herzog and converted to a funeral home and residence. In later years, it was alternately a private residence and an apartment building.

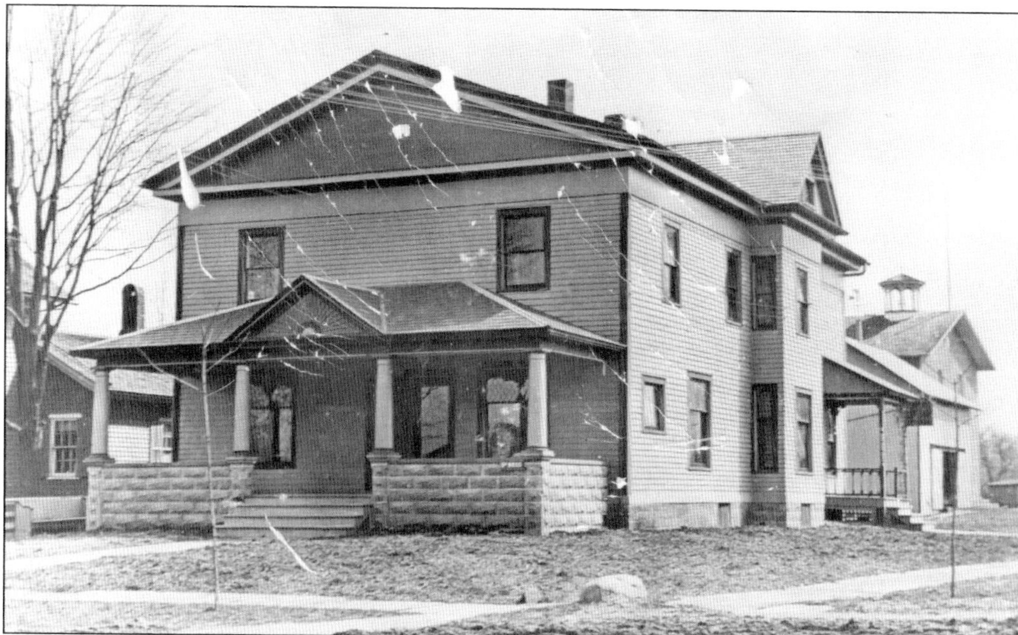

This home was once the Congregational church. It was built in 1845 and is located on Main Street in Birmingham. Over the years, it has been a residence, the doctor's office of Dr. J.W. Boss, and an apartment. As it stands today, little has changed. Behind it, the old school is visible. (Courtesy of Jason Gargasz.)

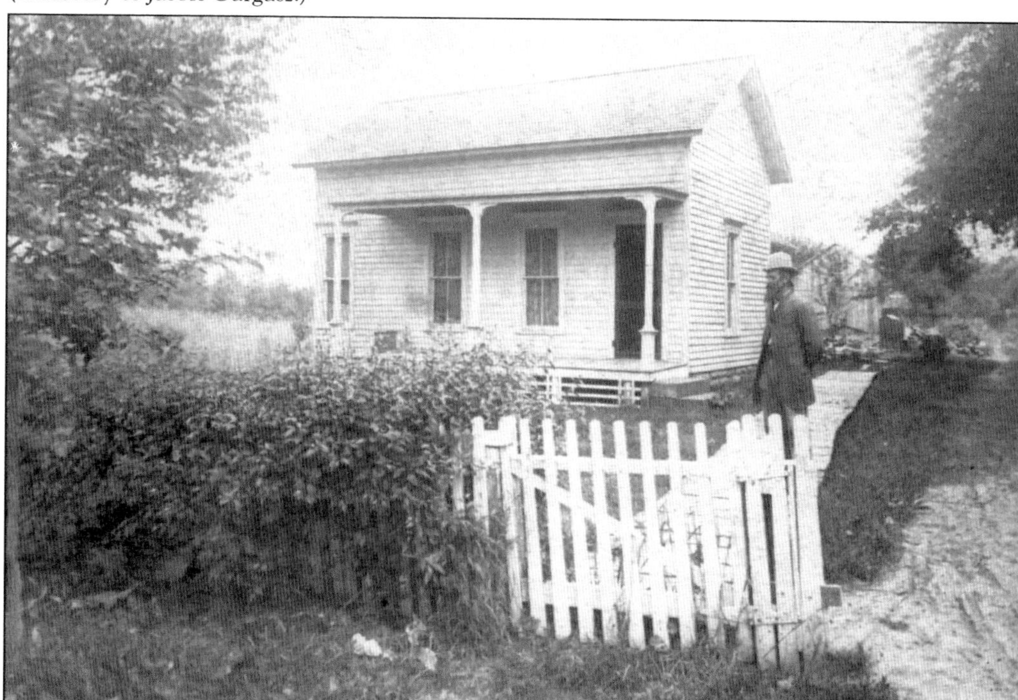

This photograph from before 1900 shows Albert Taft and his home in Birmingham. (Courtesy of Jason Gargasz.)

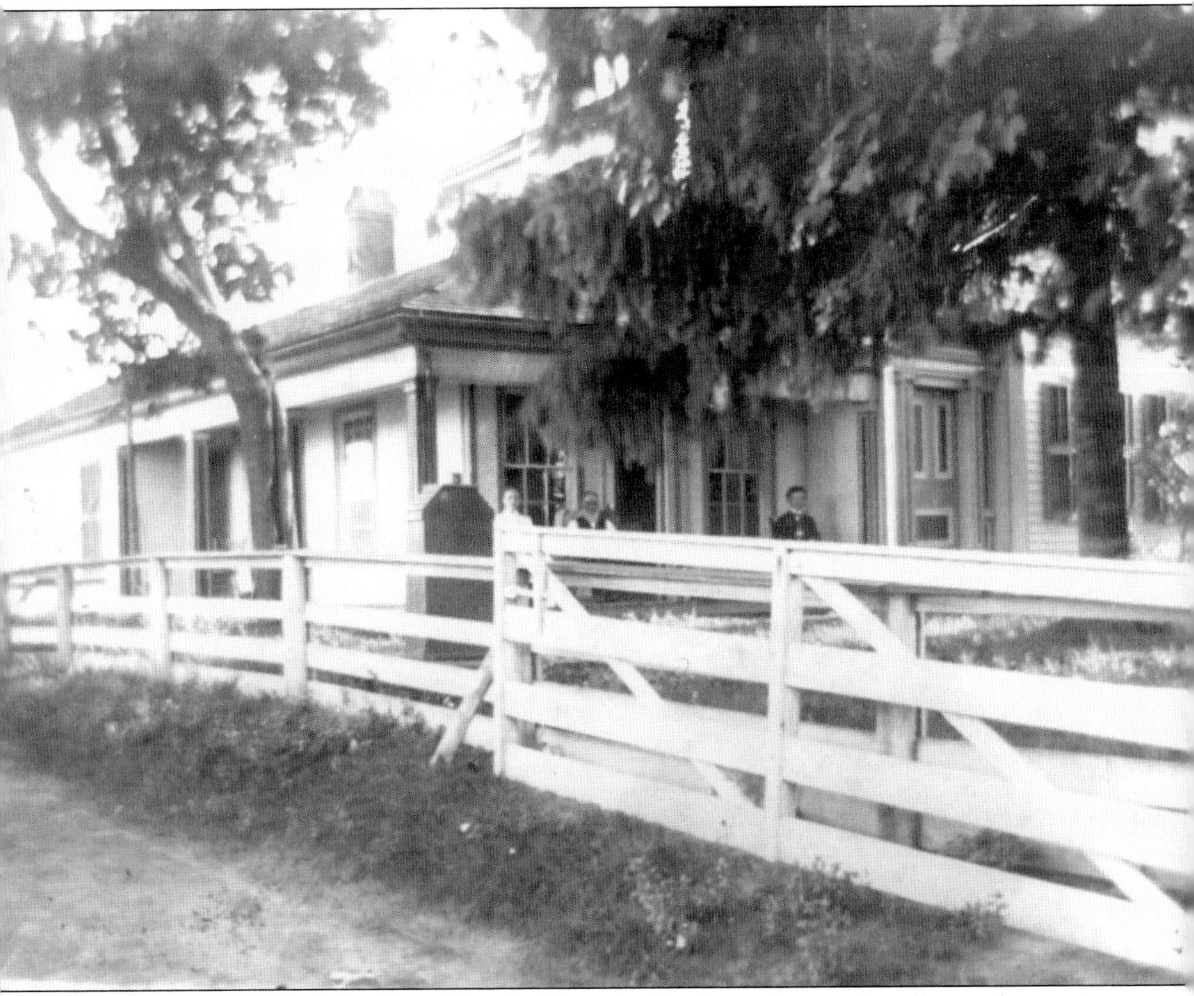

This was the home of the Bristol family. Note the family on the porch and a tombstone in the front yard. It was located on South Street in Birmingham. The building has undergone some changes, but it still stands and is now the property of nearby Birmingham United Methodist Church. (Courtesy of Jason Gargasz.)

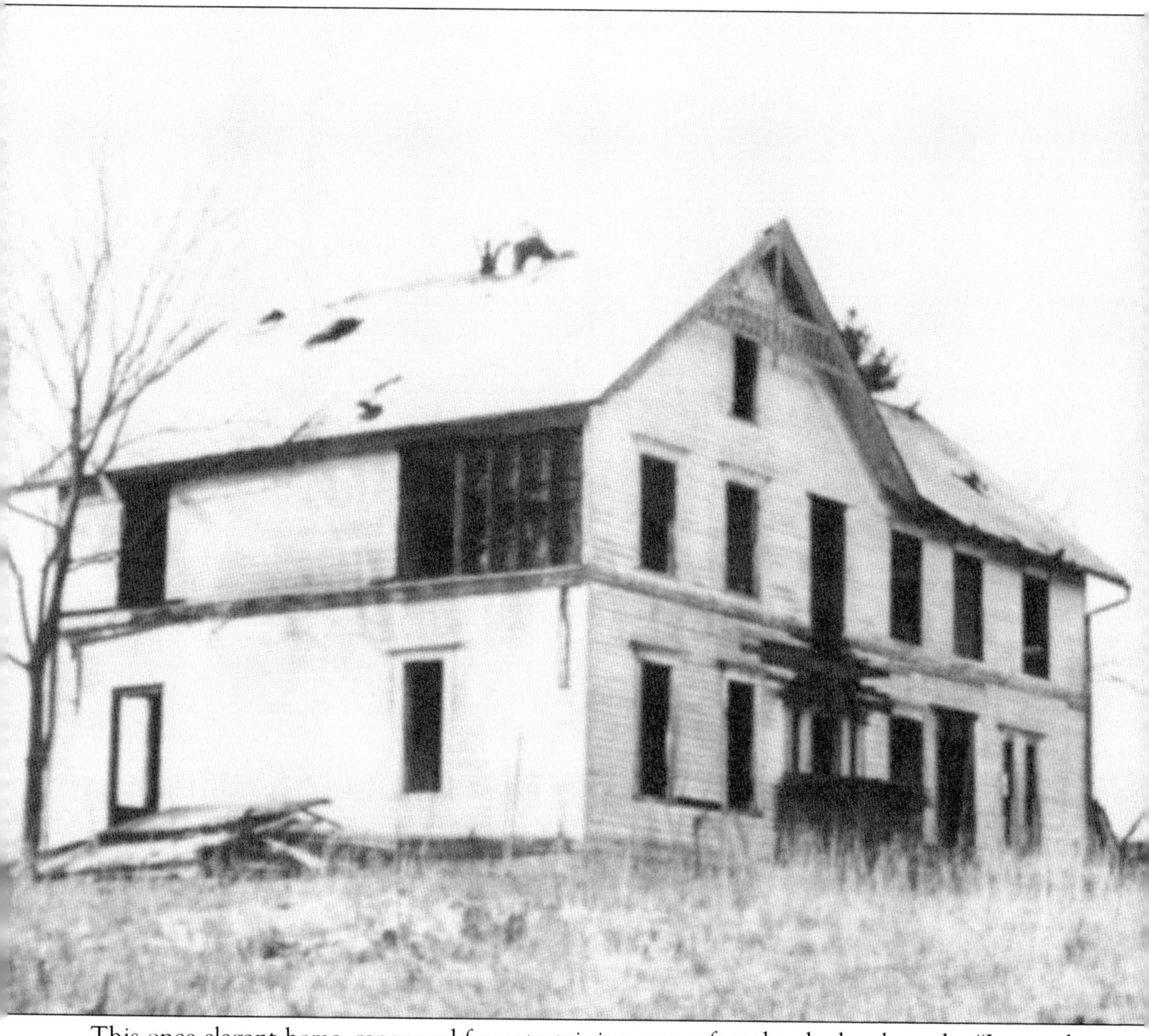

This once-elegant home, renowned for entertaining, was referred to by locals as the "Leonard House." It was built in the 1880s by the Leonard family, who owned a large orchard. The family later moved in 1898 to Fresno, California, to grow grapes. The house had several subsequent owners but eventually fell into disrepair and was demolished in 1965. It stood on Route 113 east of Birmingham. (Courtesy of Jason Gargasz.)

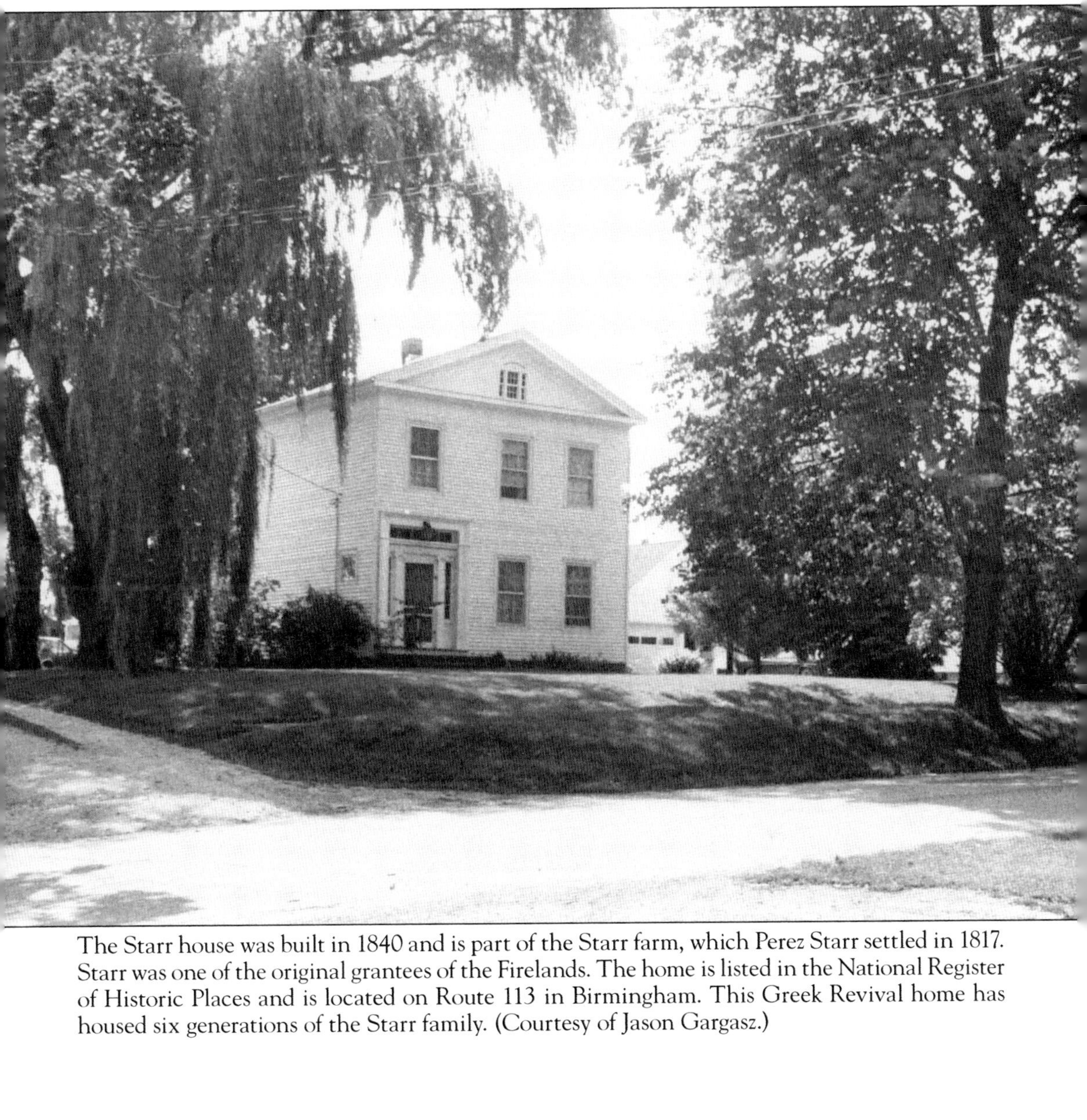

The Starr house was built in 1840 and is part of the Starr farm, which Perez Starr settled in 1817. Starr was one of the original grantees of the Firelands. The home is listed in the National Register of Historic Places and is located on Route 113 in Birmingham. This Greek Revival home has housed six generations of the Starr family. (Courtesy of Jason Gargasz.)

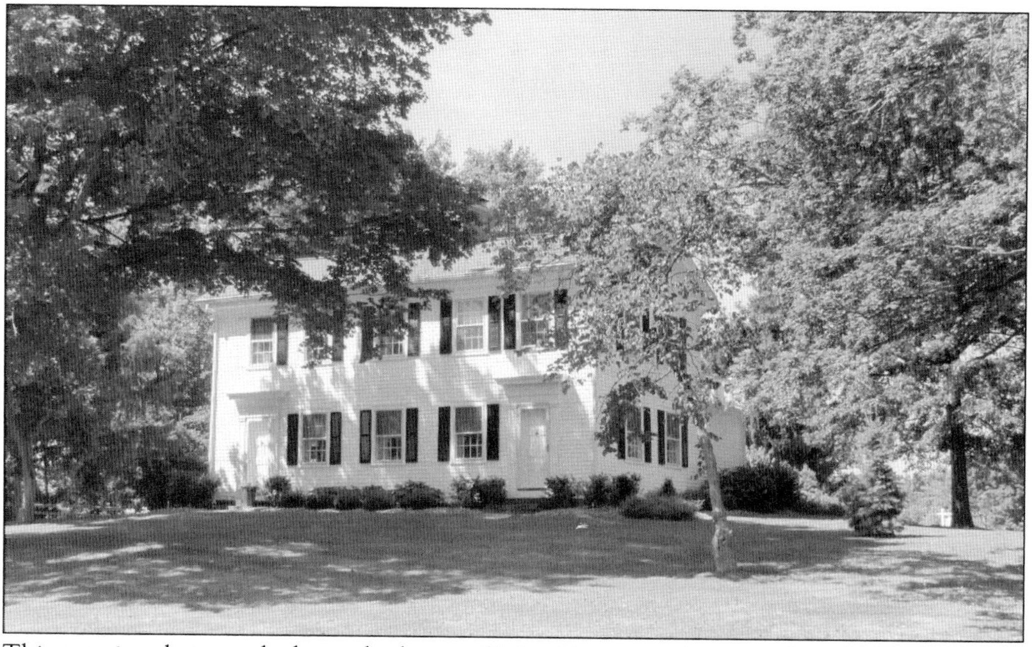

This exterior photograph shows the home of John Denman, who settled in the Firelands and had 14 children with his wife Marinda. Denman bought 160 acres for $3 each in 1816. His family lived in a log cabin until he built this beautiful house in 1834 using materials from his own land. Denman was a successful farmer, producing wool and maple syrup in great quantities. He was born in England, immigrating to America at the age of four, but never became an American citizen because he objected to slavery. The house, now called "Breeze Hill," has been in the Howe family since 1934, and they have carefully preserved and superbly maintained the property.

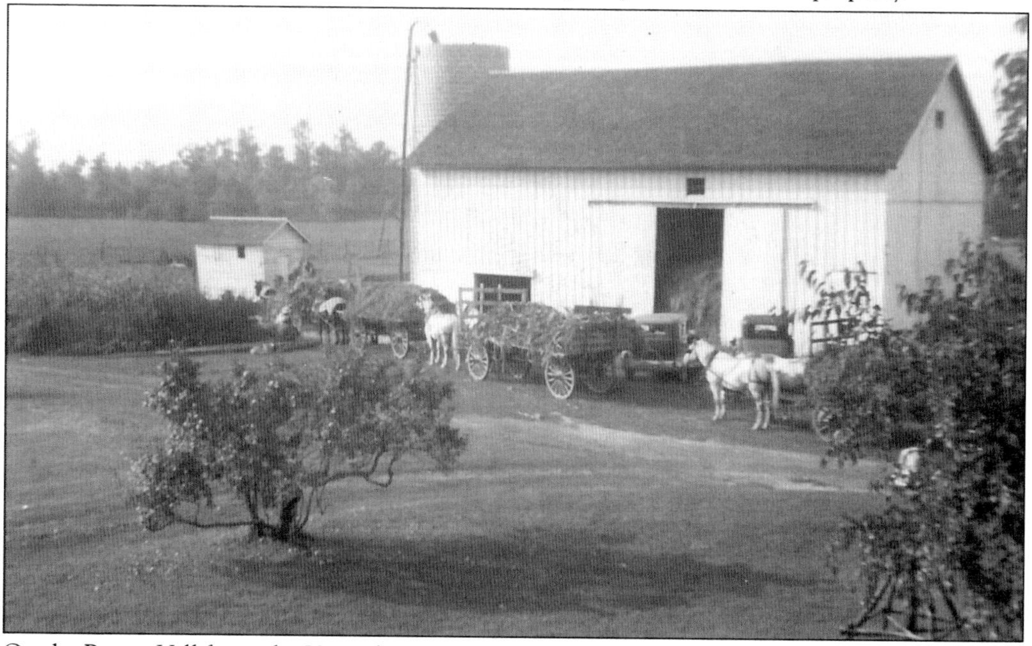

On the Breeze Hill farm, the Howe family works with neighbors to fill the silos with corn chopped into silage in this c. 1930 photograph. (Courtesy of Roger Howe.)

Eight

A Sense of Community

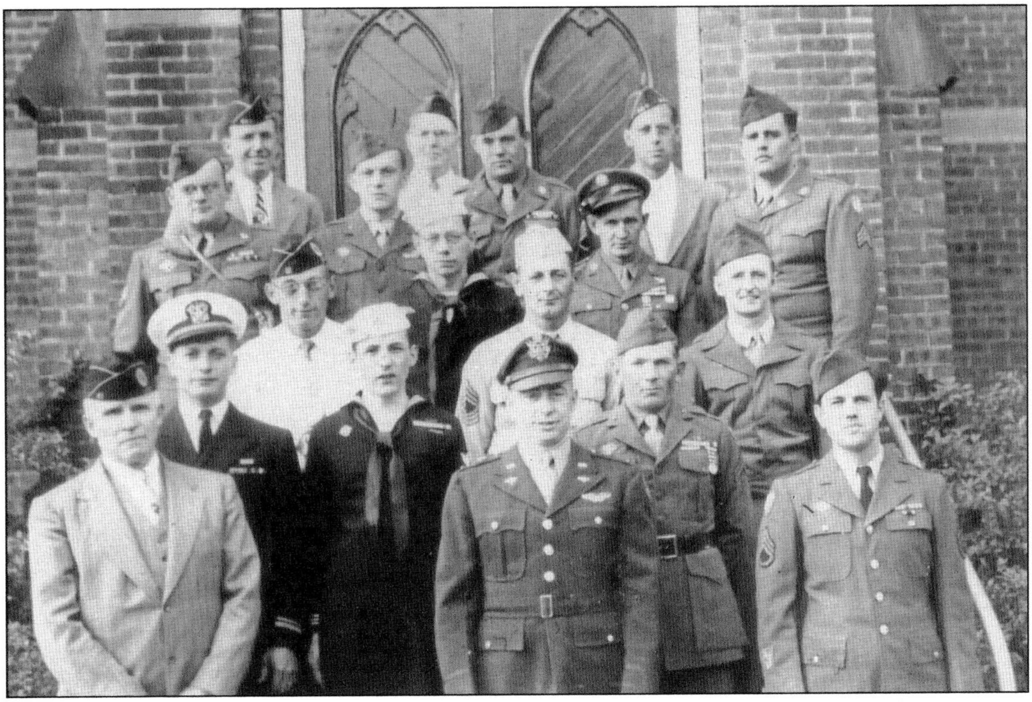

This 1950 photograph on the steps of the Congregational church in Wakeman documents a gathering of veterans. From left to right, they are (first row) Blaine Hurst, Dick Parsons, Louis Murray, Alvin Baker, Jack Potter, and Bob Bement; (second row) Don Hales, Bob Brucker, Charles Coultrip, and Bertin Keith; (third row) Jack Grady, Dick Ross, Don Snyder, Bill Miller, Ralph Jackson, Bob Jenny, Art Witzlaben Jr., and George Parker.

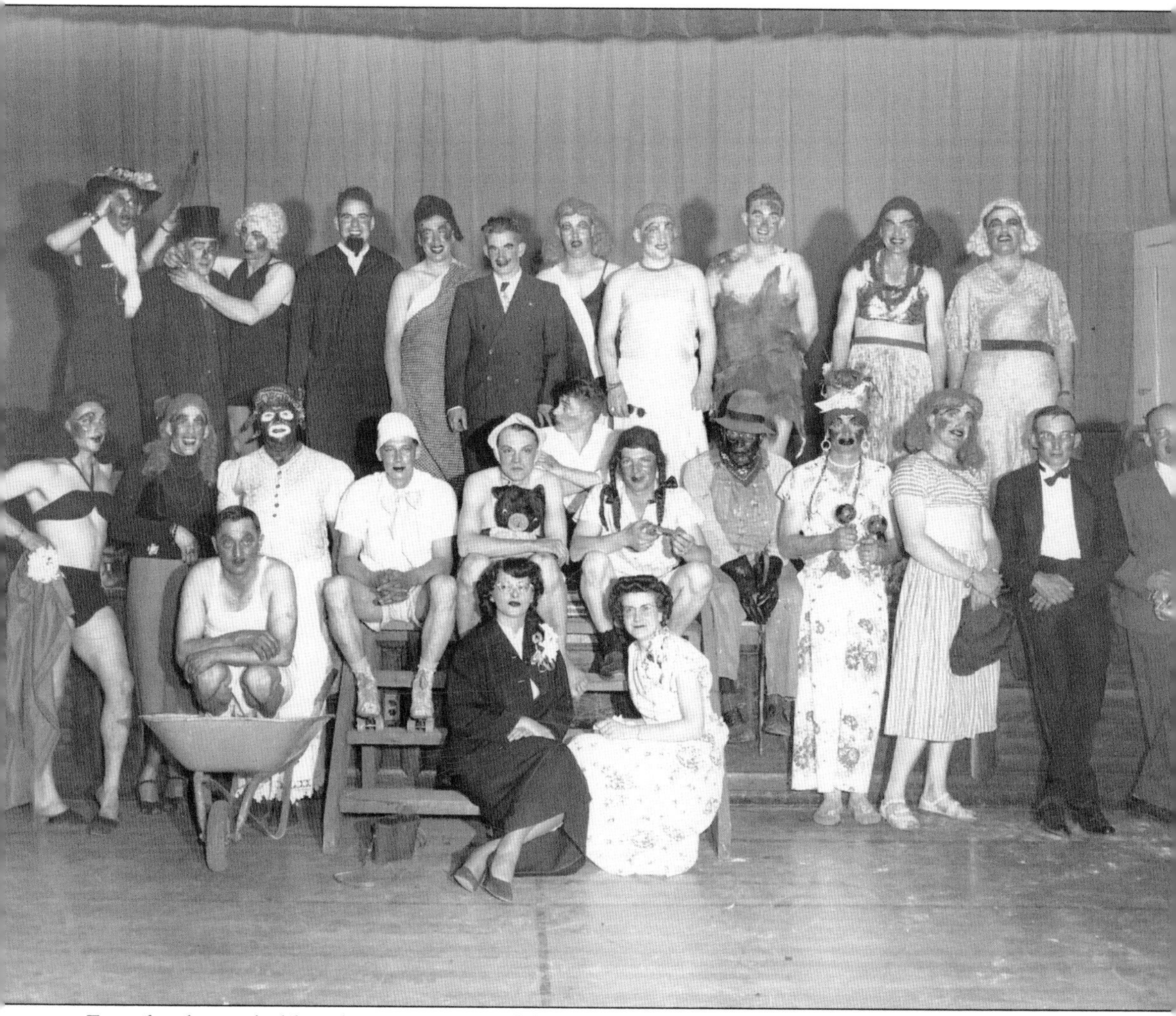

For a fundraiser held in the gymnasium of the Wakeman School, these members of the American Legion—who had all fought in World War I or World War II—dressed up for the "Beautiful Baby Contest" held in the late 1940s. Pictured from left to right, they are (first row) the traveling director and Wanda Bell Felton Hales; (second row) Dick Parsons, Louie Murray, Bob Arndt (in wheelbarrow), Bill Miller, Art Witzlaben Jr., Don Snyder, Alvin Baker, Jack Potter, Blaine Hurst, Charles Coultrip, Dick Ross, Don Hales, and Jack Grady; (third row) Maynard Clark, Ben Humm, unknown, Dave Wheeler, Andy Ortner, Bob Jenny, Ralph Jackson, Fremont Holmes, Jim Busek, Charles Shelton, and Bob Bement.

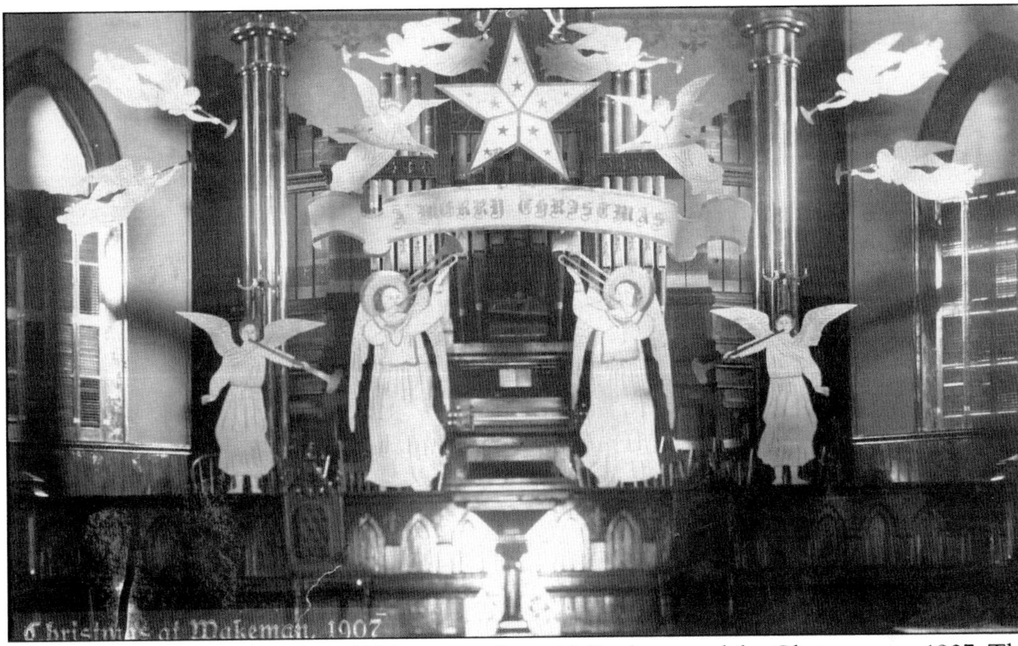

The Congregational church in Wakeman is beautifully decorated for Christmas in 1907. The church houses the original Hook and Hastings tracker organ.

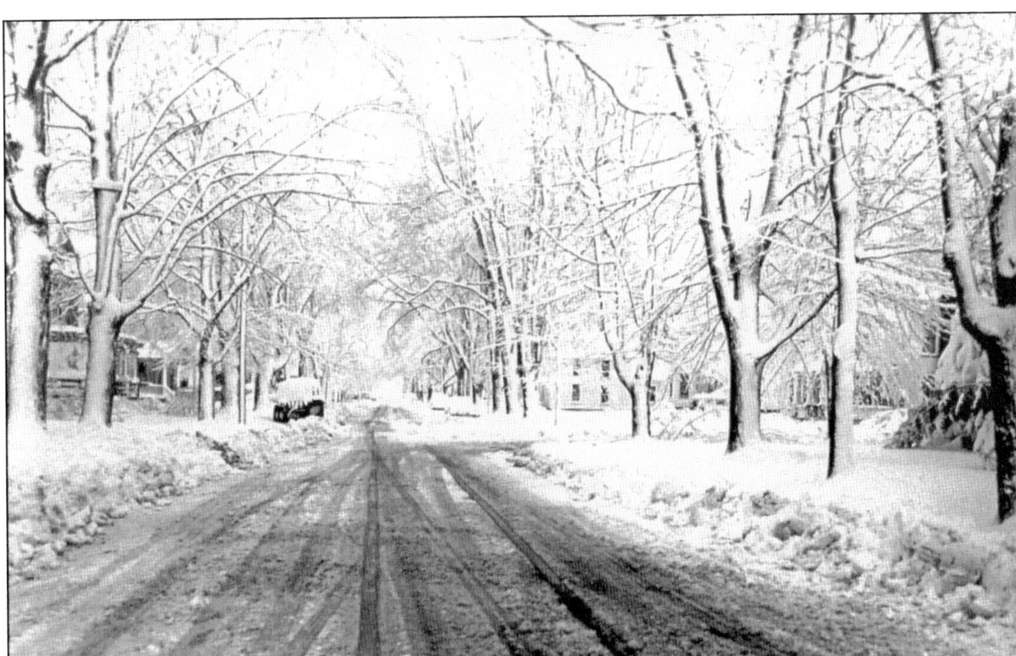

The infamous March 1954 snowstorm blankets Pleasant Street in Wakeman. The storm closed Route 20, a main highway, and stranded many truck drivers and travelers who sought refuge in private homes and the Grange Hall in Wakeman.

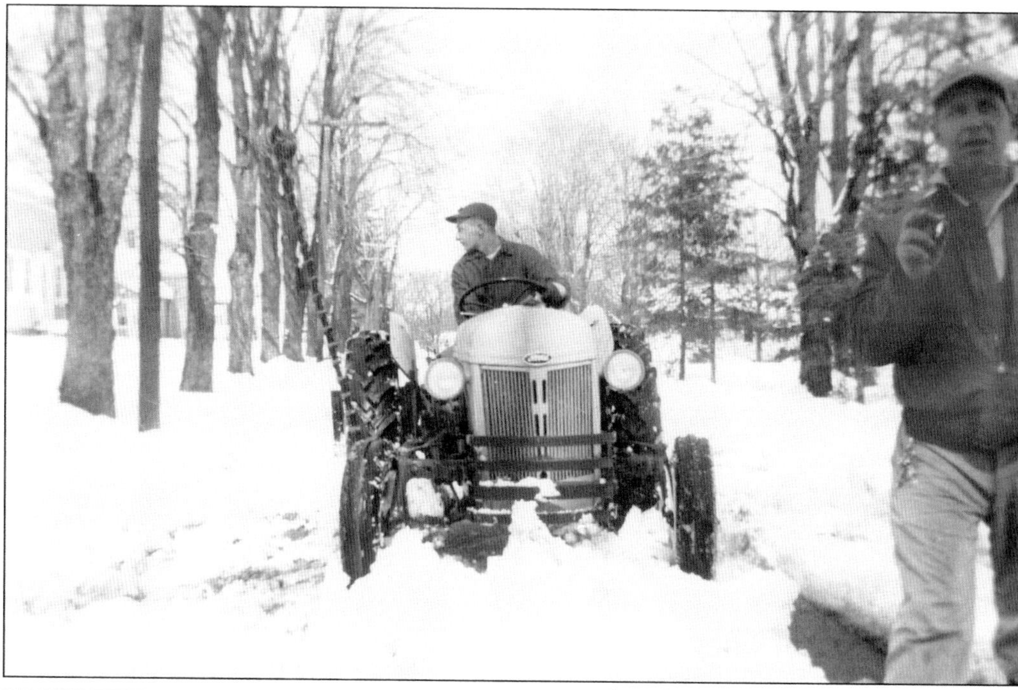

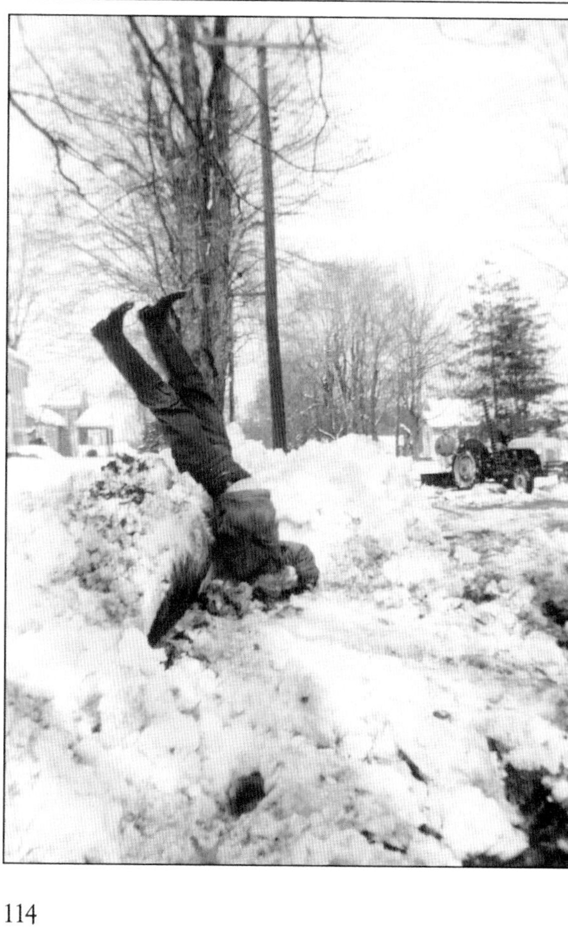

A 1954 snowstorm in Birmingham brought out resident Bill Logan on a Ford tractor to help clear the streets. The Logan family had its roots in Wakeman, but also had many members in Birmingham. Many of the members of the Logan family were in construction and trades. (Courtesy of Guy Schieve.)

Clearing snow is not all work, as Bill Logan demonstrates in this 1954 photograph. (Courtesy of Guy Schieve.)

A blanket of snow rests on a car in Birmingham after the snowstorm. During the first week of March 1954, the storm began with over 10 inches on March first and continued for several days. Five more inches fell by the end of the week. (Courtesy of Guy Schieve.)

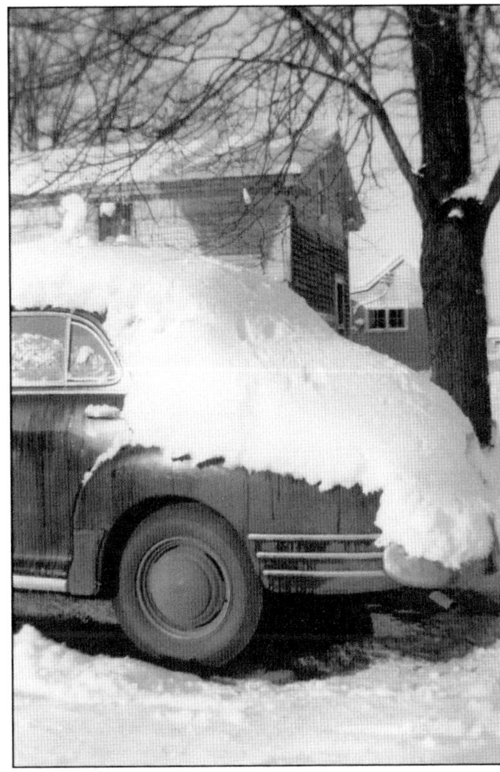

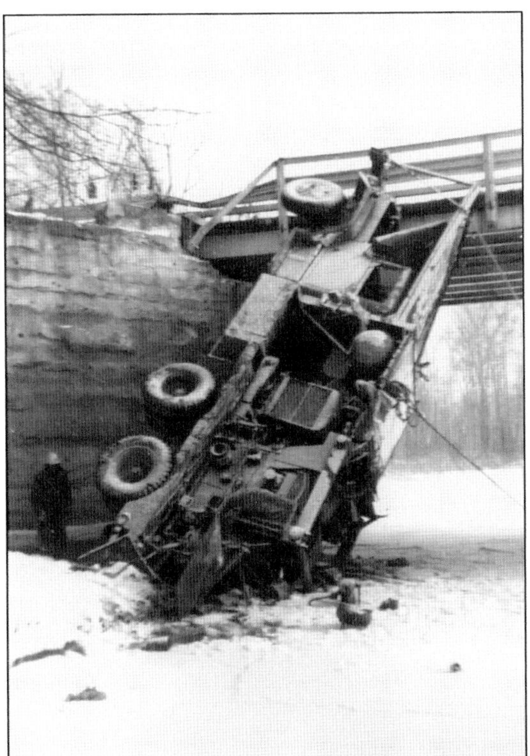

Icy roads and bridges created a dangerous situation for this truck driver. The frozen Vermilion River in Birmingham is snow-covered. (Courtesy of Guy Schieve.)

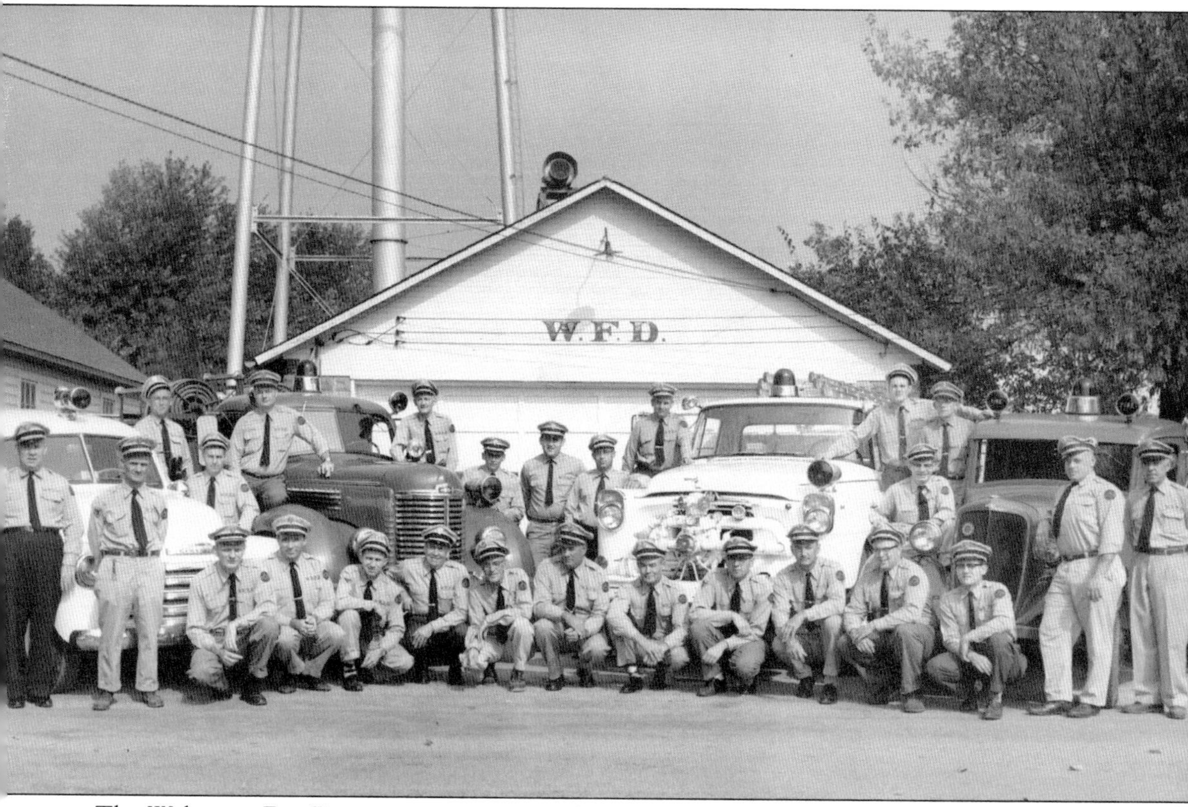

The Wakeman Fire Department appears in dress uniforms with their fleet of trucks in front of the old fire station on Pearl Street in this late 1950s photograph. The department constructed a new station on Route 303 at the end of Pleasant Street in 2001. From left to right, they are (first row) Al Vanfossen, Otto Robinson, Norman Nestor, General Divers, Nelson Green, Glenn Morey, Weezer Millhouse, Theo Timbs, Ralph Jackson, Jack Graves, Kenny Waldron, Neal Timbs, Don Graves, Albert Tuttle, and Harry Sengstock; (second row) Hank Opfer, Earl Soper, Carl Gerber, Charlie Bement, Junior Morey, Glaydon Pickworth, Art Witzlaben, AJ Steinwagner, Bill Bement, Lloyd Hurst, and Bob Miller. (Courtesy of the Wakeman Fire Department.)

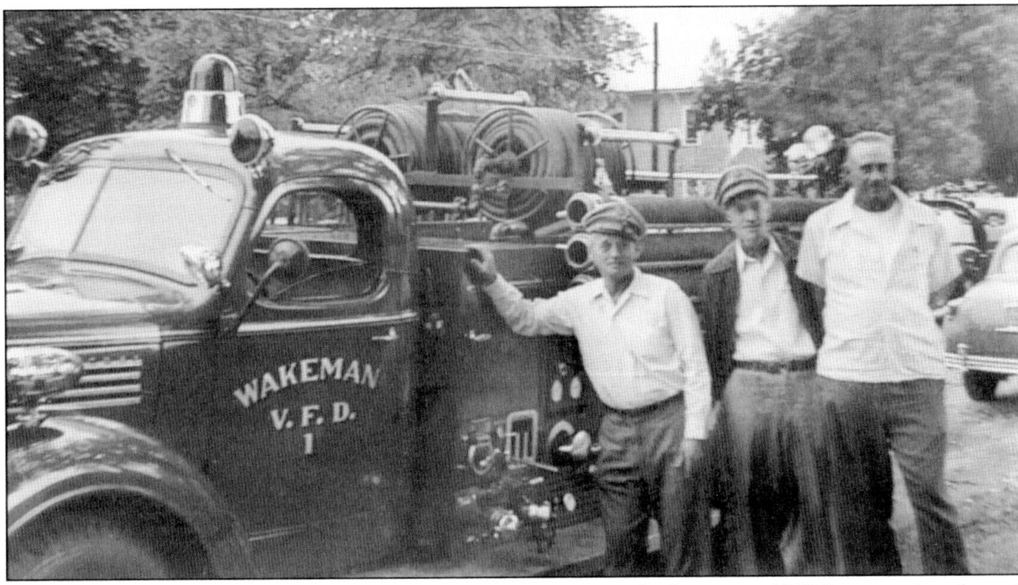

Three members of the Wakeman Fire Department pose with their new 1949 International truck the year it came to town. From left to right, they are Fred Graves, Weezer Millhouse, and Theodore Timbs.

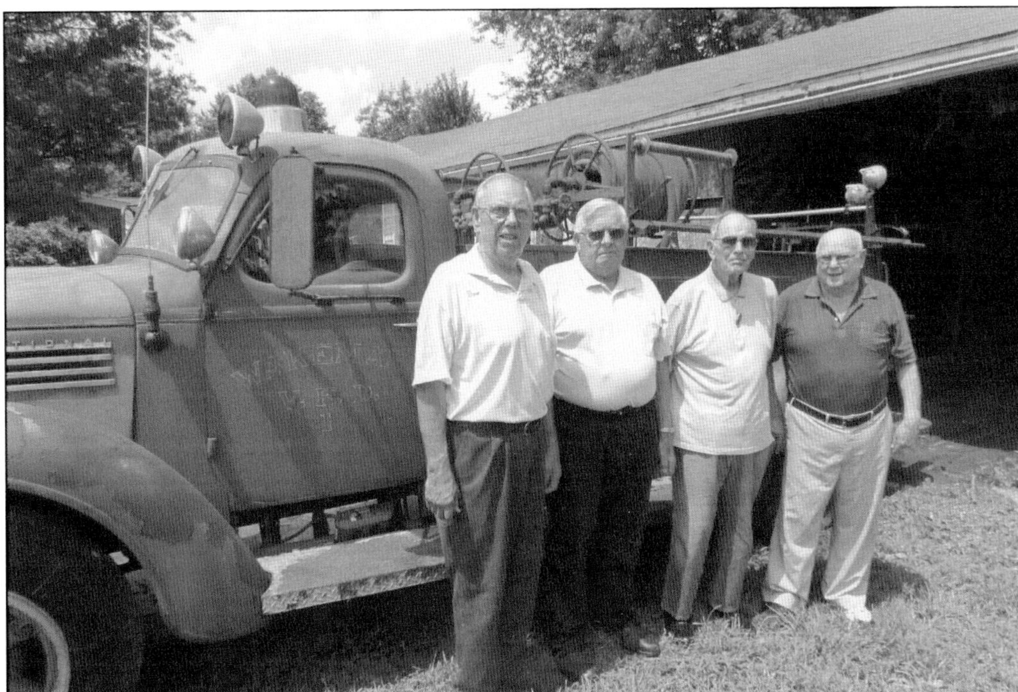

Replicating the 1949 photograph above, descendants of the three original men pose with the same truck on August 5, 2011. From left to right, they are David Graves, Jack Graves, Ronnie Millhouse, and Neal Timbs. Both Graves brothers served for many years on the department and held leadership positions, like their father. David Graves owns the 1949 truck now and plans to restore it.

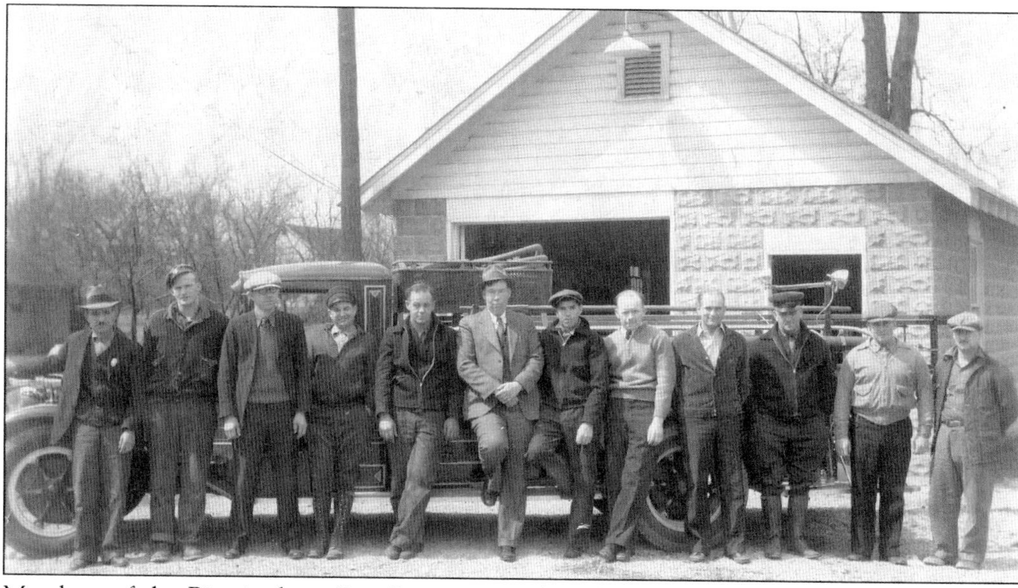

Members of the Birmingham Fire Department, later known as the Florence Township Fire Department, stand in front of their 1935 Diamond T fire truck. From left to right, they are Joe Angelo, Norris Fleming, Carl Ives, Ed Howe, Ed Prince, Thad Wilson, unidentified, Red Knott, unidentified, Charles Croft (chief), Paul Knott Sr., and Frank Griffin. (Courtesy of the Florence Township Fire Department.)

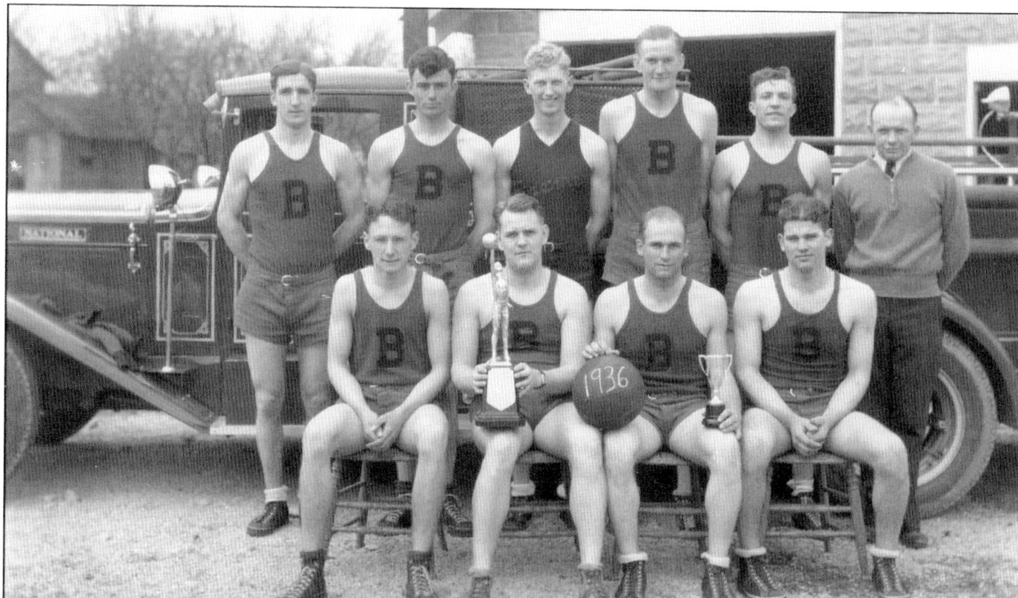

The Birmingham Fire Department's basketball team was the winner of the 1936 Cleveland Inter-City Competition. From left to right, the nine players are identified as (first row) Lyle Kingsley, George Reinhart, Clarence Johannsen, and Bob (Shorty) Hostetler; (second row) Joe Yarza, Stew Fairchild, Harold Davis, Donald (Cobb) Wasem, and Willis (Bud) Wasem. The coach is Red Knott. (Courtesy of the Florence Township Fire Department.)

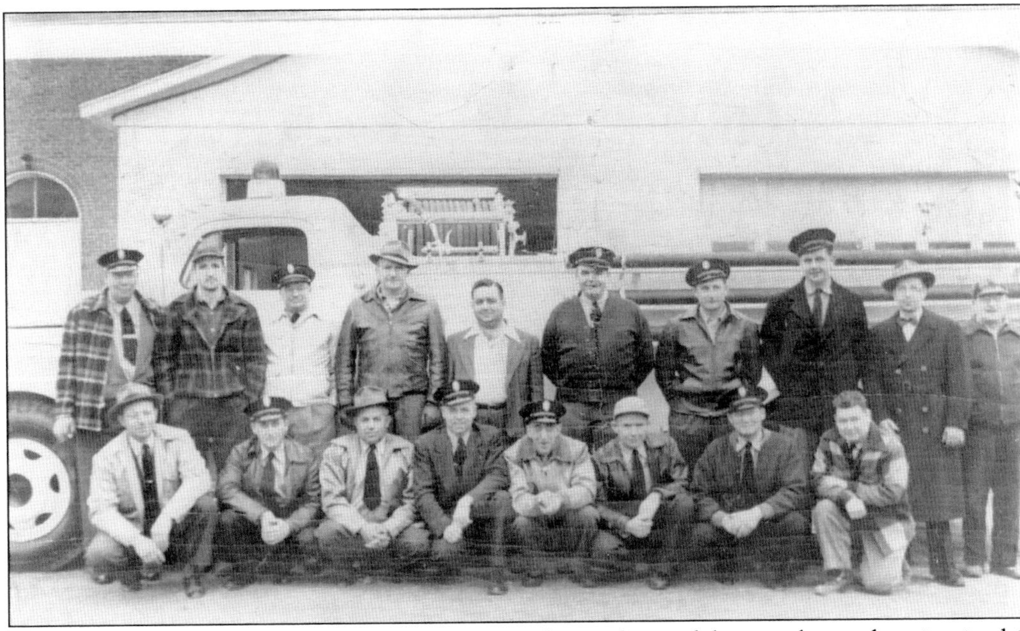

Members of the Birmingham Fire Department gather in front of their tanker and station in this early 1950s photograph. (Courtesy of the Florence Township Fire Department.)

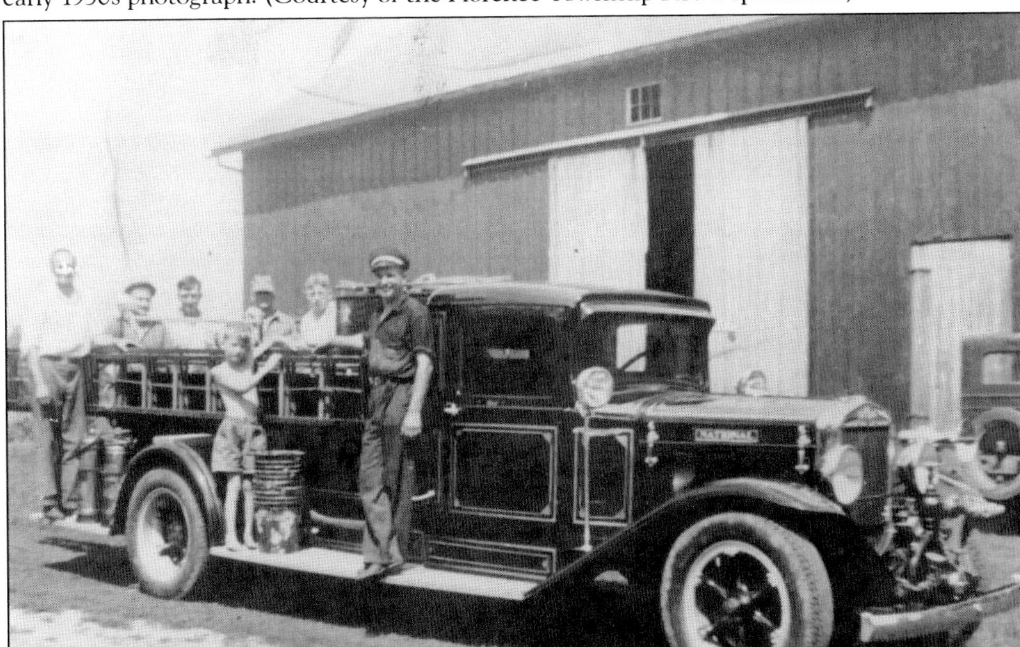

In this 1935 photograph, department and family members stand on their new Diamond T truck. From left to right are (first row) son Edwin Howe and father Edwin Howe; (second row) Lee Andrews, Frank Griffin, Paul Knott, Reuben Wenzel, and Clarence Johannsen. (Courtesy of Roger Howe.)

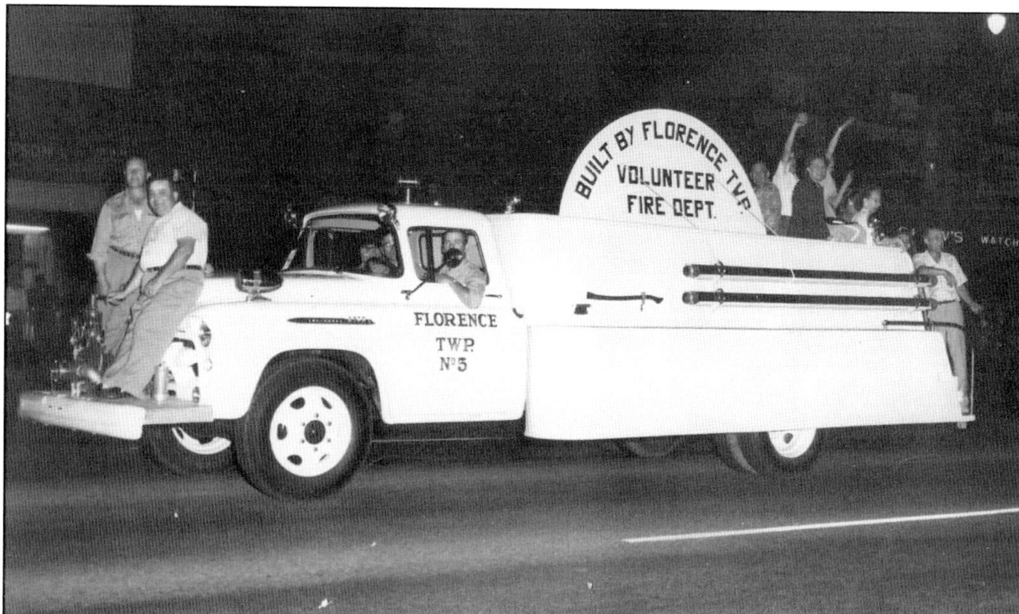

This photograph, taken at the Northwest Ohio Firemen's Convention in 1956 or 1957, shows the tanker truck that members of the department pitched in and constructed. Using a 1956 Chevy chassis, department members Charles Persons, Edwin Prince, Richard Prince, Robert Prince, Keith Jarrett, Paul Knott Sr., Merrill Peasley, and Rosell Angelo built, painted, and wired it. (Courtesy of the Florence Township Fire Department.)

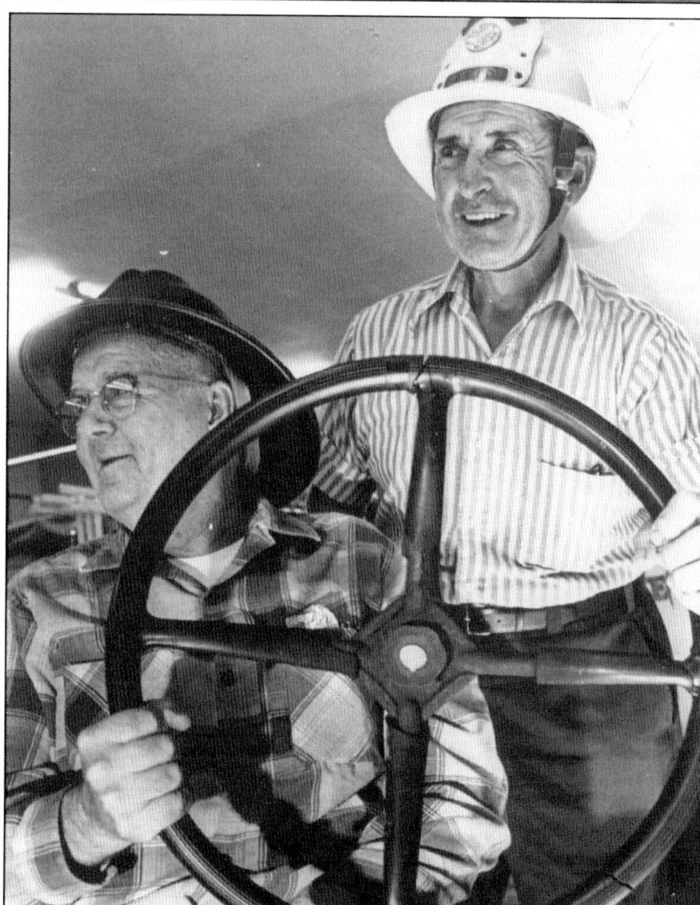

Ralph Prince and Paul Knott Sr., both former chiefs of the Birmingham Fire Department, are honored for their years of service in this 1972 photograph. (Courtesy of the Florence Township Fire Department.)

On April 4, 1949, Bill Simpkinson's gasoline truck crashed into the bridge on the section of Route 60 that spans the Vermilion River in Florence Township. The impact knocked down the bridge, and the truck landed in the river. (Courtesy of Guy Schieve.)

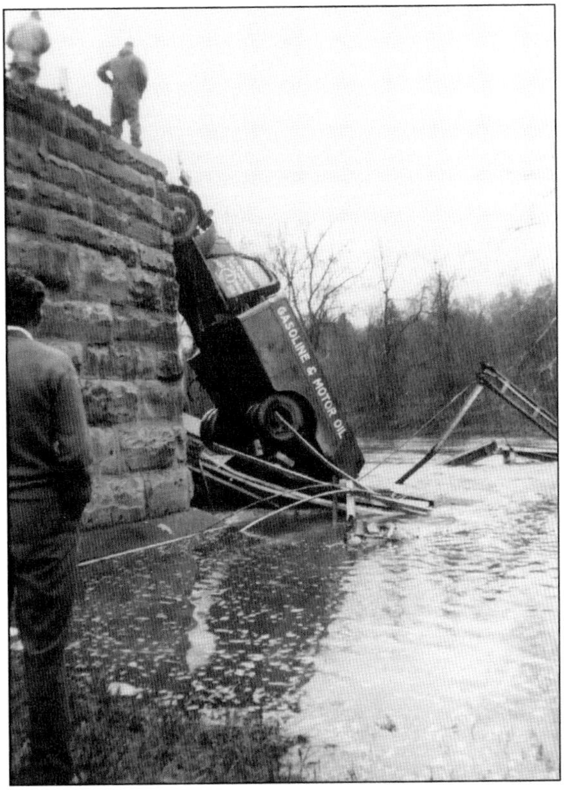

Bud McCoy, with the wrecker service from nearby Norwalk, Ohio, pulls the gasoline truck from the river and secures it to the wrecker truck. (Courtesy of Guy Schieve.)

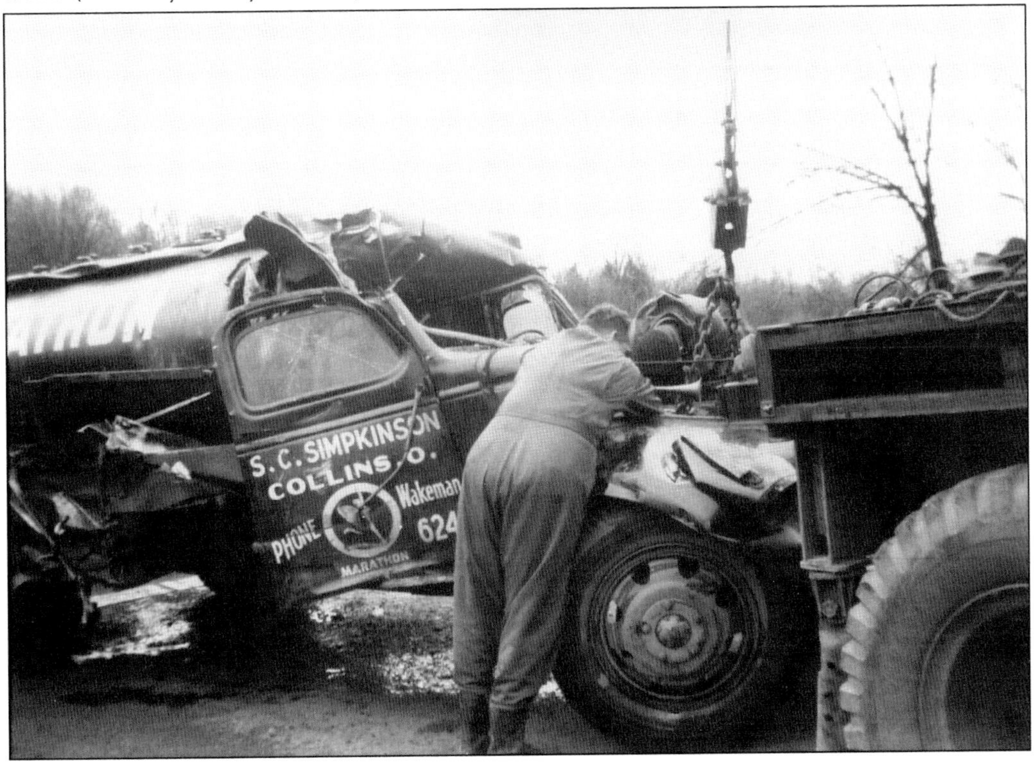

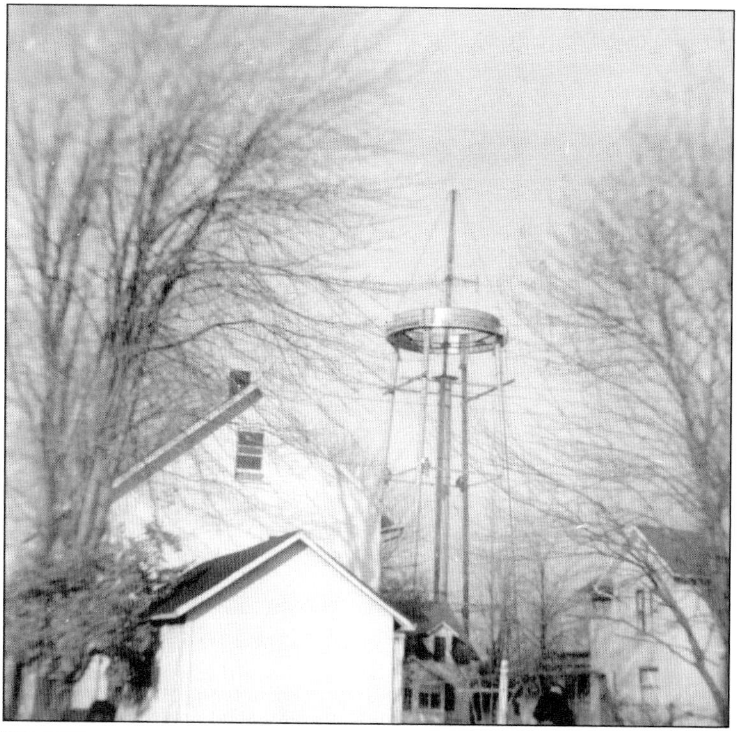

In 1954, Wakeman got its first water tower, located behind the old fire station on Pearl Street. It still stands and remains in use. An Indian tribe from New York, which traveled the country installing water towers, put the tower up. The fire siren for the Village of Wakeman was hung about halfway up the tower and called volunteer firefighters for over 50 years.

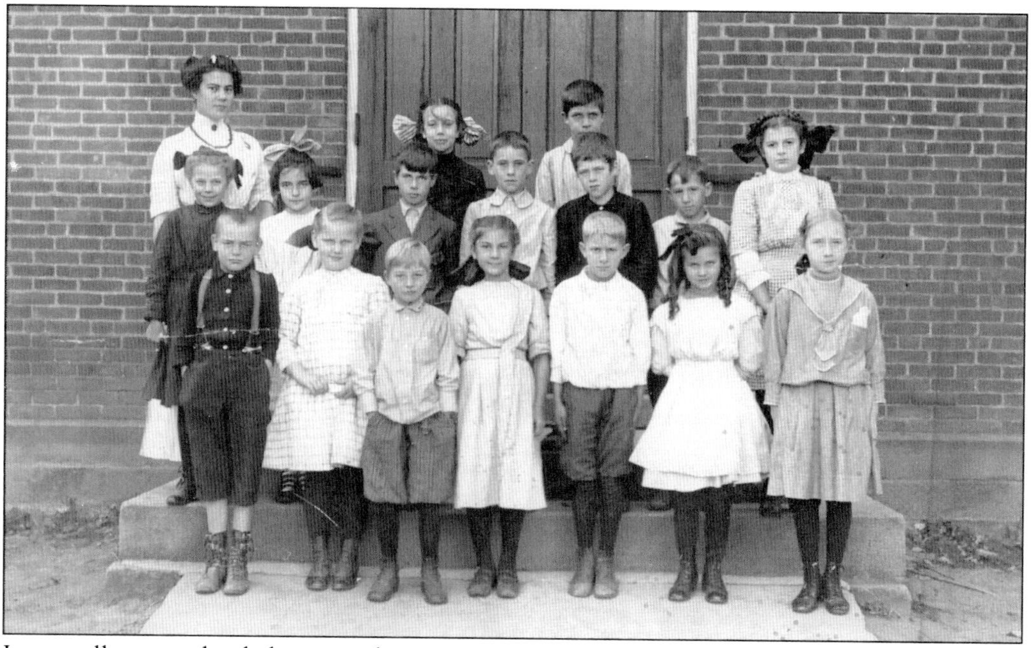

In a small town, school classmates have an important community bond. This 1912 photograph shows members of the third-grade and fourth-grade classes at Wakeman Elementary. Pictured from left to right, they are (first row) Earl Perkins, Mary Shelton, Gaius Scott, Rosie Beam, Lewis Loken, Gladys Anderson, and Nellie Cole; (second row) Mildred Fletcher, Anna Loftus, Kenneth Hurst, Harold Whitney, ? Harrigan, Merwin Kenyon, and Anna Cooley; (third row) Edna Seely (teacher), Dorothy Grover, and Merle Hurst.

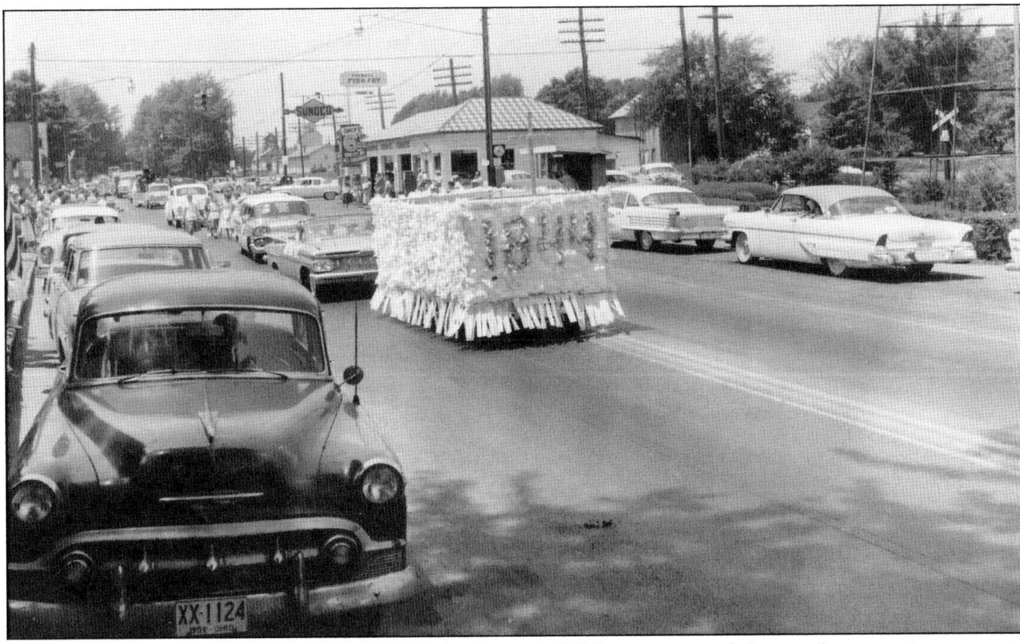

This parade was held June 20, 1959, in downtown Wakeman to celebrate the sesquicentennial of the Firelands area. There is a VW Beetle under the float for the Wakeman Congregational Church. The large tower to the right of the photograph was built in 1917 to celebrate the centennial anniversary of Wakeman's founding, but it was torn down later in the afternoon following this parade because of its age and safety concerns. Note the XX license plate on the car in the foreground. Many Wakeman residents still retain an XX plate on their vehicles.

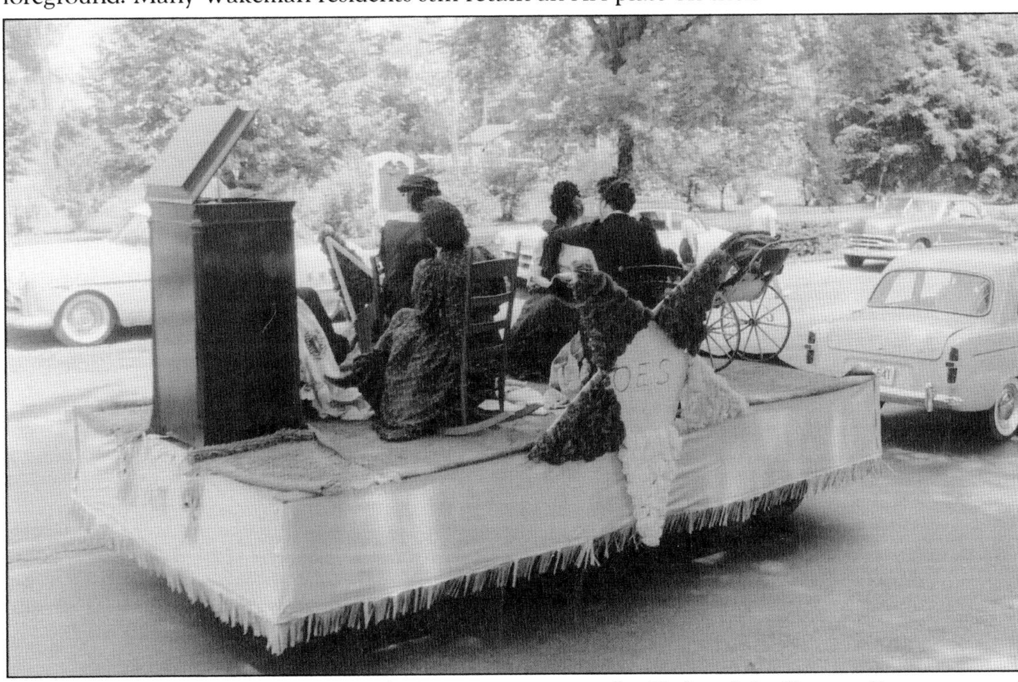

This float was also in the 1959 parade. It commemorates the Order of the Eastern Star, a women's group affiliated with the Masons.

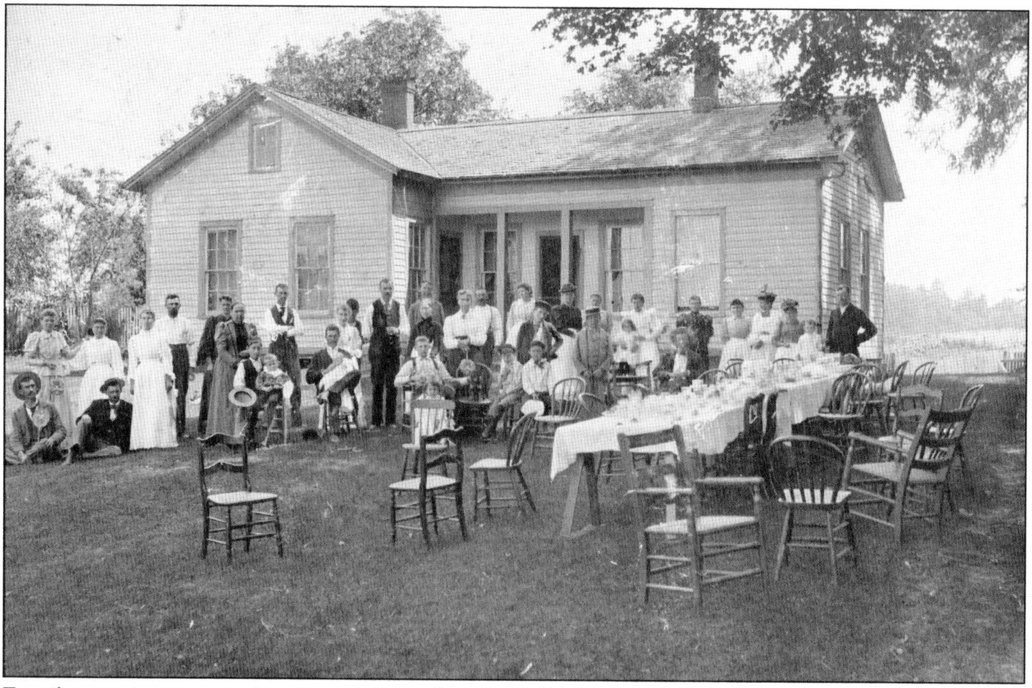

Family reunions are an important part of many communities. This is the Henry family reunion in Florence Township. This photograph was probably taken in the 1890s, and a note on the back says that the house was later moved across the street. (Courtesy of Jason Gargasz.)

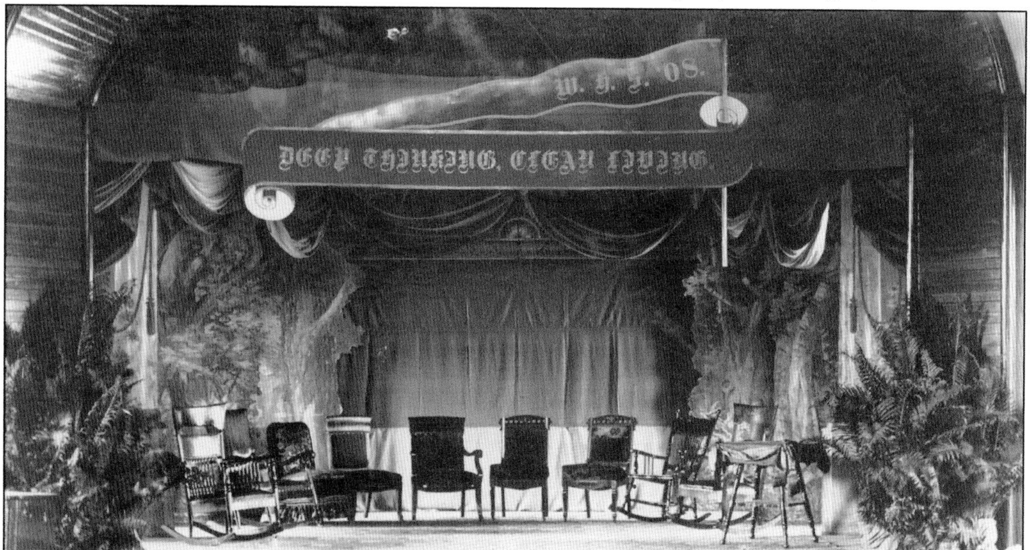

The stage is set in 1908 for a Wakeman High School event in the town hall. The town hall, also known as the opera house or the Masonic Lodge, was frequently used for basketball games, plays, concerts, and ceremonies. The top banner reads "W.H.S. '08." The bottom banner is a mystery. The elaborate bunting on the stage implies a formal occasion.

This photograph from about 1900 is labeled "Henry Peck and C.H. McMann." Both of their families were well represented in numbers in Wakeman. McMann became the president of the Wakeman Bank and held that position for many years. (Courtesy of the Wakeman Community Library.)

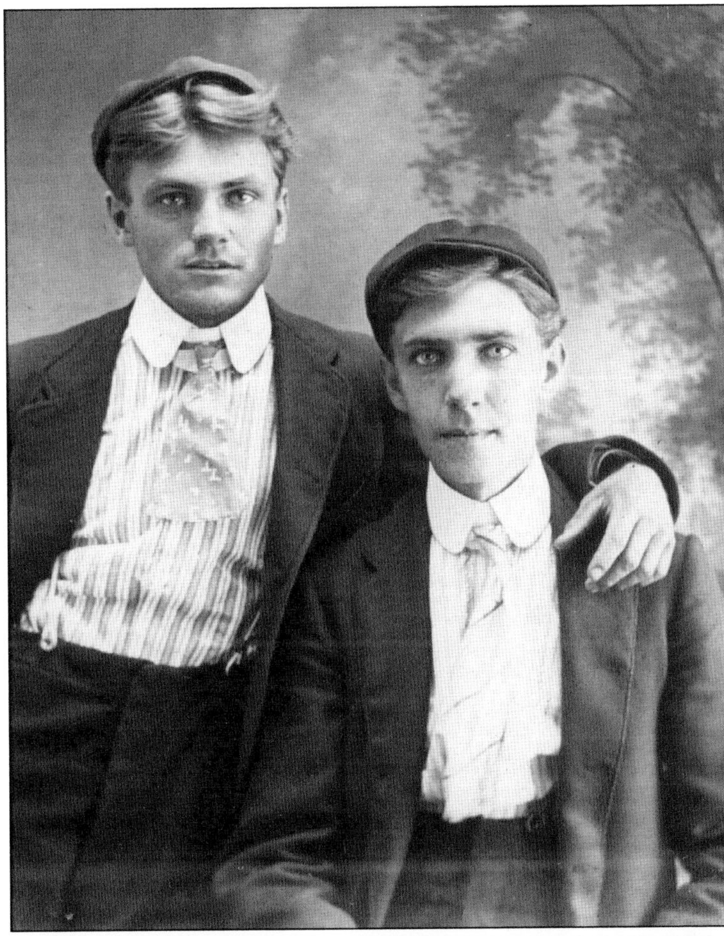

Schools are a strong force in fostering a sense of community. This postcard, depicting a Wakeman area school, has a note on the back that says, "I thought you would like to see me and mine at school."

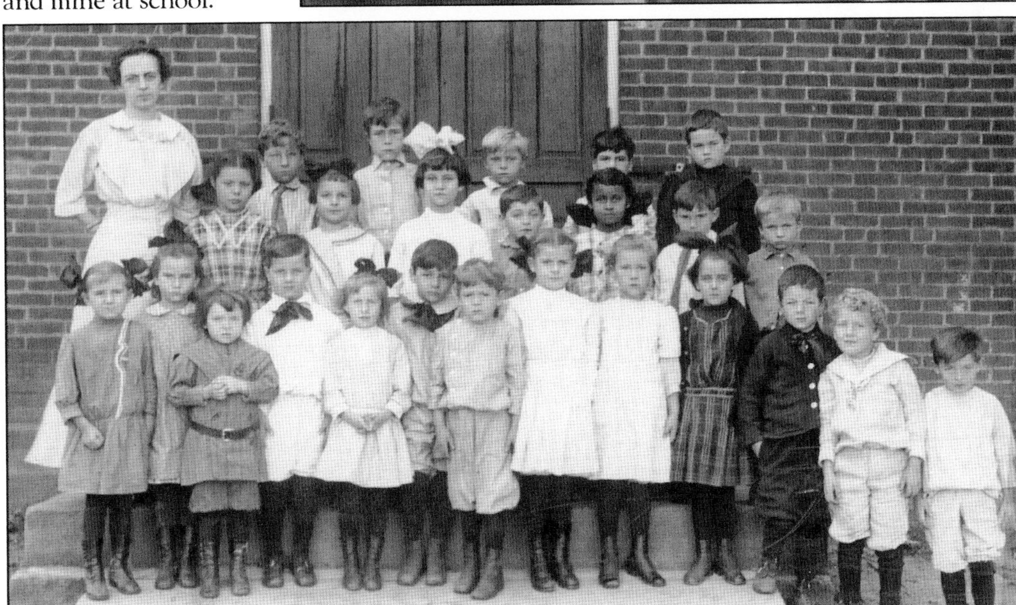

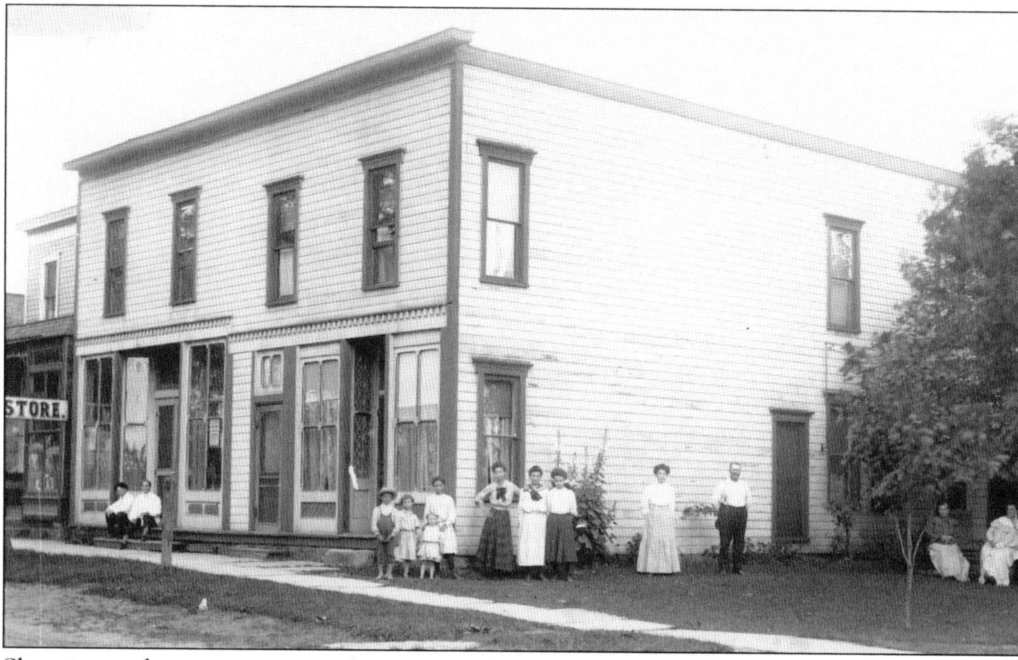

Shopping and visiting are part of community life. In this c. 1895 photograph, men, women, and children gather in front of a store in downtown Wakeman.

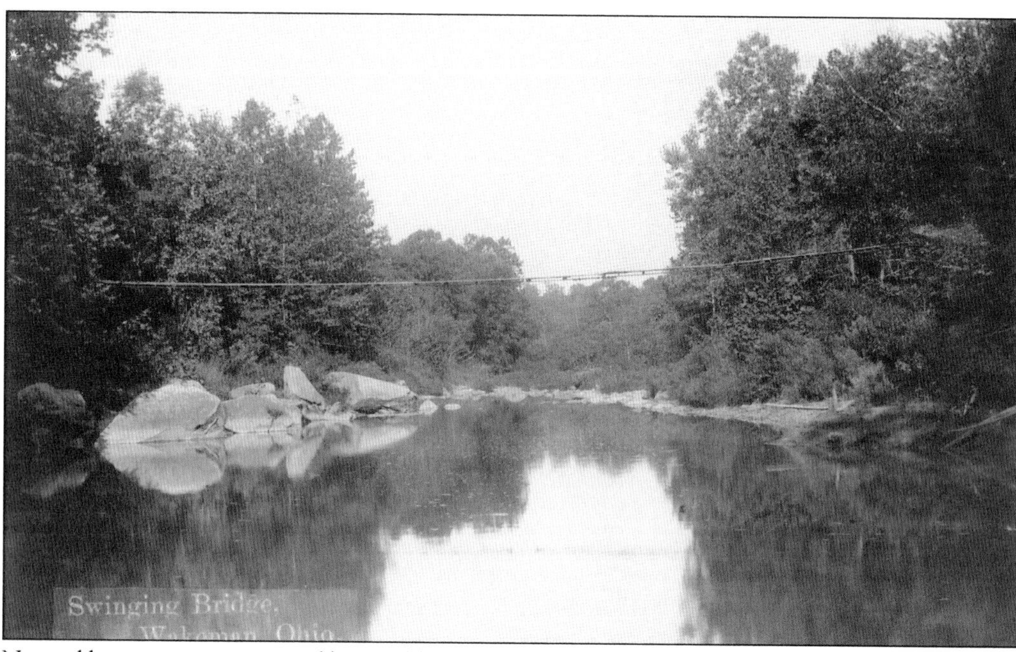

Natural beauty, recreation, and being able to get to the other side are important community assets. This swinging bridge to Herman Ott's sugar bush would not be for the fainthearted.

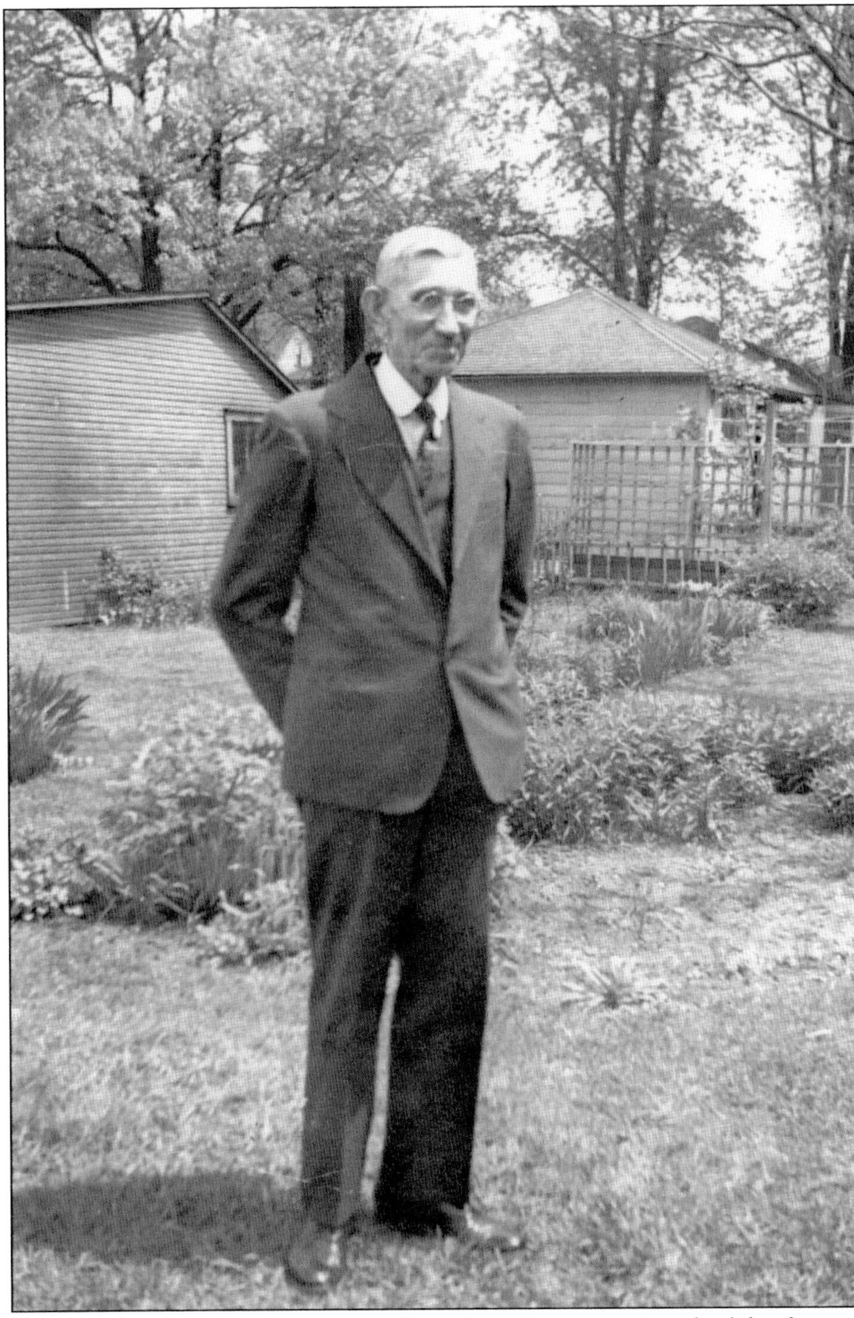

Sometimes a single person can be a compelling force for preserving the life of a community. F.A. Denman (1866–1960) lived in Wakeman and was passionate about eggs, roses, and recordkeeping. Pictured behind him at his home on Pleasant Street in this 1955 portrait are his gardens and chicken coops. For many years, he drove a weekly route into Lorain and Cleveland to deliver eggs to restaurants and hotels. He was also a local historian in his generation. He took many photographs and kept a daily journal for 20 years. Many of his photographs appear in this book, and his photo albums and journals are an important source of information he was diligent about gathering in his 93 years.

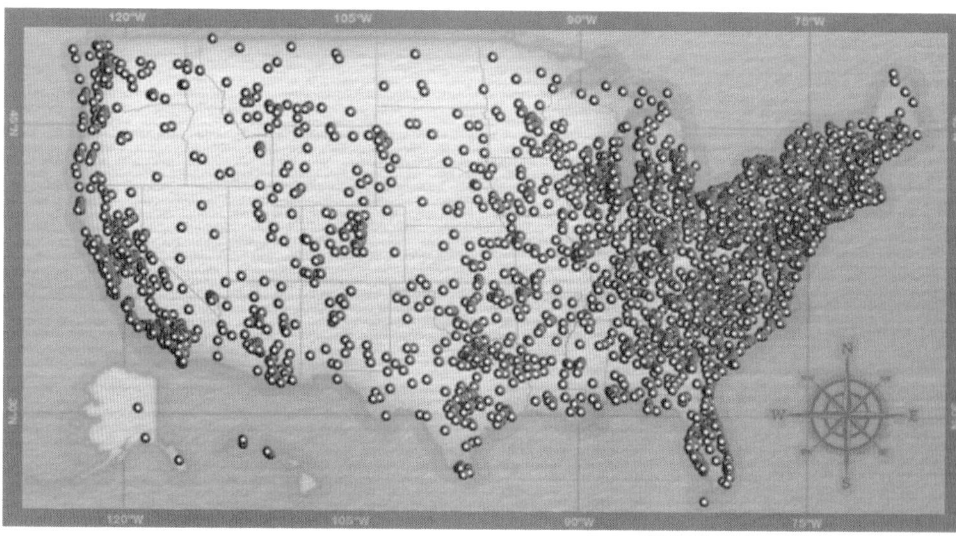